OUR SEA TURTLES

A Practical Guide for the Atlantic and Gulf, from Canada to Mexico

Blair and Dawn Witherington

Pineapple Press, Inc.
Sarasota, Florida

To all who work to save our sea turtles

Front Cover Photographs

Background: Open-sea juvenile green turtle
Juvenile green turtle eye
Adult green turtle rear flipper
Loggerhead sea turtle eggs in nest
Juvenile hawksbill face
Adult loggerhead sea turtle's open mouth
Loggerhead sea turtle nesting track
Hatchling leatherback on beach
Subadult Kemp's ridley

Back Cover: Hatchling loggerhead sea turtle

Title Page: Hatchling loggerhead sea turtle

Page 7: Juvenile hawksbill

Page 272: Hatchling loggerhead sea turtle

Inquiries should be addressed to:
Pineapple Press, Inc.
P.O. Box 3889
Sarasota, Florida 34230

www.pineapplepress.com

Library of Congress Cataloging-in-Publication Data

Witherington, Blair E., 1962–
Our sea turtles : a practical guide for the Atlantic and Gulf, from Canada to Mexico / Blair and Dawn Witherington.
pages cm
Includes index.
ISBN 978-1-56164-736-1 (pbk. : alk. paper)
1. Sea turtles—North Atlantic Ocean. 2. Sea turtles—Mexico, Gulf of. I. Witherington, Dawn. II. Title.

QL666.C536W568 2015
597.92'8—dc23

2014049117

Design by Dawn Witherington
Printed in China

Contents

Part One: Understanding Our Sea Turtles

The Species

Sea Turtle Form and Function

Life Cycle and Life History

Ecology

Part Two: Experiencing Our Sea Turtles

Our Sea Turtles on Land

Our Sea Turtles in the Water

Our Sea Turtles in Captivity

Part Three: Saving Sea Our Turtles

Acknowledgments and Photo Credits

For their gracious help and contributions, we are indebted to:

Dave Addison, Jim Angy, Dean Bagley, the Baldwin family, Zoe Bass, Aaron Barleycorn, Barbara Bergwerf, Michael Bresette, Kendra Cope, Carlos Diez, Scott Eastman, Matthew Godfrey, Jonathan Gorham, Stacy Hargrove, Tomo Hirama, Inwater Research Group, Steve Johnson, Ken Lohmann, Chris Long, Charles Manire, René Márquez, Adrienne McCracken, Philip Miller, Richie Moretti, Mote Marine Lab, Cody Mott, Maddy Mullenger, the Neff family, Cynthia Nielson, George and Suzy Pappas, the Pekmezian family, Ed Perry, Paul Raymond, the Rodriguez family, Kirt Rusenko, Kate Sampson, Michelle Tanya Scharer, Brian Shamblin, Donna Shaver, Brian Stacy, The Turtle Hospital, Toni Torres, University of Central Florida Sea Turtle Program, Robert P. van Dam, Ryan Welsh, Larry Wood, Mary Wozny, and Bette Zirkelbach.

This book greatly benefitted from thoughtful reviews by:

Karen Bjorndal, Grant Bush, Jeff Bush, Allen Foley, Kate Mansfield, Anne Meylan, Peter Meylan, Barbara Schroeder, Rachel Smith, and Jeanette Wyneken.

Photographs and Illustrations are © Blair and Dawn Witherington unless listed.

Page 8, 3rd and 4th images, Florida FWC
Page 9, middle, University of Georgia
Page 18, top, © Brian Stacy
Page 31, © Peter Leahy/Shutterstock
Page 40, top, © Kirt Rusenko
Page 41, © Robert P. van Dam
Page 42, top, © Amanda Nicholls/Shutterstock
Page 42, middle, © Rich Carey/Shutterstock
Page 43, © Amanda Nicholls/Shutterstock
Page 45, bottom, © Robert P. van Dam
Page 47, © Adrienne McCracken
Page 53, © Toni Torres, Gladys Porter Zoo
Page 55, top, © Aaron Barleycorn
Page 56, top, © Diana J. Lira Reyes, Gladys Porter Zoo
Page 57, bottom, © Ed Perry
Page 66, middle, © Philip Miller
Page 67, bottom © Michael Patrick O'Neill/SeaPics.com
Page 91, bottom, © Mote Marine Laboratory
Page 103, middle, © Inwater Research Group
Page 110, top, © Dean Bagley
Page 110, middle, © Inwater Research Group
Page 121, top, NASA Scientific Visualization Studio
Page 122, bottom, © Amanda Nicholls/Shutterstock
Page 123, 3rd image, © Dean Bagley
Page 127, © Shigetomo Hirama
Page 128, bottom, © Inwater Research Group
Page 129, bottom, © Inwater Research Group
Page 131, top, © Steve Johnson
Page 131, 3rd image, © Zoe Bass
Page 134, 2nd image, © Brian Lasenby/Shuterstock
Page 134, 3rd image, © Zoe Bass
Page 139, © Jim Angy
Page 142, middle, © Adrienne McCracken
Page 150, right, © Ed Perry
Page 151, left top, © Ed Perry
Page 151, left bottom, © Anne Meylan
Page 152, right, © Adrienne McCracken
Page 155, middle, © Stacy Hargrove
Page 155, bottom, © Shigetomo Hirama
Page 157, bottom, National Park Service
Page 161, bottom, © Inwater Research Group
Page 162, bottom, © Mary Wozny
Page 167, top, © Scott Eastman
Page 167, middle, © Shigetomo Hirama
Page 167, bottom, © Anne Meylan
Page 170, bottom, © Zoe Bass
Page 171, 3rd image, © Dave Addison
Page 173, 4th image, © Dave Addison
Page 176, right, © Adrienne McCracken
Page 179, bottom, © Kirt Rusenko
Page 186, middle and bottom, © Adrienne McCracken
Page 187, top, © Zoe Bass

Page 193, top, © Thomas Barrat/Shutterstock
Page 193, 2nd image, © Jeanne Mortimer
Page 194, top, © Zoe Bass
Page 195, 2nd image, © Scott Eastman
Page 195, 3rd image, © Zoe Bass
Page 196, 3rd image, © Jim Angy
Page 198, bottom, Creative Commons Americasroof
Page 202, top, © The Turtle Hospital
Page 202, middle, © Donna Shaver
Page 202, bottom, © Matthew Godfrey
Page 203, top, © South Carolina Aquarium
Page 214, 2nd image, © The Turtle Hospital
Page 216, bottom, © Adrienne McCracken
Page 221, 2nd image, © Inwater Research Group
Page 228, middle, © Amanda Nicholls/Shutterstock
Page 228, bottom, © BlueOrange Studio/Shutterstock
Page 229, left, © DJ Mattaar/Shutterstock
Page 229, middle, © Matt9122/Shutterstock
Page 229, bottom, © Khoroshunova Olga/Shutterstock
Page 230, © Kate Sampson, NOAA
Page 231, middle, © Loggerhead Marinelife Center
Page 231, bottom, © Inwater Research Group
Page 232, middle, © Inwater Research Group
Page 233, middle, © The Turtle Hospital
Page 235, top and 3rd images, © Shigetomo Hirama
Page 236, top, NASA
Page 243, top, © Barbara Schroeder
Page 243, middle, NOAA
Page 246, top, © University of North Carolina Chapel Hill
Page 246, middle and bottom, NOAA
Page 247, © Bette Zirkelbach, The Turtle Hospital
Page 248, middle and bottom, © The Turtle Hospital
Page 249, left, top, and middle, © The Turtle Hospital
Page 250, middle and bottom, © The Turtle Hospital
Page 252, top © BlueOrange Studio/Shutterstock
Page 252, top inset, © Walt Disney World
Page 252, bottom, © Adrienne McCracken
Page 256, © Inwater Research Group
Page 258, top, Sala (1879) *Paris Herself Again in 1878–9*
Page 258, middle, State Archives of Florida
Page 259, top and middle, State Archives of Florida
Page 259, bottom, © Michelle Tanya Scharer
Page 262, top, © Paul Raymond
Page 262, middle, © Kelly Stewart
Page 262, bottom, © Alan Bolten
Page 263, top, © Dean Bagley
Page 263, middle, © Boone family
Page 264, top, USFWS
Page 264, middle, © A. E. Montoya/INAPESCA
Page 264, bottom, © Paul Raymond
Page 265, © Jim Angy
Page 267, top, © Coastal Cleanup Corporation

An Introduction to Our Sea Turtles

The pages that follow describe *our* sea turtles. They are yours, mine … ours. That's right, not just possessive, but inclusive. We chose the book's title to focus on the unique relationship we have with sea turtles, and on the special obligation we have to protect them.

What kind of relationship could we have with a wild animal of the open sea? Can there really be a connection between us? Some of you may already realize such a connection. Our physical links to the natural world are obvious, and many of us have emotional connections as well. Could these connections be mutually beneficial? For most of the wild creatures that tread our earth and swim our seas, finding mutually beneficial connections is not easy. But sea turtles are unique. They stand out because we have access to them. The turtles present themselves, tolerate some of our advances, and mysterious as they are, they regularly crawl into our world. Oh yes, and they are awesome animals! Our access to them contributes positively to the human experience. That is, sea turtles can make us happy.

But what do the sea turtles get out of it? Perhaps, a little understanding … and some accommodation. Like it or not, our sea turtles find themselves with a potentially obtrusive roommate, with our obtrusiveness having everything to do with our sea turtles' prospects for life.

As in all worthwhile relationships, this one will take work. If we accept our connection with sea turtles, then we should take on the responsibility this implies. The benefits of enjoying our sea turtles come with requirements for their stewardship. We are all in this together.

A green turtle returns to the sea after laying her eggs. To reproduce, sea turtles must crawl into our world

Audience and Guide Organization

This book is for anyone who is the least bit curious about sea turtles. We've added detail that would help a student of biology or wildlife conservation, but we've tried not to overwhelm. To ease into various subjects, we present sea turtles in bite-size installments. We've tried to softly introduce the sea-turtle jargon needed to tell their story, realizing that many readers with enthusiasm for nature will only dimly recall their introduction to the life sciences. **Bold text** will show where new terms are represented in adjacent images.

The story is in three parts—*Understanding, Experiencing,* and *Saving* our sea turtles. We want you to come to know sea turtles, we want you to realize your connections to them, and we want you to sense an obligation to help them out.

Our Region

Our regional focus is the Atlantic Ocean and Gulf of Mexico from Canada to Mexico. But sea turtles don't recognize these boundaries, and neither do we. Much of the story we tell also applies to sea turtles living in the Caribbean Sea and the broader Atlantic, and most of the concepts we introduce are universal to sea turtles living anywhere. The principal gap a reader might recognize is that we only briefly mention two sea turtle species that are either rare or unknown in our region—the olive ridley (*Lepidochelys olivacea*, rare here) and the Australian flatback (*Natator depressus*, not here). The map of "**Our Region**" below shows many features we'll refer to often, including surface currents (light blue lines).

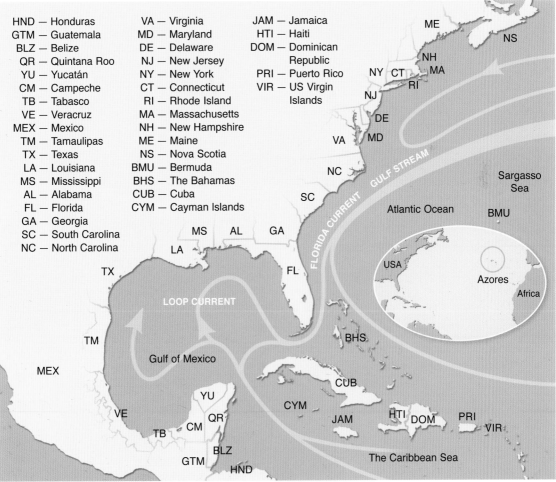

"Our Region" showing the area covered by this book. Yet many of our sea turtles live part of their lives south and east of this map

Part One: Understanding Our Sea Turtles

This is your introduction to sea turtles and their world. We begin with what sea turtles are and where they came from, and we offer portraits of each of the five species that live in our region. Then, we describe sea turtle form and function. This is what makes a sea turtle different from other animals, including the special adaptations that allow sea turtles to live in their world. Next, we introduce the life story of sea turtles—how they begin their lives, and how they develop, grow, survive, breed, and move around from place to place. Lastly, we describe the relationships that sea turtles have to other living things, namely, what sea turtles eat, what eats them, and what other roles they play in the natural world.

Part Two: Experiencing Our Sea Turtles

This section highlights our connections to sea turtles. We describe the ways that sea turtles contribute to our life experience and we decipher many of the biological clues that sea turtles leave for us. We describe connections and experiences with sea turtles on land, at sea, and in captivity. Descriptions on land include sea turtle nesting, what nesting beaches are like, and interpretations of the many signs in the sand that turtles leave behind for us on beaches. On land, sea turtles have their closest connections to us, including many things we do to threaten them. In the water, sea turtles seem to be distant from us, and indeed, their lives at sea retain many mysteries. But we are much more closely connected to turtles at sea

Seeing a young-of-the-year loggerhead sea turtle within an offshore seaweed patch can be part of a boater's wilderness experience

A hatchling loggerhead sea turtle reflects on its prospects

than we might think. Our presence at sea is profound, and some of the most important ways we connect to sea turtles occur in the water. We have numerous opportunities to experience turtles in their marine world, sharing some of their secretive lives as we gaze out to sea, snorkel, dive, or putter about in boats. Wild sea turtles that become sick or injured are often brought into captivity. These turtles establish meaningful connections to us, and they provide us with unique opportunities to experience them. In the last section of Part Two, we describe sea turtles in captivity—how they got there, what care they receive, and how they fulfill their role as ocean ambassadors.

Part Three: Saving Sea Our Turtles

Sea turtles are threatened with extinction. As splendid as they are, and as interesting as they make our world, we run the risk of losing them forever. But not to worry—you have the potential to ensure that this doesn't happen. Some of the smallest things we do day-to-day can either help sea turtles or hurt them. Many of these decisions we make as individuals are easy. But for all of us collectively, doing the right thing for sea turtles can seem overwhelming. In this part of the book, a little optimism is offered. Conserving sea turtles is a big challenge, but there are numerous opportunities. We'll describe our incentives to save sea turtles, challenges met and those that lie ahead, the dedication of those working to save sea turtles, and the ways these conservationists operate. This is the part of the book that is meant to instill hope. We'd like for you to know how to feel good about your relationship with sea turtles.

PART ONE

Understanding Our Sea Turtles

Above: A green turtle carries part of the beach on her back after leaving her eggs in the sand, carefully buried and camouflaged. After she slips beneath the waves, she will be back in her element. Millions of years have shaped the traits that allow her to live a life at sea

Left: A walnut-size loggerhead sea turtle hatchling has its first big swim. The dispersal away from its natal beach begins a journey that will span many decades and tens of thousands of ocean miles

A land turtle—gopher tortoise, Gopherus polyphemus

A pond turtle—Florida red-bellied turtle, Pseudemys nelsoni

A sea turtle—green turtle, Chelonia mydas

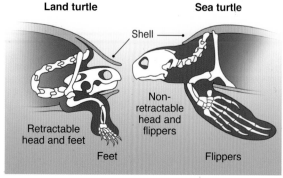

Sea turtles cannot fully retract their head or limbs

The Essence of Being a Turtle

Like us, turtles have four limbs bound by bony girdles to a column of vertebrae leading to a neck topped by a skull with movable jaws. We are vertebrate animals. Among the most notable differences seen in turtles is their unique ability to hide within their own rib cage (see pages 78–80). Their ribs are fused with broad dermal bones to form a bony carapace, which along with external platelike scales makes up a tough, armored shell that protects most of the indispensable parts of a turtle. In **land turtles** and **pond turtles**, most everything that could be chewed on by a predator can be withdrawn into the shell.

What Makes a Turtle a Sea Turtle?

Not all turtles in salty waters are **sea turtles**. In our region, the Florida softshell turtle and diamondback terrapin can be found near the sea, but these turtles don't prefer the full saltiness of seawater and lack essential adaptations for marine life. The sea turtles are truly marine animals. One of their principal adaptations is a modification of the archetypal turtle shell. A rigid box of fused bone is too confining for sea turtles, so they've evolved a more flexible shell in which carapace (upper shell) and plastron (lower shell) are joined by a bridge of supple cartilage. For a more streamlined form, sea turtles have given up the ability to pull their head and limbs inside (although they can still withdraw their neck). In comparison to their helmet-shaped relatives, sea turtles have shells that are a flattened teardrop shape, with roundness and tapering that vary between species.

A sea turtle's limbs are modified into flippers. Although they are used for a number of tasks, the principal force that has driven their form is the need for undersea flight. Like flight in air, fluid propulsion and control in water requires both power and steerage. For power, sea turtles use their front flippers, which are distinctly winglike, although narrower than a bird's wing (except the penguin's wing, which they greatly resemble). The rear flippers are shaped like broad rudders, and they are used as such; subtle rear-flipper movements are one way a swimming turtle changes course.

Land turtle Sea turtle

Shell

Non-retractable head and flippers

Retractable head and feet

Feet Flippers

Diamondback terrapins live in brackish coastal saltmarsh and protected bays from Cape Cod Bay, to the Florida Keys, to Texas. Terrapins are pond turtles (Family Emydidae) that have adapted to the estuarine environment. They have salt glands that are not as good as a sea turtle's at excreting excess salt, but terrapins do have a helpful ability to drink fresh rain water off the surface of saltier waters. They have strong jaws for eating marine snails and clams.

Diamondback terrapin, Malaclemys terrapin

Florida softshells often stray into estuarine waters from adjoining rivers. They are found in the coastal plain from South Carolina to Alabama and throughout Florida. The turtle's carapace is flexible and covered with skin rather than hard plates (scutes). The females reach 29 in (74 cm) in carapace length. Softshells eat fish, insects, crustaceans, and snails.

A Classification of Living Sea Turtles

Like other living things, sea turtles are classified within a hierarchy according to shared characteristics that best reveal their evolutionary history (their phylogeny):

Florida Softshell, Apalone ferox

KINGDOM: Animalia

The animals

PHYLUM: Chordata

Animals with a flexible rodlike "notochord" supporting the axis of their bodies, includes sea squirts, fishes, amphibians, reptiles, birds, and mammals

CLASS: Reptilia

The reptiles, animals with scaly skin and a unique skull structure. Most lay eggs

ORDER: Testudines

The turtles, animals with shells supported by fused spinal and rib bones. Turtles have no teeth

SUBORDER: Cryptodira

Turtles with "hidden-necks" that form a vertical S-shape when withdrawn

SUPERFAMILY: Chelonioidea

Sea turtles—turtles with fused digits within winglike limbs

FAMILY: Cheloniidae

Hard-shelled sea turtles—the ridley sea turtles, loggerhead sea turtle, hawksbill, flatback, and green turtle

FAMILY: Dermochelyidae

Leatherback sea turtle

Ancient Origins

Roughly 75 million years before the first humans, a proto-Atlantic was just broadening with volcanic fits and starts between a splitting Gondwana super-continent. The island India was still separated from Eurasia by a vast ocean, most of Europe was underwater, flowering plants were a novel introduction to the world, and a diverse array of dinosaurs enjoyed dominance on land. In this world of the Cretaceous Period, the Atlantic was merely a thin seaway that snaked between the Americas and Africa, and at its northern extent, a rich, shallow Niobrara Sea covered the center of North America east of the Rocky Mountains. In this sea swam *Archelon ischyros*, an immense sea turtle named with Greek roots for primitive turtle and strength.

Archelon was indeed robust, with flippers spanning almost 17 ft (5 m), a head more than 2 ft wide (0.6 m), and an estimated weight of almost 5000 pounds (2200 kg). It was a turtle more massive than many modern automobiles, and its home included the sunlit sea that once covered South Dakota. There, the enormous turtle pursued large Cretaceous cephalopods of various flavors, seizing them with its powerful curved beak. This great turtle bore the stiff winglike fore-flippers and had the smooth hydrodynamic form of our modern sea turtles, but differed enough to be categorized in a separate family. The closest archelon relative living today is the leatherback turtle, *Dermochelys coriacea.*

Archelon and the leatherback share a number of adaptive characteristics. These include an incompletely boned shell and relatively rapid growth. This latter trait is inferred from the vascular, blood-rich growing ends of their large flipper bones. Archelon probably had narrow food tastes. As such a specialist, the great turtle would have had trouble coping with the cataclysmic world changes that took place during the late Cretaceous. These changes extinguished the once wildly successful dinosaurs, many other large vertebrates, and every other marine reptile at the time except the forebears of our present-day sea turtles and one marine crocodile.

An archelon eating an inking belemnite (an extinct squidlike cephalopod) in a world we would barely recognize as our own

A Sea Turtle Family Tree

Sea turtle origins lie deep. Turtles have persisted with their distinctive shelled form since the Triassic Period, 210 million years before present. Marine-adapted turtles would not appear for another 10–50 million years or so, during the Jurassic Period, when members of two distinct turtle families (Plesiochelyidae and Thalassemyidae) began to live in the shallow seas covering Europe. These earliest sea turtles had only partially modified limbs for stroking in shallow waters. They were not the forebears of the sea turtles we know today, and disappeared long before our most recent

ocean-living turtles appeared in the Cretaceous. The Cretaceous was the heyday for sea turtles, and all the species we know today have their roots in this period. Between 110 and 65 million years ago there were dozens of species among four (or by some opinions, three) families: Toxochelyidae, Protostegidae (the family of Archelon and other large turtles), Dermochelyidae, (relatives of the leatherback), and Cheloniidae (relatives of our modern hard-shelled sea turtles). These turtles lived in diverse marine environments, from shallow coastal waters to the deep sea.

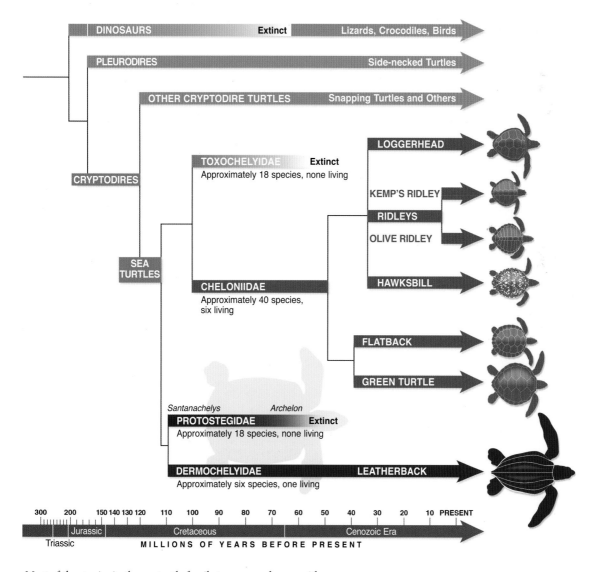

Most of the species in the sea turtle family tree are no longer with us

5

Basic Sea Turtle Parts

Before we start describing differences between the types of sea turtles and how they each make a living in their world, we thought it would be good to cover some of their basic parts. The diagrams below show a green turtle, which is nicely representative of the hard-shelled sea turtles.

Dorsal (Top) Anatomy

A sea turtle's mouth has a beak. The upper shell is called a carapace and is covered with large scales known as scutes. The turtle's limbs are known as flippers.

Carapace
(upper shell)

Beak

Flipper scales

Tail

Front flipper

Carapace
scute

Rear flipper

← Anterior

Posterior →

Ventral (Bottom) Anatomy

The lower shell of a sea turtle is called a plastron. Like the upper shell, it is plated with scutes. The turtle's head and flippers are covered with scales, but the rest of the turtle's skin is soft, with few scales.

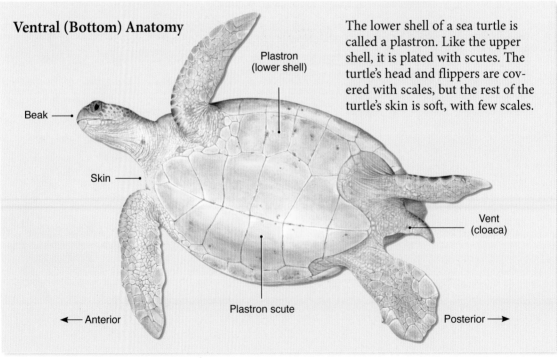

Plastron
(lower shell)

Beak

Skin

Vent
(cloaca)

Plastron scute

← Anterior

Posterior →

The Species

A typical immature loggerhead sea turtle (Caretta caretta)

An immature hawksbill turtle (Eretmochelys imbricata)

Loggerhead-hawksbill hybrid with a loggerhead-like carapace

Loggerhead-hawksbill hybrid with a hawksbill-like carapace

What is a Species?

In biology, the species is a fundamental category of classification within a system that describes relatedness. In this system (called taxonomy), the rank of species is categorized below the rank known as genus. The species unit is fundamental because it is the lowest category containing all the individuals capable of interbreeding and producing fertile offspring. But it's not always that simple.

How Many Sea Turtle Species?

Worldwide, there are seven, although some believe there are more. It is a debate that reaffirms the evolving nature of science. One controversial species is the black turtle (east Pacific green turtle), *Chelonia agassizii* (or just a unique population of *Chelonia mydas*), which does not occur within the range of this book. In our region, we have five sea turtle species commonly found, and an additional rare visitor. We introduce them to you within the pages that follow.

Sea Turtle Hybrids

Sea turtles occasionally break the species rules. They hybridize. Reports describe wild turtles that are offspring of green turtles and loggerheads, green turtles and hawksbills, loggerheads and hawksbills, and loggerheads and Kemp's ridleys. And in some instances, these hybrids reproduce. Weird, huh?

Depending on the pairing, these hybrid offspring had mothers and fathers whose lineages have been separated for ages, equivalent to the time span separating dogs and cats. Sea turtles may be distinguished among the vertebrates in having the most distantly related lineages capable of producing fertile hybrids in nature.

Hybrid sea turtles from the same two species don't necessarily look the same. In the images to the left, compare the head and carapace appearance of a typical loggerhead and hawksbill to two different-looking hybrids. In one hybrid, carapace shape and head coloration says hawksbill. In the other, carapace shape indicates a hawksbill influence, and a reddish color reveals loggerhead genes.

Sea Turtle Genetics

Sea turtles are faithful, with a loyalty to place that spans generations. Little turtles learn to recognize the beach where they hatched, and decades later they return to nest there with other members of their clan. This persistence of natal memory is key to understanding the patterns of relatedness within sea turtle populations. The practical science behind this understanding is conservation genetics—the study of diversity within a species so that variety can be conserved. Variety in a population is explained by family histories, which are revealed by DNA. This genetic material can be amplified from a small sample of blood or skin and examined for the information it contains—its combinations of base pairs. Special DNA a daughter receives only from her mother (mitochondrial DNA) traces patterns of inheritance at nesting beaches. Females nesting on the same beach are more closely related to each other than they are to turtles nesting farther away. This confirms the idea of natal beach faithfulness, and it allows us to describe the natal origins of turtle groups at sea.

This loggerhead's blood sample will provide its DNA identity

DNA identification reveals how turtles are related

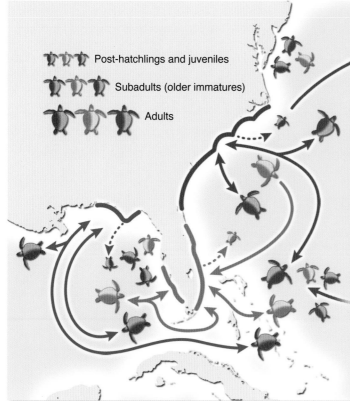

Post-hatchlings and juveniles

Subadults (older immatures)

Adults

A Loggerhead Family Reunion

Loggerheads don't have the social units of family, but they do often associate with their kin at "home." Like other sea turtles, loggerheads show natal homing (natal philopatry), or the faithful return of nesting females to the home stretch of beach where they hatched. Yet in the decades between hatching and nesting, loggerheads mix it up with a variety of family groups. In this diagram, three colors represent three separate genetic stocks (subpopulations). Any given foraging area may contain multiple stocks. In conservation, these stocks are often termed "recovery" or "management" units.

The Green Turtle

Scientific Name: *Chelonia mydas*

The name comes from the Greek word for "turtle" (chelone) and the modifier "wet" (mydos)—a wet turtle

Other Common Names

English: green sea turtle, greenback turtle, soup turtle, edible turtle
Spanish: tortuga verde, tortuga blanca
Haitian Creole: vèt tòti

Size and Weight

Most adult female green turtles have a shell straight-length of 31–47 in (90–110 cm) and weigh 265–485 lbs (120–220 kg). Adult males are slightly smaller than females.

Distribution

Green turtles occur worldwide in tropical and warm temperate marine waters. Nesting occurs on beaches mostly in the tropics and subtropics.

Summer foraging range in our region extends throughout the Gulf of Mexico and along the Atlantic coast north to Cape Cod, Massachusetts.

Diet

Except for the smallest juveniles, these turtles eat seagrasses and algae.

Above: An adult female green turtle returns from nesting on a central Florida Atlantic beach

Left: An immature green turtle from the Florida Keys glides over seagrass

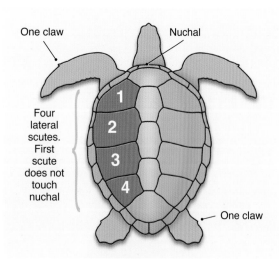

One claw

Nuchal

Four lateral scutes. First scute does not touch nuchal

1
2
3
4

One claw

Dorsal view showing carapace

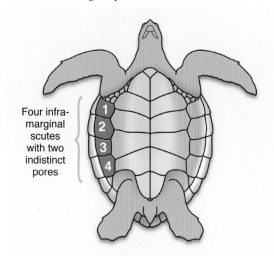

Four infra-marginal scutes with two indistinct pores

1
2
3
4

Ventral view showing plastron

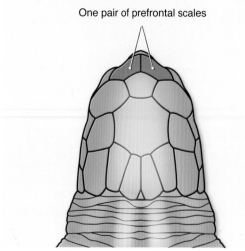

One pair of prefrontal scales

Head showing prefrontal scales

Appearance

Green turtles are sleek, powerful swimmers and grow to the largest size of the hard-shelled sea turtles. Although their name suggests otherwise, green turtles are mostly brown. Their common name comes from a description of their appearance on the inside. The turtle's fatty tissues have a greenish hue. The name is testament to how green turtles first came to be known, namely, as food.

On the outside, green turtles are lovely animals. Their teardrop-shaped shells are often unfouled by barnacles or other clinging creatures, which allows the coloration of their patterned carapace to be clearly visible. The carapace is smooth, with scutes that do not overlap. In most green turtles, the scales crowning the head and on the upper surfaces of the flippers match the colors of the carapace. Areas of skin between the scales (the seams) are lighter than the scales themselves. These bright olive or yellow scale "outlines" may be lighter than the skin covering the shoulders and neck, which has sparsely scattered, small, smooth scales. All green turtles have a blunt head and a rounded leading edge to their beak. Their lower jaw sheath is coarsely serrated and has a sharp cusp at its tip. The upper beak is more weakly serrated. Together, the cutting edges of the jaws make an efficient set of seagrass clippers.

Scute Diagnostics

A unique combination of scute and scale counts set green turtles apart from our other sea turtle species. Green turtles have four **lateral** (also called costal) scutes on either side of the midline of their carapace. Four **inframarginal scutes**, without conspicuous pores, line the sides (bridges) of their plastron. Their head scales are also distinctive in that there are only two elongate **prefrontal scales** between the turtle's eyes. Green turtles have a single **claw** protruding from the leading edge of each flipper.

Life Stages

Green turtles change in appearance as they grow to adulthood.

Hatchlings

Hatchlings are dark blue-gray on their upper surface and pure white below. Carapace and flippers are thinly rimmed with white.

Juveniles

The carapace develops earth-toned sunburst patterns within each scute. Open-sea juveniles are darker above and immaculate white below.

Coastal juveniles are lighter above and butter yellow underneath.

Subadults

Older immature turtles may lighten in skin color as they begin to forage in slightly deeper waters away from bright sunlight.

Adults

Carapace and upper portions have a brown or olive background blotched with lighter patches and spattered with dark brown or black.

Hatchling
1 oz (25 g)

Open-sea juvenile
1–3 years old,
2–35 oz (1000 g)

Coastal juvenile
3–10 years old,
2–55 lb (1–25 kg)

Subadult 10–30 years old,
55–200 lb (25–91 kg)

Adults reach 70+ years old,
average 310 lb (140 kg)

Distribution and Movements

Green turtles swim in all of the world's warm-water oceans and are most common in waters not far from the tropics. Their principal nesting beaches are also at warmer latitudes. Most green turtle nesting within our region is in southern Mexico, southern Cuba, and southeastern Florida. Juvenile green turtles in our region may have hatched on regional beaches, but also may have come from the densely nested beaches of Caribbean Costa Rica. Hatchlings departing our beaches grow up in coastal waters primarily off Florida, Texas, Bermuda, Cuba, The Bahamas, and Mexico.

Worldwide Nesting Beaches

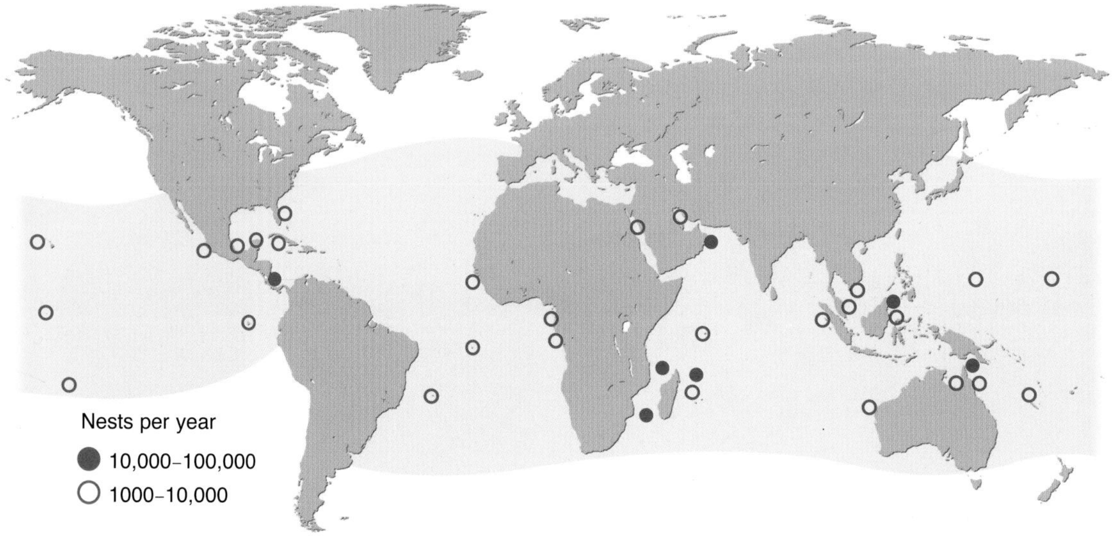

Nests per year
10,000–100,000
1000–10,000

Regional Distribution

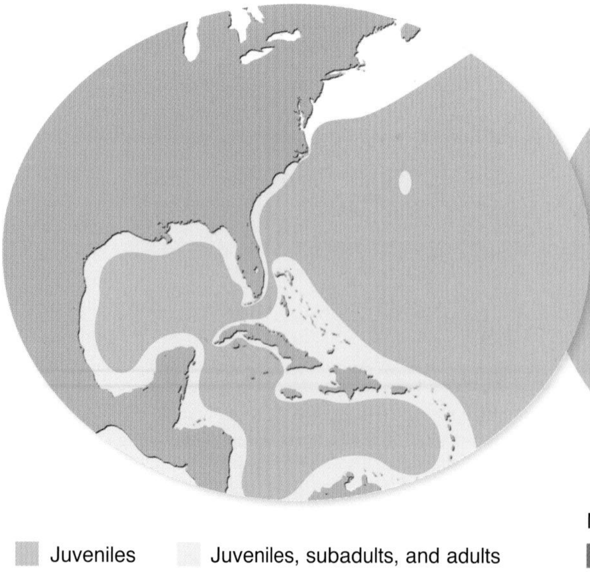

Juveniles
Juveniles, subadults, and adults

Young juveniles are in the open sea. Older juveniles inhabit shallow coastal waters. Subadults and adults move to deeper coastal waters

Regional Nesting Beaches

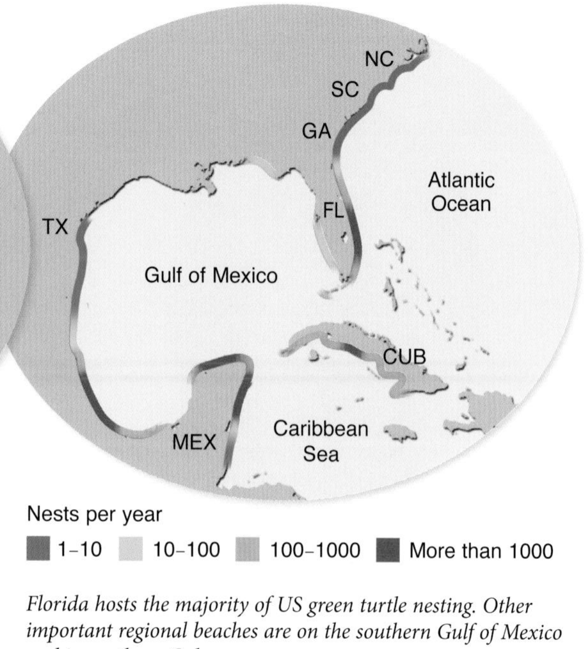

NC
SC
GA
FL
TX
Atlantic Ocean
Gulf of Mexico
CUB
MEX
Caribbean Sea
Nests per year
1–10
10–100
100–1000
More than 1000

Florida hosts the majority of US green turtle nesting. Other important regional beaches are on the southern Gulf of Mexico and in southern Cuba

Life History

A green turtle may travel thousands of miles through many different habitats during the two to four decades required to reach adulthood. Habitats they require include sand beaches; oceanic surface fronts and pelagic sargassum; and shallow coastal waters with seagrass pastures, nearshore reefs, and drift algae. Older green turtles occupy more tropical and slightly deeper coastal foraging areas. Adults migrate between foraging areas and their nesting beaches.

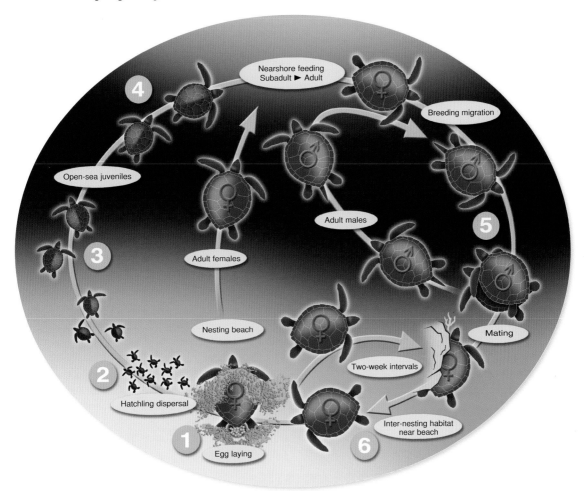

1. Nests average 135 eggs, which incubate under sand for 50–60 days. Warm sands (86° F, >30° C) produce mostly female turtles and cooler sands (82° F, <28° C) result in mostly males.

2. A few days after they hatch, the hatchlings emerge together from the nest at night, scramble to the surf, swim out to sea, and are dispersed by ocean currents.

3. Juveniles live near the surface of deep ocean waters and are carried widely by currents.

4. At about three to five years of age, juveniles swim into nearshore waters and inhabit reefs and seagrass pastures. Subadults nearing maturity move into slightly deeper and more tropical waters.

5. Adults mate along migration routes between foraging and nesting areas and immediately off the nesting beach.

6. About every two years, adult females migrate to the beach where they hatched and make about four nests at two-week intervals.

Maturity and Reproduction

Based on growth rates of wild turtles from Florida and The Bahamas, green turtles reach reproductive size in 20 to 40 years. In addition to maturing at different ages, green turtles also mature at different sizes. Juveniles that grow fast mature quickly and are larger at adulthood. After an unknown pubescent period, adult females migrate from their foraging grounds to the nesting beaches where they hatched. Males mate with females along migration routes or near the beach and depart early in the nesting season. During the nesting season, females deposit about four egg-clutches separated by two-week intervals. Eggs are laid within nests the female covers with sand.

Green turtle nests produce hatchlings well into the fall months

Courtship and Mating

Most males migrate each season to waters off nesting beaches. Courtship begins a few weeks before females nest and continues during the initial nesting season. A male will initiate courtship by nuzzling and nibbling, mount a receptive female, and remain attached to guard against interlopers (see pages 98, 110). Females intercepted in the surf are sometimes pushed onto the beach with males attached. Despite this paternity insurance, egg clutches often have two to three fathers. Males are likely to mate with several females.

Where Green Turtles Nest

Female green turtles prefer steeply sloped beaches with prominent vegetated dunes. Highest density areas are away from human development, lights, and inlets. Green turtles typically nest high on the beach close to the toe of the dune. Peak nesting areas in Florida are south Brevard through Broward Counties.

The Nesting and Hatching Season

Green turtles come ashore to nest at night, with peak activity around midnight. First nests of the season are in late May and the latest nests are in October. During the warmest months, nests incubate for about 55 days before producing hatchlings. Late-season nests incubating in cooler sands have incubation periods that may be over 70 days.

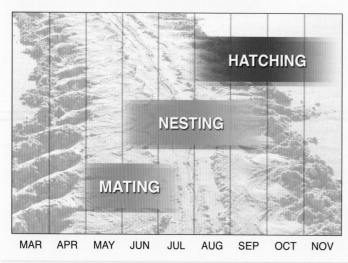

HATCHING

NESTING

MATING

MAR   APR   MAY   JUN   JUL   AUG   SEP   OCT   NOV

Fast Facts

- Most females migrate to nesting beaches every other year

- Mating takes place along migratory corridors and near the beach

- Females make an average of four nests separated by two-week intervals

- Nests contain an average of 135 eggs

- Hatchlings typically emerge in 50–60 days

It's all about the eggs. As adults, green turtles grow very slowly, putting nearly all of the energy not required for survival into reproduction. It takes a lot. A green turtle ready to breed will depart her foraging grounds and swim hundreds of miles to the waters off her nesting beach. There, she will mate with one or more males and ovulate her first clutch of eggs for the season. When the eggs are fertilized and have their shells, the female will crawl up the beach to the base of the dune, blast out a body pit with all four flippers, dig a chamber for her eggs, deposit her clutch, bury it, and spend the remainder of the two-hour nesting process throwing sand over her clutch. She will move about a ton of beach sand before she is finished.

After the green turtle leaves the beach, she will have about two weeks to prepare for the next nesting. By the end of her season, she will have nested as many as seven times (average about four). At an average of 135 eggs per clutch, a typical nest contains 15 pounds (6.8 kg) of eggs. With as many as seven installments, this reproductive burden adds production of over 100 pounds of eggs to the energy spent excavating sand on the beach, and to the hundreds of miles traveled since she last ate. Yes, for the two to three months required for her nesting season, our female does not feed. It's no wonder that females will typically take at lease one year off between reproductive seasons.

The biennial cycle of breeding (two-year remigration interval) in green turtles from our region sets up distinct high and low nesting seasons. Although it is not known how the turtles conspire, two consecutive years will often have green turtle nest counts that differ by a factor of five to ten.

A female green turtle throws sand to camouflage her nest on a Florida beach

A pelagic juvenile green turtle caught feeding on blue buttons

Coastal juvenile green turtles graze on turtle grass

Diet

For most of their lives, green turtles are facultative herbivores. This means that they eat plants, but they are not likely to pass up easily captured animal prey. The youngest green turtles eat mostly animal material, and make a profound shift in diet along with an equally abrupt change in the habitats they forage in.

Post-hatchlings and Pelagic Juveniles

Green turtle hatchlings swimming away from their natal beach are fueled by the residual energy in their internal yolk sac. But at the end of their frenzied swimming offshore, a little turtle must eat. Food available at the surface of the wide-open sea is largely restricted to oceanic fronts where currents press together floating stuff, including denizens of the pelagic sargassum community. Within this habitat, post-hatchling and juvenile green turtles opportunistically munch on a wide variety of small, slow-moving animal prey. These include tiny **hydroids**, crustaceans, bryozoans (moss animals), and **jelly animals** common within the floating patches of golden sargasso weed adrift on Gulf and Atlantic currents. Many preferred prey are wind-dispersed drifters with whimsical names like **blue buttons** (*Porpita*), by-the-wind sailors (*Velella*), and purple sea snails (*Janthina*). Small turtles also favor **dead insects** that accumulate in these concentrations of floating material.

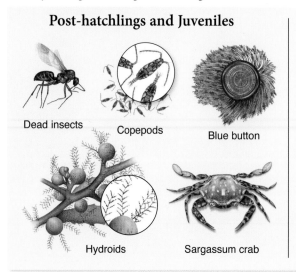

Post-hatchlings and Juveniles

Dead insects

Copepods

Blue button

Hydroids

Sargassum crab

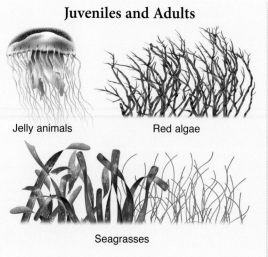

Juveniles and Adults

Jelly animals

Red algae

Seagrasses

Coastal (Neritic) Juveniles

When juvenile green turtles depart the open sea and settle into coastal waters, they take up a largely vegetarian diet. As herbivores, green turtles feed on a variety of **algal** and **seagrass** species. The rich community of microbes that the turtles maintain in their gut aids digestion of this plant material. Just like animals that graze on land, green turtles cannot break down plant cellulose by themselves, and without the tiny symbiotic organisms living within them, they would starve. The bacterial and protozoan gut flora of green turtles is thought to be specific to the cellulose of particular plant groups. Because of this, individual green turtles typically specialize on only algae or on only seagrasses. Although they seldom mix their salads, green turtles are happy to accept an occasional jellyfish treat along with other opportunities for animal protein.

Subadults and Adults

As green turtles approach adulthood, they leave the shallow foraging pastures they occupied as juveniles and arrive at more southerly pastures in slightly deeper waters. This marks a habitat shift from bays, sounds, lagoons, and nearshore reefs in both tropical and temperate climates, to seagrass pastures in tropical and subtropical waters. For adult green turtles that nest in our region, these foraging grounds are the expansive turtle grass *(Thalassia)* pastures of the Florida Keys, The Bahamas, Cuba, and the northern Caribbean Sea.

Coastal green turtles in the wild consume small invertebrates only occasionally. But when given the opportunity to eat animal protein in captivity, green turtles can survive for years on nothing else. These captive turtles grow quickly but can become pathologically obese.

A juvenile green turtle grazes on red algae growing on a nearshore reef off eastern Florida

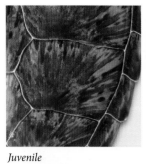

Juvenile

Juvenile

Juvenile

Juvenile

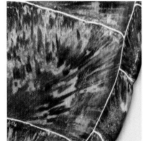

Subadult

Subadult

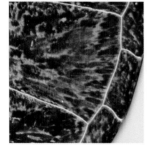

Subadult

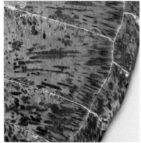

Adult

Adult

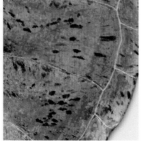

Adult

Unique Traits

Among the sea turtles, the green turtle is the largest of those with hard shells, it is the only herbivore, and it has endured the most extensive commercial and subsistence harvest for food. Some additional characteristics that make the species unique include the green turtle's variety in coloration and its underwater athleticism.

Color Variation

Green turtles display intriguing variation in their carapace color patterns. Juveniles are vibrant with streaks of brown, olive, gold, black, or reddish brown, which radiate as sunbursts from the rear margin of each scute or blur into a noisy scatter of color. Adults are less vivid but almost as variable, with a brown or olive background spattered with dark brown or black. Variation in this pattern includes mottling of brown, yellow, olive, and gray throughout nebulous background color.

The green turtle may be the world's fastest turtle

A Turtle Fleet of Flipper

For a turtle, green turtles are really fast. A juvenile or subadult green turtle can swim for short stretches at more than 13 miles per hour (21 kph) when in a rush to outrun a predator. This translates to a little over ten body lengths per second for a typical young green turtle. By comparison, Olympic gold-medalist swimmer Michael Phelps can't quite reach 5 mph (8 kph) in his shortest race, which for him is about one body length per second.

Conservation Status

The green turtle is listed under the US Endangered Species Act as Threatened. Until recently, the Florida nesting population was separately listed as Endangered. The species is also officially protected from harvest in Mexico, Cuba, Bermuda, and The Bahamas. Regional countries are signatories to the Convention on International Trade in Endangered Species of Wild Fauna and Flora (CITES), an international treaty that lists the green turtle as protected from commercial trade. The International Union for Conservation of Nature (IUCN) has the species on its Red List as Endangered.

Green turtles are believed to have been one of the most common large animals on the planet. Millions of green turtles once grazed the seagrass pastures of the wider Caribbean. Today, they are much rarer following extensive declines. Green turtles have been eaten by people for thousands of years, but we can be relatively sure that the last few hundred years have taken the greatest toll. Over this period, human population growth, technological advancement, and commercial harvest of green turtles have increased the species' risk of extinction.

Nesting Trends

Lately, things are looking up for our green turtles. **Nest counts** over the last 25 years on Florida beaches show that green turtle nesting has increased exponentially. Although the long-term trend is up, the **annual variation** in green turtle nesting is extreme. Nest counts in consecutive high and low years can vary by a factor of ten. This noisy scatter of annual nest counts is due to variation in the proportion of total females that have decided to nest in a given year. A two-year cycle often repeats, but in recent years, green turtle nesting has skipped a beat in some years, surprising biologists who thought they had figured out the pattern. Despite the messiness of nesting data, the upward trend is certain to represent an increase in female members of the whole population. The trend reveals an unprecedented conservation success story.

Our green turtles have shown recent increases

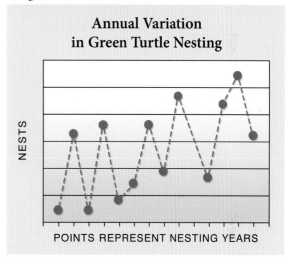
Typical biennial nesting variation with some recent beat-skips

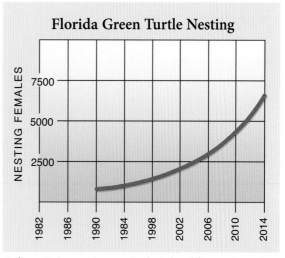
A dramatic increase in green turtles inferred from nest counts

21

The Loggerhead Sea Turtle

Scientific Name: *Caretta caretta*

Caretta is a New Latin modification of the French "caret" for turtle.

Other Common Names

English: loggerhead, logrit (Caribbean)
Spanish: caguama, cabezón
French: caouanne

Size and Weight

Most adult female loggerheads have a shell straight-length of 31–43 in (80–110 cm) and weigh 150–375 lbs (70–170 kg). Weight varies greatly with body condition. Adult males weigh less than females.

Distribution

Temperate marine waters and into the tropics, but only occasionally within 8° latitude of the equator. Most nesting is on warm temperate beaches or on those just inside the tropics. Summer foraging range in our region extends throughout the Gulf of Mexico and along the Atlantic coast north to Cape Cod, Massachusetts.

Diet

Larger turtles eat jellies, sponges, and hard-shelled invertebrates.

Above: An adult loggerhead surfaces to breathe. The turtle's strong jaws allow it to crush hard-shelled prey

Left: At home on a patch of south Florida reef, a subadult loggerhead moves amongst soft corals and sponges

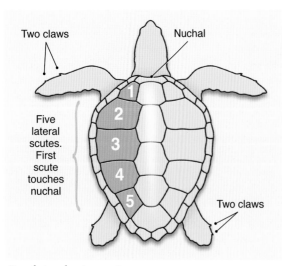

Two claws

Nuchal

Five lateral scutes. First scute touches nuchal

1
2
3
4
5

Two claws

Dorsal view showing carapace

Three infra-marginal scutes without pores

1
2
3

Ventral view showing plastron

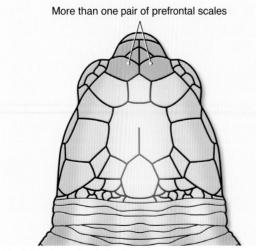

More than one pair of prefrontal scales

Head showing prefrontal scales

Appearance

Older loggerheads give the appearance of a toughened, worn, brute of a turtle. Adults are typically scarred, notched, and bedecked with barnacles, which presents a figurative and literal roughness around the edges. Yet many would argue that loggerheads have a noble beauty all their own.

Although shell coloration is often partially obscured by a carpet of macroalgae, large barnacles, and a host of clinging tagalongs, the exposed carapace is a dark reddish brown with a faint radiating pattern of orange, red, brown, and black smears within each shell scute. These scutes are often fragmented and peeling where old layers of keratin flake away as new scutes grow underneath. At whatever rate a loggerhead is able to shed its acquired load of commensal organisms by losing shell scutes, it is not frequent enough to keep many loggerheads from looking much like the sea bottom they rest on.

The loggerhead's massive head is its namesake, having a width often substantially larger than our own. A loggerhead's upper jaw sheath is highly thickened, with a curved leading edge and a blunt cusp. The lower jaw is sheathed in equally thick keratin and has a broad crushing surface at its cusped end. Bulging jowls betray a robust bony framework and strong muscles capable of pulverizing hard mollusk shells.

Scute Diagnostics

Loggerheads are distinguished from other sea turtles by having five **lateral (costal) scutes** on either side of their carapace midline, three **inframarginal scutes**, and on the head, two pairs of **prefrontal scales** between the eyes. These prefrontal scales often have one or two intervening scales for a total of four to six. Loggerheads have two **claws** on the leading edge of the front and rear flippers. One claw is conspicuous and the other is typically flush with the flipper scales.

Life Stages

A loggerhead's features and proportions change as it matures into an adult.

Hatchlings

Variable from pale brown or gray to dark brown or charcoal. Most are light below and dark above, but some are uniformly pigmented. The carapace is lumpy with raised scutes.

Juveniles

Turtles develop an amber skin and plastron, orange flipper scales, and orange-mahogany cara- pace scutes. Sharply keeled scutes line the upper and lower shell. Carapace margins are serrated.

Subadults

Keeled scutes are lost and the carapace darkens to a deep mahogany. Growth lines and partial shedding are seen in carapace scutes. Large bar- nacles and other growth may cover the shell.

Adults

Similar to subadults but without signs of carapace growth. The rear shell notch is less pronounced.

Hatchling
0.7 oz (20 g)

Post-hatchling
1–12 weeks old,
1 lb (450 g)

Juvenile
3 months to 10 years old,
1–55 lb (0.5–25 kg)

Subadult 10–30 years old,
55–200 lb (25–91 kg)

Adults reach 65+ years old,
average 260 lb (120 kg)

Distribution and Movements

Loggerheads are most common in temperate waters just outside the tropics. As an exception to this rule, loggerheads in the northern Indian Ocean nest and forage mostly within tropical waters. The majority of the world's loggerheads nest in only two places—the southeastern US and northeastern Oman. In our region, sizes of coastal foraging loggerheads increase from north to south. Adults are mostly in southern and offshore waters. Our coastal loggerheads in northern waters move south or offshore in winter.

Worldwide Nesting Beaches

Nests per year

● 10,000–100,000

○ 1000–10,000

Regional Distribution

Regional Nesting Beaches

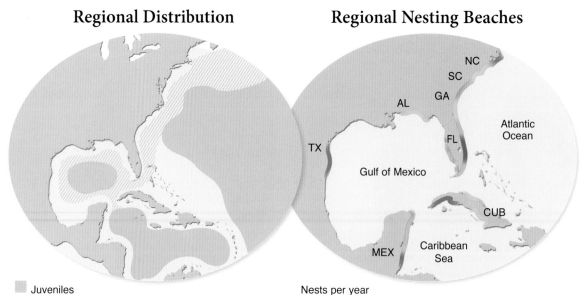

Juveniles

Juveniles and Adults   Subadults and Adults

Young juveniles live on the open sea. Subadults and adults inhabit coastal waters, but may forage offshore extensively, especially in winter

Nests per year

■ 1–100   100–1000   1000–10,000

■ More than 10,000

Florida hosts about 90% of the loggerhead nesting in the western north Atlantic

Life History

During its first ten years, a young loggerhead may circle the entire north Atlantic, perhaps more than once. After this life on the open sea, older juveniles move into coastal waters where they forage on seagrass pastures, channels, and rocky reefs. Many loggerheads move south as they mature, and at age 30 or so, they begin to make periodic breeding migrations between foraging grounds and nesting beaches. Some subadults and adults forage in offshore waters and on deep reefs.

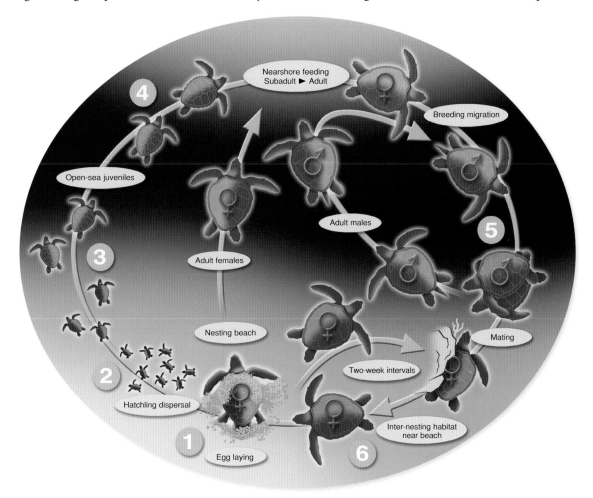

1. Nests average 115 eggs and incubate under the sand for 50–60 days. Warm sands (86° F, >30° C) produce mostly female turtles and cooler sands (82° F, <28° C) result in mostly males.

2. A few days after they hatch, the hatchlings emerge together from the nest at night, scramble to the surf, swim out to sea, and are dispersed by ocean currents.

3. Juveniles live near the surface of deep ocean waters and are carried by ocean-spanning currents.

4. At subadult size, turtles swim into nearshore waters and inhabit hardbottom reefs, lagoons, and bays. Most subadults nearing maturity move into warmer subtropical waters, out to deep reefs, or into offshore waters.

5. Adults mate predominantly along migration routes between foraging and nesting areas.

6. Every two to four years, adult females migrate to the beach close to where they hatched and make about three to six nests at two-week intervals.

Maturity and Reproduction

Judging by rates at which loggerheads grow, adult size is reached in roughly 30 years. As in most other sea turtles, loggerheads virtually stop growing in shell length when they reach adulthood. Following a pubescent period that may take years, a female makes her first nesting migration. Males intercept females to mate along migration pathways and are seldom seen near the nesting beach. Most females choose beaches close to where they hatched. During the nesting season, females deposit an average of five egg-clutches within sandy nests made at two-week intervals.

Courtship and Mating

Most adult male loggerheads breed every season. In our region, mating pairs of loggerheads are

Loggerhead hatching follows nesting by about two months

commonly seen in the spring near the edge of the Gulf Stream (Florida Current) off southeastern Florida. A male clinging to the back of a female often endures bites from rival males. This mate guarding may be effective; most loggerhead clutches have only one father, although some have two or more fathers.

Where Loggerheads Nest

Nesting loggerheads seem to prefer steeply sloped beaches with coarse sands and prominent vegetated dunes. The areas of highest nesting density are away from human development, lights, and inlets. Most loggerhead nests are on the open beach between the highest recent tide line and the toe of the dune. Peak nesting areas are in Florida between Cape Canaveral and Fort Lauderdale, although there is good nesting in southwestern Florida and near Cape Romain, South Carolina.

The Nesting and Hatching Season

Nesting is at night, with peak activity around midnight. The first nests of the season are typically in late April in south Florida and in early May for the more northern beaches. The last nests are in early September. Hatchlings emerge from nests late June into November. The incubation period for warm nests may be as short as 45 days. Cool, late-season nests may require more than 70 days to produce hatchlings.

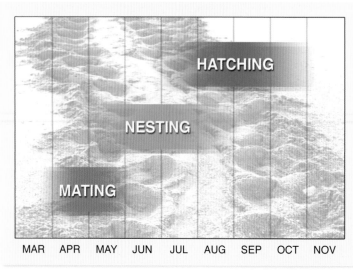

HATCHING

NESTING

MATING

MAR APR MAY JUN JUL AUG SEP OCT NOV

Fast Facts

- Females migrate to nesting beaches every two to four years

- Mating takes place along migration routes

- Average females make five nests separated by two-week intervals

- Nests contain an average of 115 eggs

- Hatchlings typically emerge in 50–60 days

A loggerhead's reproductive effort begins years before she nests. That is the time required to gain sufficient weight on the foraging grounds so that a season's worth of eggs can be produced. Females that are not nutritionally ready for reproduction will forgo breeding and wait for fatter times. Sensing readiness, a female will migrate hundreds of miles to arrive at her nesting beach, encountering her mate (or mates) along the way. During her nesting season, an average loggerhead will lay 575 eggs, an expenditure weighing more than 53 pounds (24 kg), which is about 21% of her total weight. During all this, she does not eat.

Each of the five or more nests made by a female loggerhead requires a two-week period during which yolked follicles are ovulated, fertilized with stored sperm, coated with albumen, and wrapped in eggshell. With her clutch of eggs ready to lay, a loggerhead will move into the surf zone and make her nesting attempt as nightfall arrives. An average loggerhead will abandon one nesting attempt above the recent tide line before successfully depositing her clutch in a nest. Success means crawling to a sufficiently elevated beach site, moving the top sand layer away, digging a hole, laying eggs in it, burying them, and disguising the site by scattering sand on top of it. After five or more nesting episodes, a loggerhead will migrate back to her foraging grounds. An average female will take part in nesting every 2.7 years. During lean times on foraging grounds, this remigration interval is lengthened. Some years with low numbers of nests are partly due to such privations.

A nesting loggerhead sea turtle camouflages the location of her egg clutch by throwing sand behind her

Portuguese man-o-war—a spicy loggerhead snack

The sargassum swimming crab, carapace width to 2 in (5 cm)

Diet

Loggerheads are generalist carnivores that have a talent for cracking hard-shelled prey. But they are more than willing to munch on a variety of squishy animals as well.

Post-hatchlings

After a day or more of frenzied offshore swimming and a day or two of slower oriented stroking, a hatchling loggerhead takes its first bite of food and graduates to the post-hatchling stage. At this point, the turtle has exhausted the yolk it retained from the egg and is in deep water dozens of miles from land. A loggerhead's early tastes are not discriminating. Its meals are likely to include any of hundreds of small items floating within open-sea lines where surface waters converge. The most prominent items are animals of the pelagic sargassum community, such as **hydroids**, **copepods**, bryozoans tube worms, and tiny crustaceans. Also common are wind-dispersed drifters like **blue buttons, by-the-wind sailors**, purple sea snails, and **blue glaucus** sea slugs. Other drift foods include **dead insects**.

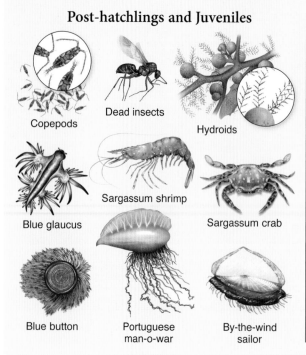

Post-hatchlings and Juveniles

Copepods

Dead insects

Hydroids

Blue glaucus

Sargassum shrimp

Sargassum crab

Blue button

Portuguese man-o-war

By-the-wind sailor

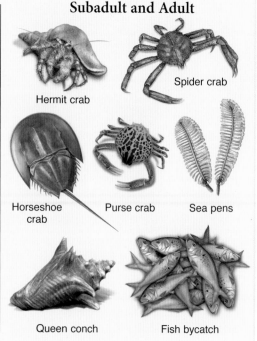

Subadult and Adult

Hermit crab

Spider crab

Horseshoe crab

Purse crab

Sea pens

Queen conch

Fish bycatch

Pelagic (Oceanic) Juveniles

As a loggerhead drifts far from its natal beach, it is no longer considered a post-hatchling. The turtle becomes a juvenile. At this stage, a logger-head is better able to dive for prey below surface waters and sargassum patches. In addition to larger surface animals like **Portuguese man-o-war** *(Physalia)*, floating sea snails, and gooseneck barnacles, juveniles make occasional deep dives to feed on jellyfish and salps (translucent, free-swimming sea squirts).

Coastal (Neritic) Subadults and Adults

After about a decade on the open sea and growth to a little over fifty pounds, loggerheads in our region swim into western Atlantic coastal waters. They are only about one-third of their way to maturity, but they have reached a size allowing them to feed on large bottom-dwelling animals. This sea-food varies across habitats, but general menu items include large invertebrate animals, most of which live closely associated with the sea bottom.

Favorite foods of coastal loggerheads include tough-shelled crunchy animals like **horseshoe crabs**, nonswimming crabs, marine snails, bivalve mollusks, and **sea pens** (plumelike colonies of coral-related animals). Loggerheads also enjoy softer foods like jellyfish, sea squirts, sea cucumbers, and anemones. To catch their food, logger-heads muscle through obstacles between them and their prey. This often means consuming the sponge and coral concealing a cowering crab, or flipper-plowing through bottom sediment to get at burrowing bivalves, a behavior called infaunal mining. Where available, loggerheads will eat (scavenge) fish. Most often, these are fish origi-nally caught in trawls or gill nets that were dumped overboard as **bycatch**. Large numbers of fish are discarded this way, so their appearance in the diet of sea turtles is not surprising. Unfortu-nately, the lure of a fish dinner may draw turtles into fishing areas where they are more likely to be captured and drowned themselves as bycatch.

A sharksucker rides beneath a subadult loggerhead cruising for food on a deep reef off eastern Florida

This post-hatchling, weeks old, is beginning to acquire tagalongs

Turtle barnacles, Chelonibia testudinaria, *a common commensal*

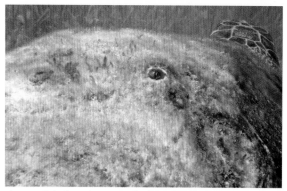

A coat of algal species covers this loggerhead's back

Many loggerheads look a lot like the sea bottom they rest on

Unique Traits

Loggerheads have extraordinarily strong jaws that provide an ability to eat armored prey, and they have an equally notable competency in defending themselves with the same equipment. But despite their capability for toughness, loggerheads are mild-mannered animals. There may be no better example of their harmonious existence than the living community loggerheads carry with them.

Commensals

Loggerheads collect commensals. These are the tagalong animals and plants that benefit from living on a turtle but have little effect upon their host. Loggerheads are exceptional for their diversity and tolerance of clinging commensal creatures: **barnacles** of several species, long tufts of colonial hydroids, amphipods that cling and lash out at tiny prey, shelled mollusks of all types, marine worms, small to hand-size crabs, sea urchins, many species of **macroalgae**, and even stony corals.

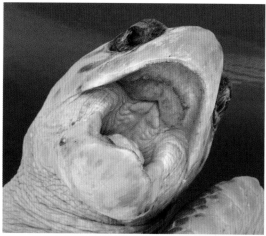

A prey-crunching capability is also helpful for defense

Powerful Jaws

An adult loggerhead can bite with the force of nearly 500 pounds (>2100 newtons). The turtles are known to advertise this to attacking sharks by presenting an open mouth. Because they are less swift than other sea turtles, turning to fight is an important option for discouraging would-be predators.

32

Conservation Status

The loggerhead sea turtle is listed under the US Endangered Species Act with a separate status for each of nine distinct population segments (DPSs). The DPS in our region, the Northwest Atlantic Ocean DPS, is considered Threatened. Loggerheads are considered Endangered within the Northeast Atlantic, Mediterranean Sea, North Indian Ocean, and Pacific Ocean, and are considered Threatened elsewhere. The species is officially protected from harvest in Mexico, Cuba, Bermuda, and The Bahamas. Regional countries are signatories to the Convention on International Trade in Endangered Species of Wild Fauna and Flora (CITES), which lists the loggerhead as protected from commercial trade. The International Union for Conservation of Nature (IUCN) currently has the species on its Red List as Endangered. Although the loggerhead is the most common sea turtle in our region, in other areas of the world the turtle is rare, and many smaller populations are in perilous decline.

Nesting Trends

Loggerheads share nesting beaches with green turtles, a species that has shown impressive increases in nest counts (see page 21). But loggerheads have not shown any definitive recovery in numbers. Only time will tell if the recent rise in **loggerhead nest counts** will persist.

In general, loggerheads have not suffered from the intense commercial harvests that some other sea turtle species have experienced. But this does not mean that loggerheads have avoided human threats. This species has had the misfortune of positioning itself between us and the seafood we fish for. Juvenile loggerheads forage precisely where longlines (series of baited hooks) are set to catch oceanic fishes, and larger loggerheads feed within areas of fertile sea bottom extensively trawled for shrimps. At these intersections, loggerheads perish by the tens of thousands each year after being accidentally captured and drowned.

Our hatchling production is good, but threats at sea remain

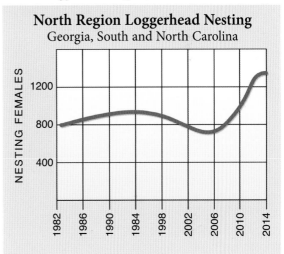
Annual nesting loggerheads inferred from nest counts

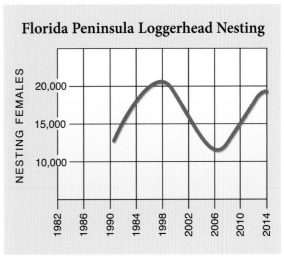
Florida loggerhead nesting has had its ups and downs

The Hawksbill Turtle

Scientific Name: *Eretmochelys imbricata*

Named for the Greek roots for "rowing turtle" (turtle with oars) and the Latin root for "bearing overlapping scales" (a reference to the hawksbill's shingled shell scutes)

Other Common Names

English: hawksbill sea turtle, hawksbill
Spanish: carey (ka-RAY)
French: tortue imbriquée

Size and Weight

Most adult female hawksbills have a shell straight-length of 30–35 in (75–90 cm) and weigh 100–150 lbs (45–70 kg).

Distribution

Hawksbills are found in tropical and subtropical seas. Their nesting occurs almost exclusively on tropical beaches. Hawksbills trace the distribution of coral reefs and stray only occasionally into temperate waters.

Diet

Larger juveniles and adults eat mostly sponges and soft reef invertebrates.

Above: A juvenile hawksbill from the Florida Keys

Left: This juvenile hawksbill in the deep blue Gulf of Mexico will spend a couple of years drifting with seaweed until it reaches dinner-plate size and settles upon a shallow tropical reef

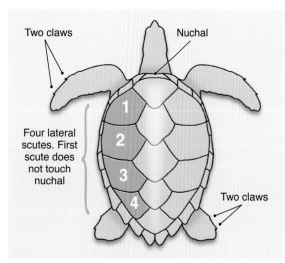

Dorsal view showing carapace

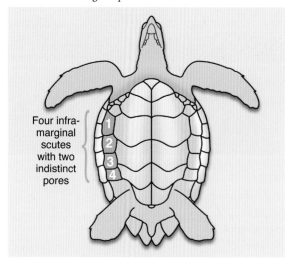

Ventral view showing plastron

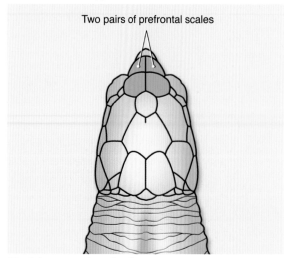

Head showing prefrontal scales

Appearance

Hawksbills are strikingly beautiful. Their shell colors seem magnified by the thickness of the translucent scutes covering their carapace. The tough, plasticlike scute plates are as thick as about 20 book pages and are imbedded with a myriad of colors. From a distance, hawksbill shells range in appearance from blonde with chocolate drippings to black with golden sunbursts.

Typically, a hawksbill's underside is much paler than its topside. In many young hawksbills, the scutes covering the plastron are a patternless, thick cream color, although these belly scutes may have dark corners in some turtles. In adults, the plastron becomes deep amber. Depending on the life experiences of an individual turtle, some of the beauty of a hawksbill's shell may be hidden by coarse, sandpaperlike scratches from rocks and coral. Hawksbills also occasionally acquire barnacles, but they seldom bear the heavy fouling load that many loggerheads show.

A narrow raptorlike beak is the hawksbill's namesake. With the slightly cusped bill arching into an overbite and extending about half the length of the turtle's head, a hawksbill's profile is decidedly birdlike. The beak is strong, sharp, slender, and in a narrow form adapted for probing and extracting sponges and other invertebrates from coral crevices.

Scute Diagnostics

A hawksbill's carapace and plastron shell scutes are imbricate, meaning that, like roof shingles, each slightly overlaps the scute behind it. The center-line vertebral carapace scutes overlap the most, such that they taper rearward into sharp Vs or Ws. Hawksbills have four **lateral (costal) scutes** on either side of their carapace midline, four **inframarginal scutes**, and on the head, two pairs of **prefrontal scales** between the eyes. There are two distinct **claws** on the leading edge of each of the front and rear flippers.

Life Stages

Hawksbills change in form as they mature.

Hatchlings

Most are a light to medium-dark brown above, although dry hatchlings can appear charcoal gray. Their lower surface is typically lighter. The carapace is lumpy with raised scutes.

Juveniles

As the turtles grow they quickly develop imbricate shell scutes with complex color patterns. Their carapace margins become serrated.

Subadults

The carapace is smooth except for overlapping scutes, which show growth bands. Scratches and barnacles indicate habitation of shallow reefs.

Adults

Similar to subadults but without signs of carapace growth. The shell margins are smooth, the rear shell notch becomes less pronounced, and in some (perhaps older) adults, the shell scutes no longer overlap.

Hatchling
0.5 oz (15 g)

Open-sea juvenile
1–3 years old,
to 35 oz (1000 g)

Juvenile
3–10 years old,
2–46 lb (1–21 kg)

Subadult 10–25 years old,
46–101 lb (21–46 kg)

Adults reach 45+ years old,
average 130 lb (59 kg)

Distribution and Movements

Hawksbills swim in tropical and subtropical seas, don't undergo extensive seasonal movements, and rarely stray into temperate waters. Most hawksbills in the continental US are found in southern Florida. The majority of the world's hawksbills nest on tropical beaches. In our region, nearly all nesting occurs in the southern Gulf of Mexico and Caribbean. Although numerous scattered nesting colonies remain, hawksbills do not nest in great abundance anywhere.

Worldwide Nesting Beaches

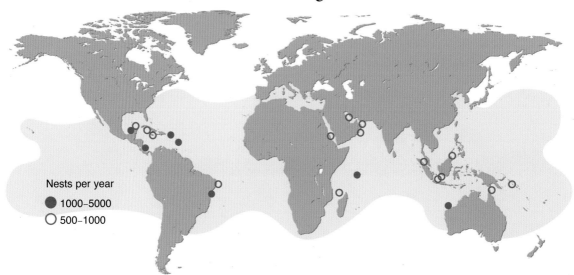

Nests per year
- 1000–5000
- 500–1000

Regional Distribution

Juveniles

Juveniles, subadults, and adults

Young pelagic juveniles live at the surface of the open sea. Larger juveniles and adults inhabit warm, shallow (neritic) coastal waters

Regional Nesting Beaches

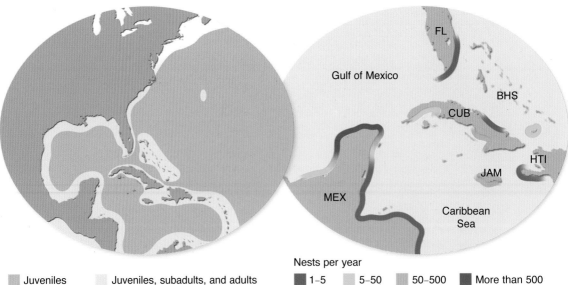

Nests per year
- 1–5
- 5–50
- 50–500
- More than 500

Mexico's Yucatán Peninsula hosts our largest regional nesting assemblage of hawksbills. Puerto Rico and Panama also have good nesting

Life History

After swimming away from the beach where it hatched, a hawksbill will spend three to five years at the surface of the open sea. After this pelagic or oceanic stage, older juveniles move into coastal waters where they forage on shallow reefs and seagrass pastures. Larger immature turtles and adults occupy slightly deeper reefs. At age 25 or so, hawksbills mature and take part in periodic breeding migrations between foraging grounds and nesting beaches.

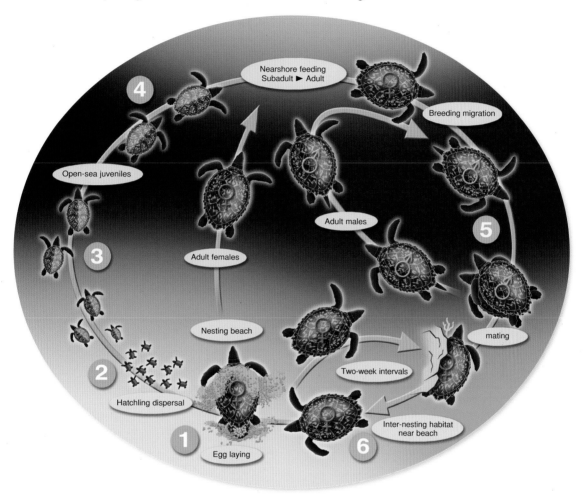

1. Nests average 140 eggs, which incubate under sand for 55–75 days. Warmer sands produce mostly female turtles and cooler sands result in mostly males.

2. A few days after they hatch, the hatchlings emerge together from the nest at night, scramble to the surf, swim out to sea, and are dispersed by ocean currents.

3. The youngest juveniles live near the surface of deep ocean waters and are carried by ocean currents.

4. At about four years of age, juveniles swim into nearshore waters to inhabit reefs and other shallow habitats. Subadults may occupy deeper reefs.

5. Adults mate along migration routes between foraging and nesting areas and off the nesting beach.

6. Every three to four years, adult females migrate to the beach where they hatched and make about three to five nests at two-week intervals.

Maturity and Reproduction

The rates at which hawksbills grow suggest they reach adult size in roughly 25 years. Approaching adulthood, the turtle's growth slows, then virtually stops. Following a pubescent period that may take years, a female will make her first nesting migration. Males intercept females to mate along migration pathways and in waters adjacent to nesting beaches.

Courtship and Mating

Adult male hawksbills are believed to breed every season. Most observations of mating occur on reefs near beaches just as the nesting season begins. Males bite and wrestle with females, and

occasionally with other males already attached to females. Once a male secures a position on the back of a female, he clings tightly to mate with her and guard her against rivals. Perhaps because of male persistence, most hawksbill egg clutches have only one father.

Where Hawksbills Nest

Hawksbills nest on narrow sandy beaches that often grade directly into coastal forest. Their nests are typically in dense vegetation and the traces of their nocturnal activity are sometimes no more than a short track disappearing into undergrowth or accumulated beach wrack.

The Nesting and Hatching Season

Nesting is at night, with peak activity around midnight. The hawksbill nesting season is longer than that of most other sea turtles, and on some tropical beaches hawksbills nest all year long. In Mexico and the northern Caribbean, the first nesting is in late April and the last nests are in November. Hatchlings emerge from nests between late June and December. The incubation period in warm nests may be 55 days. Cool, shaded nests may require more than 70 days to produce hatchlings.

Hawksbill hatchlings emerge from nests on tropical beaches

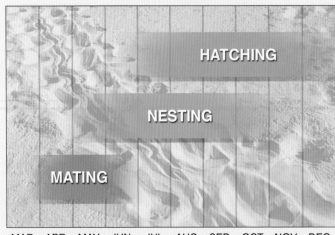

HATCHING

NESTING

MATING

MAR APR MAY JUN JUL AUG SEP OCT NOV DEC

Fast Facts

- Females migrate to nesting beaches every two to four years
- Most mating takes place near the beach
- Females make multiple nests (possibly three to five) separated by two-week intervals
- Nests contain an average of 140 eggs
- Hatchlings typically emerge in about 60 days

A female hawksbill may forage within 50 miles (80 km) of the beaches where she will nest, or she may travel as far as 1000 miles (1600 km) between her foraging and breeding sites. Like other sea turtles, a breeding hawksbill must be nutritionally ready for reproduction. A female that is not feeling sufficiently plump will skip one or more reproductive seasons. During her nesting season, an average hawksbill will lay 560 eggs in four installments separated by two-week intervals. During each biweekly inter-nesting interval, the yolked follicles to be the subsequent clutch are ovulated, then fertilized and shelled. With her clutch of eggs ready to lay, a hawksbill will move into the surf zone and make her nesting attempt as nightfall arrives.

Hawksbills are unique among sea turtles for their ability to deal with obstacles on the beach. One function of a hawksbill's thick shell scutes may be to protect them from the jabs they are likely to get as they climb over the gothic projections from the fossil reef-rock that often fringes their nesting beaches. Once on a beach, hawksbills are even less intimidated by the tangle of branches and vines on the upper beach where eggs can incubate away from the tide. Hawksbills surpass other sea turtles in their maneuverability on land, and can do something the other species can't do. If turned on her back in the sand, a female hawksbill is often able to flip herself upright. Despite the difficult places where hawksbills put their eggs, the turtle's rapid pace in crawling and nesting results in a nesting process that is the fastest among the sea turtles—approximately 45 minutes in total.

Hawksbills often nest under trees, in dense vegetation, or amidst other obstructions

Hawksbills eat sponges, which have a variety of toxic defences

A hawksbill's specialized diet is unique among large vertebrates

Diet

After a couple of years of omnivorous feeding in the open sea, hawksbills become specialists on soft, tropical, bottom-dwelling invertebrates, especially **sponges**.

Post-hatchlings and Pelagic Juveniles

After their hatchling dispersal, young hawksbills take up living within oceanic fronts where currents press together a wide variety of floating animals the small turtles eat. These include residents of the pelagic sargassum community such as **hydroids,** crustaceans, bryozoans, goose barnacles, and jelly animals. It also includes wind-dispersed drifters like **blue buttons**, by-the-wind sailors, purple sea snails, and **blue glaucus** sea slugs. Small turtles also favor **dead insects** that accumulate in these concentrations of floating material.

Coastal (Neritic) Juveniles and Adults

When juvenile hawksbills leave the open sea, they settle into shallow coastal waters typically dominated by reefs, hardbottom, and occasionally, seagrasses. Although some of the smallest coastal hawksbills eat a variety of invertebrate animals and **algae**, most juveniles and adults assume a narrower diet. For most of their lives, hawksbills are spongivores—specialists in eating sponges.

Post-hatchlings and Juveniles

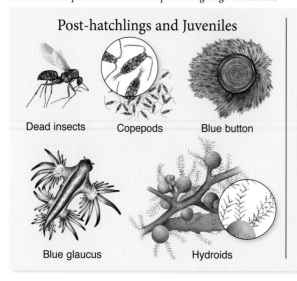

Dead insects   Copepods   Blue button

Blue glaucus   Hydroids

Juveniles and Adults

Colonial anemones   Red algae

Geodia spp. sponges   Chicken liver sponge

Sponges are an unusual food choice. These colonial animals tend to possess substantial defenses against would-be predators. By lacing themselves with toxic chemicals and dangerously indigestible silica spicules, sponges make themselves among the least favored marine menu items. For most animals, eating a silica sponge can be a lethal mistake. Yet young hawksbills quickly acquire a taste and tolerance for sponge, and after a short initiation period, sponges are likely to make up 95% of their diet. A limited number of sponge species belonging to the order of demosponges are the hawksbill's favorites. Some of the sponges in this order are soft, like the familiar bath sponges. But these pleasant sponges made of flexible spongin are generally shunned by hawksbills. Most of the demosponges eaten by hawksbills are held together by lacy, glasslike silica spicules that you would no more want near your bare skin

than shredded glass. A hawksbill's tolerance for a diet of glass is largely a mystery. Occasionally, hawksbills do eat less toxic fare such as **colonial anemones** (zoanthids), sea cucumbers, mollusks, jelly animals, and algae, but the rarity of these diet substitutes points to a clear preference for sponge. It is a wonder what benefits a hawksbill could get from eating sponges that would outweigh the difficulties of such a diet.

In larger hawksbills, the majority of diet items, including sponges, are part of the coral reef fauna. The hawksbill too is a quintessential coral reef animal with a number of adaptations for foraging on encrusting animals tucked within the nooks and crannies of stony reefs. These include the turtle's narrow birdlike jaws, long neck, and thick protective shell scutes.

Anxious French angelfish wait to feed on the soft insides of a tough-skinned Geodia *sponge opened by a subadult hawksbill.*

This image and below: Color variation in juvenile hawksbills

Some individuals are dark

Others are blonde

A pelagic juvenile that has yet to have its shell scratched

Unique Traits

Many of the traits unique to hawksbills fit the turtle's lifestyle of reef living.

Thick, Variably Patterned Scutes

Thick scutes are a likely deterrent to sharks' teeth, but the defense may also help hawksbills avoid damage from sharp coral during their search for food. The thick shell plates are uniquely iridescent. Up close in daylight, a hawksbill shell can be seen to have colors such as cream, amber, rusty reds, browns, and black. The colors blend together in rich patterns ranging from overlapping bursts and radiating zigzags to irregular superimposed splotches. Given this variation, no two hawksbills look quite the same.

A long neck helps a hawksbill probe reef crevices for its food

Stop, Don't Eat That Hawksbill!

Other than the remorse one should feel from eating an endangered species, there are other reasons not to select a hawksbill turtle for your next dinner party. Consuming hawksbill meat has resulted in cases of chelonitoxin poisoning. The toxins are thought to be associated with sponges in the turtle's diet, toxins that bio-accumulate in proportion to the amount of toxic sponge a turtle has eaten. Chelonitoxin poisoning is known to cause burning sensations, nausea, chest pain, swallowing difficulty, skin rash, liver enlargement, coma, and death.

Conservation Status

The hawksbill turtle is listed as Endangered worldwide under the US Endangered Species Act. The species is also officially protected from harvest in Mexico, Cuba, Bermuda, and The Bahamas. Regional countries are signatories to the Convention on International Trade in Endangered Species of Wild Fauna and Flora (CITES), which lists the hawksbill as protected from commercial trade. The International Union for Conservation of Nature (IUCN) currently has the species on its Red List as Critically Endangered. Because most of the hawksbills in our waters have come from nesting beaches in Mexico and the Caribbean, another important treaty for this species is the Inter-American Convention for the Protection and Conservation of Sea Turtles (IAC).

Nesting Trends

Informed guesses by biologists are that the world's hawksbills have declined by 80% or more during the past century. Because hawksbills are widespread in the tropics, there is an illusion that the species is holding its own. Most of these populations are mere shadows of their former abundance. The Caribbean now has about a third of the world's hawksbill nesting. In this region, **nesting trends** are mixed. The plot to the right describes estimated trends in annual nesting females based on four nests per turtle per year.

Like the green turtle, the hawksbill has suffered the fate of a commercially harvested species. For many decades, hawksbills have been harvested for their shell scutes. These scutes as a trade commodity are known as tortoiseshell, bekko, or carey. The malleable, plasticlike plates are fashioned into jewelry, hair combs, eyeglass frames, and varied ornaments. Shell scutes from 30,000 or more hawksbills per year were imported into Japan alone during the period of 1970–1992. Currently, trade in tortoiseshell has diminished following adherence to an international convention (CITES) to protect endangered species, but substantial illegal harvest and trade still occurs.

The hawksbill's beauty has contributed to its endangered status

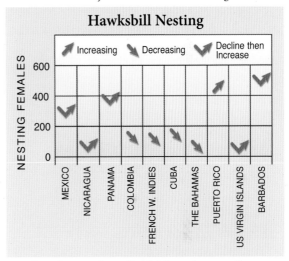

Mixed trends in numbers of hawksbills nesting annually

Threats to hawksbills and their population status vary by region

Kemp's Ridley Turtle

Scientific Name: *Lepidochelys kempii*

Named for the Greek roots for "scaly turtle" and the proper name "Kemp" with the Latin genitive ending (from Richard Kemp, a fisherman who submitted the type specimen)

Other Common Names

English: Atlantic ridley, bastard turtle, ridley (from the vernacular of fishermen, who considered the turtle's identity to be a riddle)
Spanish: tortuga lora

Size and Weight

Most adult female Kemp's ridleys have a shell straight-length of 24–28 in (60–70 cm) and weigh 75–100 lbs (34–45 kg).

Distribution

The Gulf of Mexico and warm temperate waters of the western North Atlantic. Most nesting is in north-eastern Mexico, but recently there have been increasing numbers of nests in Texas.

Diet

Larger juveniles and adults feed on crabs, tunicates, and other bottom-dwelling invertebrates.

Above: An adult female Kemp's ridley covers her nest on a Texas beach

Left: A subadult ridley rests within a mixed habitat of seagrass and hardbottom in the eastern Gulf of Mexico off Florida

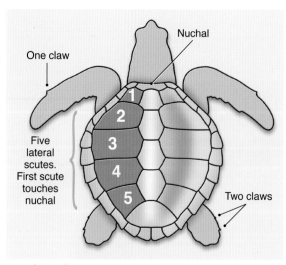

Dorsal view showing carapace

Dorsal view showing carapace

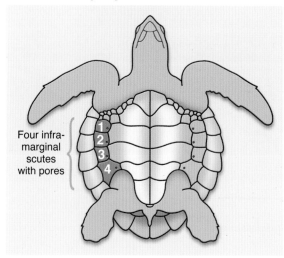

Ventral view showing plastron

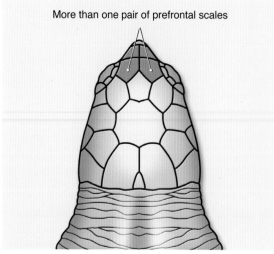

Head showing prefrontal scales

Appearance

Kemp's ridley is our smallest sea turtle, reaching the weight of a large dog. The turtle's coloration is light gray to drab olive above and yellowish cream underneath. Turtles from turbid waters seem to have the palest coloration. Ridleys have a triangular head and a cusped parrotlike beak, giving the turtle a unique profile. Their shell is more circular in shape than the shells of other sea turtles. The carapace has flanged edges and is typically wider than long in larger turtles. The impression given by a passing Kemp's ridley is that of a ghostlike gray disk gliding by.

Hatchling Kemp's ridleys are dark gray all over. Fresh from the nest, the average ridley hatchling is slightly larger than a hawksbill and slightly smaller than a loggerhead, although there is substantial size overlap with these species. As ridley hatchlings grow, they develop three ridges down the length of their carapace and two ridges on their plastron. The ridges, especially the sharp, finlike crests of the center carapace ridge, are most prominent in juveniles. As turtles near adulthood, only a thin remnant of the center carapace ridge remains. An adult's carapace is smooth. At all life stages, ridleys seldom have significant numbers of barnacles and other fouling organisms. Turtles in clear, shallow waters occasionally have thin patches of algae coating their head and shell.

Scute Diagnostics

Like loggerheads, Kemp's ridleys most often have five pairs of **lateral (costal) scutes** on either side of their carapace midline, and five vertebral scutes along the center length of their shell. Kemp's ridley has four **inframarginal scutes** to the loggerhead's typical number of three. These scutes in the ridley each bear a **pore** (see page 56) that is distinct in most turtles larger than post-hatchling size. Ridleys have two pairs of **prefrontal scales** on the head and only rarely have additional intervening prefrontal scales as loggerheads often do. Ridleys have one **claw** on the leading edge of each front flipper and two **claws** on each rear flipper.

Life Stages

Kemp's ridleys get wider, smoother, and greener as they mature.

Hatchlings

There is little color variation in the charcoal gray pattern, above and below. Wet hatchlings appear darker. The carapace is lumpy with raised scutes.

Juveniles

Finlike crests form a ridge on center scutes, and two additional ridges line lateral scutes. Carapace margins become slightly serrated and pale.

Subadults

The carapace lightens to gray or olive. Ridges diminish leaving only the center. Serrated carapace margins disappear.

Adults

Similar to subadults but without signs of any carapace ridges. The shell margins are smooth and the rear shell notch becomes less pronounced.

Hatchling
0.6 oz (17 g)

Post-hatchling
1–12 weeks old,
1 lb (450 g)

Juvenile
3 months to 2 years old,
1–7 lb (0.5–3 kg)

Subadult 3–12 years old,
7–85 lb (3–39 kg)

Adults reach 30+ years old,
average 85 lb (39 kg)

Distribution and Movements

Most Kemp's ridleys swim in the Gulf of Mexico, but the turtle is also known from bays and sounds along the Atlantic US. In the summer, significant numbers of ridleys forage as far north as Cape Cod Bay, MA. These Atlantic coast ridleys tend to be small juveniles, which move south as the water cools in the late fall. Records of ridleys from the eastern Atlantic are rare. Most nesting takes place in the state of Tamaulipas, Mexico, with significant nesting also in southern Texas.

Kemp's Ridley Most Visited Nesting Beaches

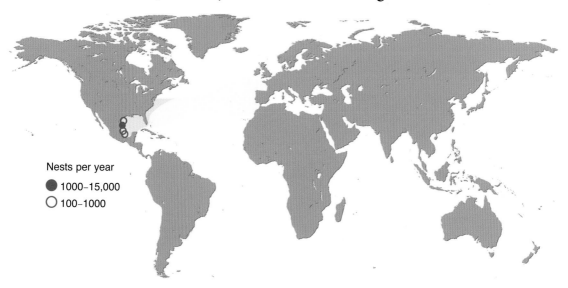

Nests per year
- ● 1000–15,000
- ○ 100–1000

Regional Distribution

Regional Nesting Beaches

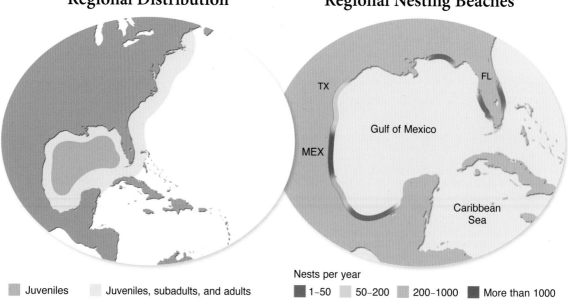

Juveniles   Juveniles, subadults, and adults

Nests per year
- ■ 1–50   ■ 50–200   ■ 200–1000   ■ More than 1000

Young pelagic juveniles live at the surface of the open sea. Larger juveniles and adults inhabit warm, shallow (neritic) coastal waters

Northeastern Mexico hosts the majority of the world's nesting population of Kemp's ridleys

Life History

Hatchling ridleys disperse from their natal beaches in the western Gulf of Mexico and spend the next two to three years at the surface of the open sea. After this pelagic or oceanic stage, older juveniles move into estuaries and other coastal waters where they forage near channels, oyster reefs, seagrass, and muddy sediment. At about age 12, ridleys mature and begin periodic breeding migrations between foraging grounds and nesting beaches.

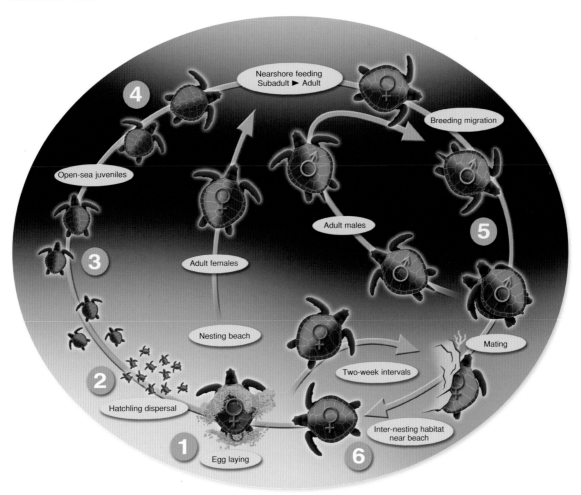

1. Nests average 103 eggs. Most successful nests produce hatchlings in 48–62 days. Warmer sands produce mostly female turtles and cooler sands result in mostly males.

2. A few days after they hatch, the hatchlings emerge together from the nest at night, scramble to the surf, swim out to sea, and are dispersed by ocean currents.

3. The youngest juveniles live near the surface of open gulf waters. Some exit the gulf by the Florida Current and Gulf Stream.

4. At about two years of age, juveniles swim into nearshore waters to inhabit a variety of estuarine and other shallow coastal habitats.

5. Adults prefer coastal gulf waters that are slightly deeper and more open. Mating occurs off nesting beaches.

6. Every one to three years, adult females migrate to their nesting beach and make two to three nests at intervals of two to three weeks. Nesting is synchronized within mass events called *arribadas*.

Maturity and Reproduction

Growth rates of wild Kemp's ridleys and the sizes of immature turtles with known ages suggest that an average ridley reaches maturity in about 12 years. At adulthood, growth nearly ceases. For females, adulthood means the start of periodic breeding migrations that can take place each spring if the turtles are well fed. Ridleys that are less ready for the demand of migration and nesting may skip one or two breeding seasons.

Courtship and Mating

There are few observations of male and female Kemp's ridleys hooking up, so their courtship behavior is unclear. Tracking studies reveal that

A Kemp's ridley hatchling crawls to the sea

many males live near the main nesting beaches. Genetic analyses of sibling hatchlings show that one male fertilizes the majority of eggs in a clutch, but some clutches have as many as four fathers.

Ridley Beaches and Their *Arribadas*

Most Kemp's ridleys nest during daylight and in a crowd. These synchronized nesting events are called *arribadas,* Spanish for "arrivals". The most popular place for these mass nesting events is a stretch of beach backed by grassy dune and swales in northeastern Mexico. We'll have more about *arribadas* later on.

The Nesting and Hatching Season

Because ridley nesting is triggered by variable environmental cues not completely understood, the first nests of the season are difficult to predict. Nonetheless, the first nesting is generally in April and most nesting concludes by early July. Unlike our other sea turtles, the principal nesting time is during daylight, although some nesting does occur at night. Hatchlings emerge from nests between late May and early September in departures that lag roughly 55 days behind each mass-nesting arrival. During the warmest months, incubation averages only 48 days, but an average nest during cooler months will incubate for 62 days.

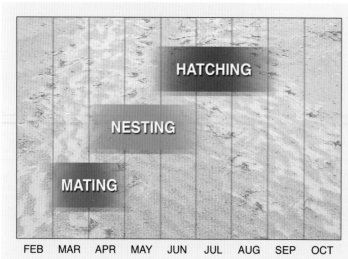

HATCHING

NESTING

MATING

FEB MAR APR MAY JUN JUL AUG SEP OCT

Fast Facts

- Females migrate to nesting beaches every one to three years
- Mating takes place offshore from the nesting beach
- Average females make two to three nests separated by two to three week intervals
- Nests contain an average of 103 eggs
- Hatchlings emerge in about 55 days

From their principal foraging areas spanning coastal gulf waters from western Florida to the Yucatán Peninsula, female Kemp's ridleys converge on the waters off their nesting beaches in the far western gulf. Sufficiently healthy turtles may make this migration every spring. Others may skip breeding if they are feeling lean. For a Kemp's ridley female lingering off her nesting beach, waiting to nest means waiting on the same environmental cues that will prompt the hundreds of other females also prepared to emerge from the sea and lay their eggs.

No one knows for certain what triggers an *arribada* event or how the participants orchestrate the alliance. One thing the events tend to have in common is that they occur on days with a strong onshore wind. These winds are generally from the northeast and accompany a change in barometric pressure. Of course, to be ready when the conditions say the time is right, the females have to coordinate an anticipatory gathering. One hypoth-

esis describes that the communication needed in advance of an *arribada* may be by pheromones. These chemical cues might be secreted by the Rathke's glands that ridley turtles have, glands that empty through pores in their four pairs of inframarginal scutes. Evidence for chemical communication is that the larger an *arribada* is, the more organized it is (with fewer stragglers). This organization aside, some ridleys end up nesting outside the main *arribada* beaches in solitary attempts.

Because Kemp's ridleys nest on blustery days, their track and nest site is often blown away after the turtle leaves the beach. Although an *arribada* of hundreds of turtles could last many hours, each individual nests in less than an hour. The females that nest will lay 200–300 eggs over two to three beach visits separated by variable intervals of two to three weeks. Eggs that are ovulated, fertilized, and shelled, must wait in suspended animation while the female awaits the right time to revisit the beach.

The majority of the world's breeding Kemp's ridleys emerge in an arribada *to nest on a beach in northeastern Mexico*

A juvenile ridley parting pelagic sargassum to find food

A ridley searching for food in dense seagrass

Diet

Ridleys are nimble turtles with the ability to chase down relatively fast-moving crustaceans.

Post-hatchlings and Pelagic Juveniles

After they disperse seaward as hatchlings, post-hatchling Kemp's ridleys begin to feed within the surface convergence zones that assemble the pelagic sargassum community. The turtles remain there until about the age of two, feeding on **hydroids**, **copepods**, bryozoans, tube worms, **dead insects**, **jelly animals**, and a variety of sargassum associates. As they grow, the turtles take larger prey items including the drifters that are also food for juvenile green turtles, loggerheads, and hawksbills *(Porpita, Velella, Janthina, Glaucus)*. Juvenile ridleys are particularly fond of pelagic crabs like the **sargassum swimming crab** and the blotched swimming crab. These crabs are relatives of the shallow-water species ridleys will seek once they recruit into coastal waters as older juveniles. To find these prey items, small ridleys part the floating mats of pelagic sargassum where they live, a behavior similar to the infaunal mining used by larger turtles in shallow sea bottom.

Coastal (Neritic) Juveniles and Adults

At the size of a large dinner plate, a juvenile ridley will leave the blue, open waters of the gulf and settle into murkier coastal or estuarine

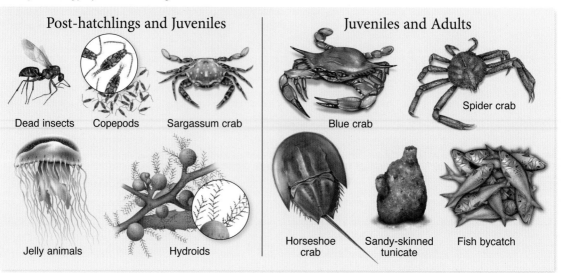

Post-hatchlings and Juveniles

Dead insects   Copepods   Sargassum crab

Jelly animals   Hydroids

Juveniles and Adults

Blue crab   Spider crab

Horseshoe crab   Sandy-skinned tunicate   Fish bycatch

waters with a sea bottom of mud banks, seagrass, or oyster bars. These habitats favor a number of crab species that ridleys love to eat, especially the

A juvenile ridley surfaces with its lunch—a horseshoe crab

blue crab, *Callinectes sapidus*, a sprightly swimming and fast-clawed resident of secluded bay waters. Catching this fast-moving swimming crab must require considerable agility in addition to a tolerance for have one's face pinched. Other crunchy critters in the ridley diet include **spider crabs**, purse crabs, and **horseshoe crabs** (not actually crabs). Additional seafood popular with Kemp's ridley includes jellyfish, solitary **tunicates** (sea squirts), slower fishes such as sea horses, and small marine snails and clams. Because balls of mud have been found in the stomachs of some ridleys, it is thought that they may take in bites of the sea bottom in efforts to consume the small invertebrates hidden in the sediment. We've witnessed examples of ridleys infaunal mining, that is, using their front flippers to part the sea bottom in front of them, perhaps to reveal hidden prey.

In addition to these naturally occurring items, a major component in the diet of many ridleys seems to be discarded **bycatch**. This includes a number of fish species commonly caught in trawl and net fisheries but not commercially valuable enough to keep. The fish make up the majority of most trawl-net contents and generally don't live after being discarded. Trawlers crisscross ridley foraging habitat and dump masses of bycatch that can lure turtles into the path of the fishery. Many Kemp's ridleys stranded dead are found to have their stomachs filled with fishes common in bycatch. These are species that are too fast for a turtle to catch when the fish was alive. Unfortunately, the crabs that ridleys love to eat occupy the same habitat of commercially valuable shrimps targeted by trawlers.

A juvenile Kemp's ridley examines a patch of sargassum for food items in the blue waters of the eastern Gulf of Mexico

Female Kemp's ridleys nesting during an arribada

Ridleys share a shape with the classic 1950s flying saucer

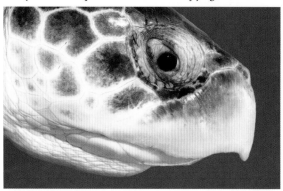

The ridley's Spanish name, tortuga lora, *means "parrot turtle"*

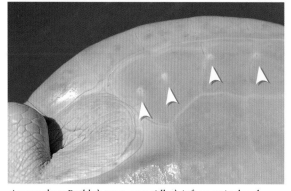

Arrows show Rathke's pores on a ridley's inframarginal scales

Unique Traits

In addition to being the world's rarest sea turtle, Kemp's ridley has a number of other unique and notable characteristics.

Nesting *Arribadas*

Only the ridleys (Kemp's, and the olive ridley, *Lepidochelys olivacea*, a turtle restricted to tropical oceans) nest in the mass arrivals known as *arribadas*. How ridleys coordinate the timing of these events is largely a mystery, and the adaptive advantage of group nesting remains speculative (see page 142).

Wide, Flattened Carapace

A carapace shape reminiscent of a classic UFO disk probably allows Kemp's ridley to swing a much tighter turning radius in comparison to the other sea turtles. This maneuverability may come in handy for chasing nimble prey like the ridley's favorite meal, the blue crab.

Parrotlike Bill

A ridley's cusped upper beak cuts a distinctive profile. The parrot-bill shape is reflected in the name the turtle goes by in Mexico—*tortuga lora* or "parrot turtle". The cusp could allow the turtle some enhanced prey-capturing ability, but this has yet to be demonstrated.

Rathke's Pores

Yet another mystery setting Kemp's ridley apart revolves around the turtle's Rathke's glands. The glands exit through distinct pores in the lower inside corners of the turtle's inframarginal scales. Granted, all aquatic turtles we know of have these glands, but they seem to be most numerous and most visible in the ridleys. Because turtles exude liquid from these glands when disturbed, one hypothesis is that the viscous fluid squirting out somehow deters predators. The glands exude proteins, lactic acid, esters, lipids, and a variety of other compounds. The conspicuous presence of Rathke's pores in ridleys has tempted some biologists to suggest they play a role in pheromonal control of ridley social behavior, namely, their *arribadas*.

Conservation Status

Kemp's ridley is listed as Endangered worldwide under the US Endangered Species Act. The species is also officially protected from harvest in Mexico, Cuba, and The Bahamas. Regional countries are signatories to the Convention on International Trade in Endangered Species of Wild Fauna and Flora (CITES), which lists Kemp's ridley as protected from commercial trade. The International Union for Conservation of Nature (IUCN) has the species on its Red List as Critically Endangered. Kemp's ridleys come from a single population with one principal nesting location. Having all eggs in one basket is a dangerous condition for any species.

Nesting Trends

One June morning on a Tamaulipas beach in 1947, a Mexican engineer named Andres Herrera witnessed a Kemp's ridley *arribada*. The film that Herrera made of this event revealed that Kemp's ridley was once an abundant sea turtle. In a systematic count and careful extrapolation from the turtles visible in the film, it is estimated that 42,000 ridleys took part in that 1947 *arribada*. Only a few years after this revelation, it became clear to biologists that Kemp's ridley was in **rapid decline**. By 1968, the *arribada* at Rancho Nuevo comprised only 5000 turtles, and by the 1980s, *arribadas* rarely involved more than 200 turtles. Kemp's ridley was slipping away. The cause? A double whammy of nearly complete egg harvest and mortality from shrimp trawling throughout the turtle's foraging areas. The cure? Protection of the nesting beach, and turtle excluder devices (TEDs) on trawl nets. Although the story is more complex than this (see pages 243, 261), the point is that concerted conservation actions resulted in success. Since the mid-1980s there has been a dramatic upturn in the number of nesting Kemp's ridleys. This increase has extended to locations where ridleys were once almost unheard of, like south Texas, where nesting has increased from a few nests per year to roughly 200. Biologists are carefully watching a recent stall in nesting that may mean a delay in the ridley's path to recovery.

Most Kemp's ridley hatchlings come from just one location

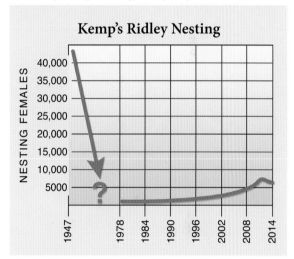

Kemp's ridley—a perilous past with an uncertain future

Kemp's ridley came dangerously close to the brink of extinction

The Leatherback Turtle

Scientific Name: *Dermochelys coriacea*

Named with Greek roots for leathery turtle and the Latin descriptor for leathery skin

Other Common Names

English: leatherback
Spanish: tortuga laúd, canal, cardón, baula, tinglar
French: tortue luth

Size and Weight

An average nesting female has a curved shell length of 5.1 ft (155 cm) and weighs about 800 lbs (360 kg).

Distribution

Virtually all oceanic and near-coastal waters outside the arctic. Nesting is mostly in the tropics.

Diet

Jelly animals, including jellyfish, comb jellies, and pelagic tunicates.

Above: An adult female leatherback returns to the sea on a southeastern Florida beach

Left: A hatchling leatherback sets off on its first big swim, beginning a lifetime journey that will span the Atlantic many times over

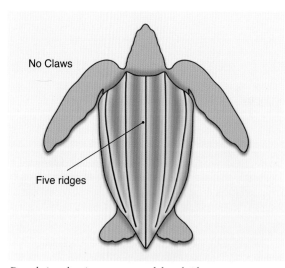

Dorsal view showing carapace and dorsal ridges

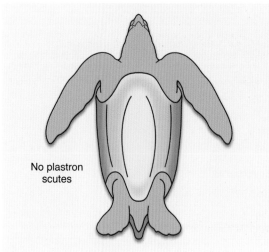

Ventral view showing plastron

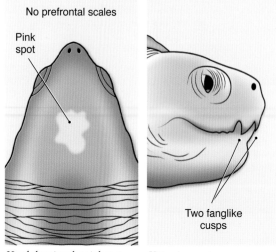

Head showing the pink spot   *Upper jaw cusps*

Appearance

Leatherbacks are grand turtles. The largest known was a male weighing a little over a ton (916 kg). Most leatherback adults weigh a little less than half a ton, which is still impressive. The turtles are also distinctive in general appearance. Leatherbacks are dark, streamlined, scaleless turtles (except hatchlings) with long, broad flippers. Their topsides are slate black to blue-black with random pale splotches, and their undersides are splotched almost equally by black and white. On a nesting beach, the turtle's light undersides are often blush. But the most conspicuous dash of color is an irregular **pink spot** (splotch) at the crown of the turtle's head. Apparently, no two spots are the same shape. A leatherback's body is a barrel-shape elongated into a streamlined teardrop. They are broad-shouldered, with the leading edge of their teardrop torso bulging with the muscle that powers their massive fore-flippers. Five distinct **dorsal ridges** (keels) extend the length of the turtle's carapace and fade together at the rear, which tapers into a bluntly pointed caudal projection. Both the stiff, winglike front flippers and the broad, rudderlike rear flippers are larger in proportion to the turtle's body than in the other sea turtles. Although front flippers are highly tapered in adults, those in hatchlings are more of a paddle shape. In larger turtles, a broad web of skin connects the rear flippers to the tail. Except in embryos and some hatchlings, none of the leatherback's flippers has claws.

The head is large and triangular, and the mouth has only a weakly keratinized beak. Yet the fit of the closed lower jaw within the upper jaw makes a set of efficient scissorlike cutting edges. Leading the upper jaw, a deep notch separates two **fanglike cusps**, and the lower jaw ends forward with a sharp point that fits inside the upper jaw. Hatchling leatherbacks are black with white highlights and are covered with tiny, thin, beadlike scales. The white highlights trace the margins of the flippers, the longitudinal ridges, and an imaginary continuation of these ridges down the turtle's neck. The fore-flippers of a hatchling span one-third greater than the turtle's length.

Life Stages

The general body shape of a leatherback changes relatively little as it grows to adulthood.

Hatchlings

Beadlike scales mark a contrasting pattern of white lines on a black background. The front flippers are broadly rounded at the tips and the head is proportionally large.

Juveniles

Most scales disappear and the front flippers become tapered. This life stage is rarely seen.

Subadults

The juvenile dorsal coloration fades into random pale splotches, although white dotted lines extending from the dorsal ridges onto the neck remain. The pink head spot becomes prominent.

Adults

Appearance is similar to that of subadults. Adults are the most commonly observed leatherback life stage.

Hatchling
1.6 oz (46 g)

Juveniles grow quickly and
are rarely observed

Juvenile,
unknown age
and growth

Subadult, unknown age and growth

Adults reach 30+ years old,
average 800 lb (360 kg)

Distribution and Movements

Leatherbacks have the broadest distribution and movements of any reptile. Adults occur worldwide from the subarctic to the subantarctic, although these northern and southern extremes are only in summer. The turtle forages in deep oceanic waters and shallower waters near coastlines, including large bays. Juveniles are largely restricted to tropical waters. Most nesting is also in the tropics. Adults are known to make seasonal movements that span the Atlantic.

Worldwide Nesting Beaches

Nests per year
- ● 1000–10,000
- ○ 100–1000

Regional Distribution

Regional Nesting Beaches

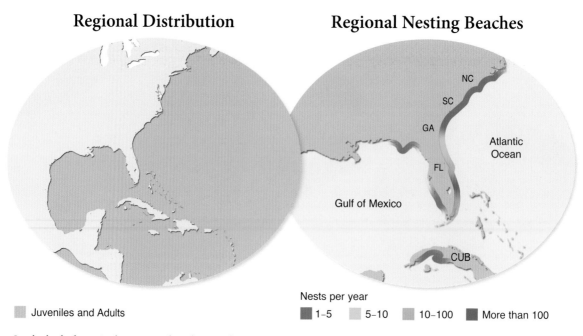

NC
SC
GA
Atlantic Ocean
FL
Gulf of Mexico
CUB

Juveniles and Adults

Nests per year
■ 1–5 ■ 5–10 ■ 10–100 ■ More than 100

Leatherbacks forage in the open sea, but also enter large deep bays. Coastal foraging north of Cape Hatteras is mostly in the summer

Although southeastern Florida hosts most of the nesting in our region, our foraging leatherbacks have come from many tropical Atlantic beaches

Life History

Leatherbacks are turtles of the open sea. Hatchlings disperse from natal beaches and grow quickly, foraging in tropical oceanic waters. Turtles are thought to reach adult size in roughly 15 years. Periodic breeding migrations are extensive, as are the seasonal sojourns the turtles make while foraging. Mating seems to take place near nesting beaches, and males are thought to migrate ahead of females. Females deposit four to seven egg clutches before returning to their foraging areas.

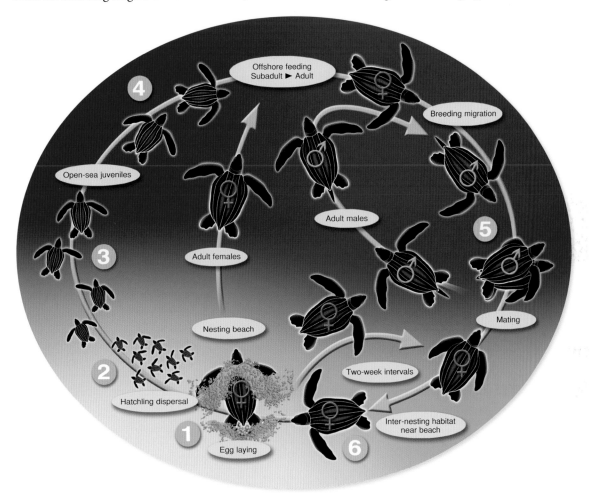

1. Nests average 80 viable eggs (with 15–50 additional smaller yolkless eggs) and produce hatchlings in 60–75 days. Warmer sands produce mostly female turtles and cooler sands result in mostly males.

2. Days after escaping their eggs, hatchlings emerge together from the nest at night, crawl to the sea, and disperse.

3. Juvenile leatherbacks forage and grow almost exclusively in tropical oceanic waters.

4. At subadult size, leatherbacks begin to occupy more temperate oceanic waters. Most evidence suggests turtles reach adult size in roughly 15 years.

5. Females migrate to waters off nesting beaches every two to three years, where mating is thought to occur.

6. Females emerge onto the beach to make approximately four to seven nests at ten-day intervals.

Maturity and Reproduction

Although leatherbacks are thought to grow quickly and mature sooner than other large sea turtles, the estimates for these rates range widely. Evidence comes from limited observations of small leatherbacks in captivity and from annual rings marking tiny bones within the turtle's eye. These studies suggest that maturity is possible in roughly five years, but a more likely estimate in wild turtles is about 15 years. Additional estimates put this age at 25 to 30 years. As an adult, a female leatherback will make periodic breeding migrations every two to three years, depositing four to seven clutches at eight to fourteen day intervals.

A leatherback hatchling from a Florida nest crawls seaward

Courtship and Mating

Males seem to converge on the waters off nesting beaches in advance of females arriving and remain there until the season peaks, although this seasonality is unclear. Few accounts describe mating, and the process by which males mount females is a mystery (the males have no fore-claws to help them hang on). Most egg clutches have only one father. Like other sea turtles, females likely store the sperm needed to fertilize multiple clutches and do not need to mate more than once.

Where Leatherbacks Nest

Female leatherbacks prefer steeply sloped beaches with prominent vegetated dunes. Most nests are made between the high tide line and the toe of the dune. Peak nesting areas are in Florida within St. Lucie, Martin, and Palm Beach Counties.

The Nesting and Hatching Season

Most leatherback nesting is at night, although several conspicuous daylight nesting events occur each year. The first nest of the season in Florida is often just after Valentine's Day, and the latest nests are in August. Early nests incubate in the coolest sands and may require 75 days to produce hatchlings. Late-season nests are warmer and can produce hatchlings in about 60 days.

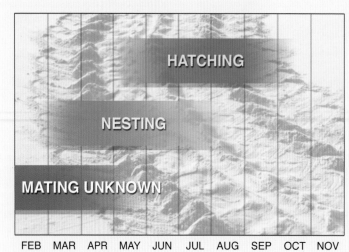

HATCHING

NESTING

MATING UNKNOWN

| FEB | MAR | APR | MAY | JUN | JUL | AUG | SEP | OCT | NOV |

Fast Facts

- Females migrate to nesting beaches every two to three years

- The mating process remains mysterious

- Females average four to seven nests separated by ten-day intervals

- An average nest contains 80 eggs and about 30 yolkless "spacers"

- Hatchlings emerge in 60–75 days

Reproductive migrations in sea turtles are generally thought of as distinct journeys between a home foraging area and a nesting beach. But for a leatherback, long ocean voyages are the norm. Although a leatherback female may travel over a thousand miles to reach her nesting beach, this trip is likely to be just one leg of a wandering path stretching many thousands of miles. Those adult females nutritionally ready for reproduction will converge on the waters off beaches in the regional vicinity of where they first entered the sea as hatchlings. During her total nesting season, she will likely lay about 400 eggs with a total weight of about 72 pounds (33 kg). Each egg is about the size of a billiard ball, which is the largest for any turtle. Toward the end of depositing each clutch of roughly 55–95 eggs, she will also lay roughly two dozen or so smaller yolkless "eggs," sometimes called "spacers," that are merely spheres of clear albumin packaged in papery eggshell. Each of the five or more egg clutches made by a female leatherback requires about ten days to produce. During this time, yolked follicles are ovulated, fertilized with stored sperm, coated with albumen, and wrapped in eggshell. Although many hypotheses advance the adaptive function of the yolkless eggs leatherbacks lay, some also believe they are simply egg-production overruns that accidently missed the critical ingredient making a viable egg.

With her clutch of eggs ready, a leatherback will crawl onto the beach. Once past the wave wash, the majority of females will continue the nesting process, which lasts about two hours. The process of nest site preparation, egg laying, and burial of eggs is similar to that of the other sea turtles. But in camouflaging their nest after eggs are laid, a leatherback will put in a much more extensive effort compared to other species. In addition to heaving sand into a broad mound over her clutch, a leatherback will typically repeat this camouflaging at one or more adjacent locations. After five or more nesting episodes like this, a leatherback will depart for foraging waters and not return for two to three years.

A female leatherback camouflages her nest. These daylight nesting events are occasional on southeastern Florida beaches

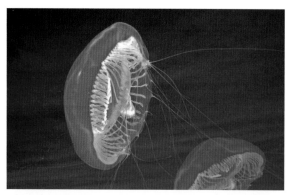

The many-ribbed hydromedusa is a popular leatherback treat

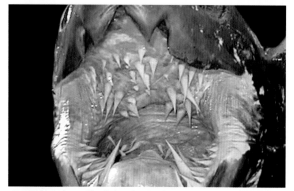

Cone-shaped papillae help a leatherback keep down its meal

The Portuguese man-o-war is a floating colonial hydroid

Diet

The world's largest turtle lives and grows on a diet of clear, watery, **jellylike animals**. The revelation is a bit like hearing from a champion weightlifter that they have never eaten anything but cucumbers. How could a leatherback be the biggest and grow the fastest by feeding on animals that are 96% water? The answer is that leatherbacks apparently eat a lot. Juvenile leatherbacks that have lived briefly in captivity were able to eat twice their body weight in jellyfish every day. It is possible that leatherbacks of all sizes in the wild are just as ravenous. Given the watery nature of the turtle's gelatinous food, quantity must make up for low nutritional quality.

Leatherbacks at all life stages seem to be specialist feeders on slippery critters including a variety of true jellyfish (Scyphozoa) such as moon jellies *(Aurelia)*, cannonball jellies *(Stomolophus)*, lion's mane jellies *(Cyanea)*, mauve stingers *(Pelagia)*, and sea nettles *(Chrysaora)*, and the jellyfish relatives (Hydrozoa) such as the **many-ribbed hydromedusa** *(Aequorea)* and the **Portuguese man-o-war**. This group of animals (Cnidaria) is famous for their tentacles armed with stinging nematocysts. Although some cnidarians have stings potent enough to send a human to the hospital, leatherbacks have acquired a tolerance, or perhaps even a taste, for these spicy species. Leatherbacks also feed on **comb jellies** (ctenophores, unrelated to true jellyfish), and on slightly firmer but similarly transparent animals like **salps** and pyrosomes.

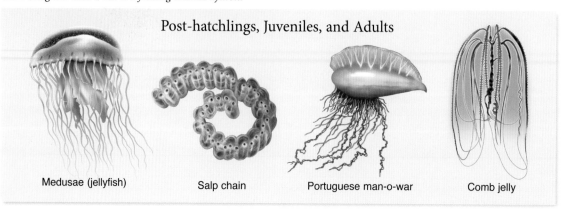

Post-hatchlings, Juveniles, and Adults

| Medusae (jellyfish) | Salp chain | Portuguese man-o-war | Comb jelly |

An adult leatherback trails tentacles from a recent meal

Leatherbacks have many adaptations that allow them to consume their squishy prey. For example, the turtle's upper and lower jaw cusps function to pierce and hold the most elusive jelly blobs. And for snacks larger than a single bite, scissorlike jaws are able to slice larger jellies into consumable pieces. This feeding method is especially important for the smallest leatherbacks, which are able to nibble off pieces of jellies much larger than they are.

Another feeding adaptation is the leatherback's ability to pre-process slippery prey once the turtle has it in its mouth. This is helped by rows of stiff, overlapping, inch-long, **cone-shaped papillae** that line the complete length of a leatherback's gullet (esophagus) and point toward the turtle's stomach. The grip of these backward-pointed spines, coupled with strong throat muscles, enable a leatherback to wring out its food and expel the excess seawater a turtle might slurp in. Limiting the ingestion of seawater with each meal is important because the excess salt a turtle would take in is toxic. Leatherbacks and other marine animals struggle to make themselves less salty than their surroundings.

Leatherbacks reach their immense size by eating tremendous volumes of low calorie food

The "pink spot" of an adult leatherback in the deep Atlantic

A blushing female leatherback exerts herself on a warm beach

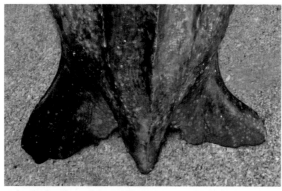

A leatherback's caudal projection

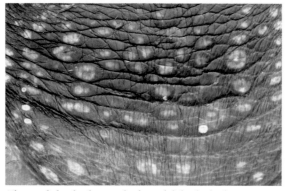

The supple but leathery neck of an adult leatherback

Unique Traits

Of all the sea turtle species, leatherbacks are least like a turtle. In fact, many of their traits are shared more with marine mammals than with reptiles.

Pink Spot

The conspicuous splotch of pink atop a leatherback's head is associated with the extension of the brain known as the pineal gland. The lack of pigment allows transmission of daylight, which is thought to modulate biological rhythms. Perhaps a keen sense of rhythm is needed to anticipate the daily vertical migrations of gelatinous macroplankton (jellyfish and pyrosomes) that leatherbacks depend on.

Warm-bloodedness

One mammalian trait leatherbacks have is a tendency toward being warm-blooded. To be more specific, leatherbacks are endotherms (their body heat can raise their body temperature) that remain poikilothermic (variable in body temperature). This trick is critical for an animal in need of vigorous activity while enveloped in near-freezing water. Although the turtle's body temperature varies, its internally generated warmth, along with a large body (high thermal inertia) and special heat-conservation measures, allow a leatherback to have a core temperature far above the surrounding seawater. The adaptations that allow this temperature regulation are detailed later (see page 103).

Caudal Projection

The teardrop shape of a leatherback's body ends in a pronounced caudal projection. This posterior extension likely helps reduce hydrodynamic drag, making a leatherback an even more efficient swimmer.

Scaleless Skin

Although hatchlings and young juveniles are covered in tiny scales, an adult leatherback is mostly surrounded by rubbery skin. The feel of this skin is more marine mammal than reptile.

Conservation Status

The US Endangered Species Act lists the leatherback turtle as Endangered worldwide. The turtle is also protected by Canada's Species at Risk Act (SARA) 2003. The species is also officially protected from harvest in Mexico, Cuba, and The Bahamas, and on various regional nesting beaches. Regional countries are signatories to the Convention on International Trade in Endangered Species of Wild Fauna and Flora (CITES), which lists the leatherback as protected from commercial trade. The International Union for Conservation of Nature (IUCN) currently has the species on its Red List as Critically Endangered. Because many leatherbacks in our waters come from rookery locations in central and south America, another important conservation treaty for this species is the Inter-American Convention for the Protection and Conservation of Sea Turtles (IAC).

Nesting Trends

Western Atlantic leatherback populations are thought to have experienced dramatic declines following World War II. But over the past two decades, **nest counts** have been increasing on our regional nesting beaches, principally eastern Florida. The increase has been exponential, although annual variation in nest counts is high. The mostly biennial pattern of consecutive high and low years can vary by a factor of two to three, and reflects variation in the proportion of total females that have decided to nest in a given year. Elsewhere in the western Atlantic, nesting at major rookeries also seems to be increasing or at least stable. These nesting colonies, like the largest western Atlantic colonies at the northern shoulder of South America in Trinidad and the Guianas, contribute most of the leatherbacks we see in US and Canadian waters. Recovery in Atlantic leatherbacks contrasts to the plight of the species in the Pacific. The species is in peril there, exemplified by nesting declines of more than 90% on Mexico's Pacific beaches, which at one time hosted roughly half the world leatherback population.

Endangered leatherback populations in the Atlantic are recovering

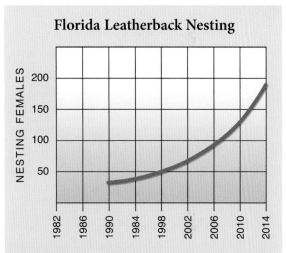

Florida Leatherback Nesting

Recent increases in leatherback nesting have been exponential

A leatherback camouflages her nest on a Florida beach

69

Sea Turtle Form and Function

In this section, we introduce how sea turtles are put together. Fundamentally, they are turtles, sharing the ancestral turtle traits. But they are also thoroughly marine animals with some highly specialized changes to the chelonian form. Life at sea demands movement through a fluid. To accomplish this, sea turtles have had to give up some of the protections offered by the ancestral shell in return for hydrodynamic efficiency. Streamlining their bodies has meant forgoing shell-space for their head and forelimbs. Pockets beneath an overhanging shell that would accommodate these extremities would create expensive drag and reduce swimming speed. So, these hollows at the neck and shoulders of other turtles are instead bulging with the powerful muscles that drive a sea turtle's swimming strokes. Their shoulders are a rounded prow covered by tight but supple skin

that blunts the turtle's leading edge between carapace and plastron. Sea turtles can withdraw their necks into their shells, but their heads remain exposed. As a remedy for this potential vulnerability to large-jawed predators, the sea turtles have evolved robust skulls roofed over with dense bone, which composes a cranium every bit as tough as the turtle's shell. That shell still protects a sea turtle, but its shape has evolved a flattened teardrop form resistant to aquatic drag. And those limbs left outside the shell? They've become flippers, modified for undersea flight.

Form and function describe a sea turtle's anatomy, their use of energy, and how they sense their world, manage water and temperature, and reproduce. These challenges are dealt with under constraints of both environment and ancestry.

Above: The strong muscles that power this green turtle's swimming are recessed within the forward quarters of its shell

Left: Even as hatchlings, green turtles show the smooth, hydrodynamic lines that reduce drag and make them efficient swimmers

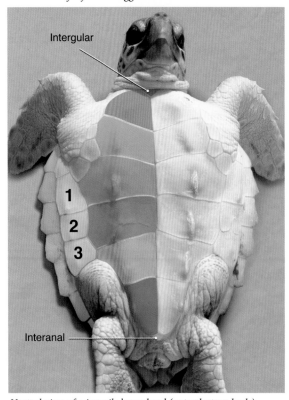

Dorsal view of a juvenile loggerhead sea turtle

Intergular

Interanal

Ventral view of a juvenile loggerhead (note plastron keels)

Scutes, Scales, Skin, and Claws

A turtle's scales are keratinized skin. This keratin is flexible, strong, and pigmented, which gives a turtle its color. Thicker keratin makes up the large scutes (plates) covering the upper and lower shell. A turtle's claws are equivalent to our nails and extend from the ends of the first (thumb) and second phalanges.

Carapace Scutes

These plates protect the shell, and are referred to by name and number. Because their number and position are relatively constant within a species, they can be used in identification. But don't rely on these characters too heavily. Sea turtles can't count and do not read field guides.

- Marginal
- Nuchal
- Costal (lateral or pleural)
- Vertebral (central)
- Pygal (supracaudal or postcentral)

Plastron Scutes

Scutes covering the plastron are similar in number among the sea turtle species, except for the inframarginals lining the bridge of the plastron. The marginals are the same scutes as seen topside. The gular and anal scutes often have an intervening scute of varied size respectively called the intergular and interanal scute. Because the plastron scutes are dependable in the positions they occupy, the scutes serve as useful anatomical landmarks.

- Marginal
- Inframarginal
- Intergular
- Gular
- Humeral
- Pectoral
- Abdominal
- Femoral
- Anal
- Interanal

Male Plastron

Adult males have an elongated area of de-keratinized scutes over a soft depression in their plastron. It's unclear how this soft "belly" patch changes seasonally, but during breeding, the cushion performs its function by allowing a male to mount firmly atop his mate's carapace.

Scute Growth and Shedding

A scute grows when the skin underneath adds a larger layer of keratin underneath. The old scute layer is eventually shed. Loggerheads may retain a few layers of scute before they are lost. In a growing loggerhead, each scute often shows growth bands encircling the offset, oldest scute layers. The loggerhead's old layers shed in ragged pieces rather than all at once.

Extra Scutes

Each sea turtle species has a set number of scutes, except when they don't. It is relatively common to find perfectly healthy turtles with abnormalities that give them extra (supernumerary) shell scutes in unorthodox patterns.

Carapace Spines

Juvenile hawksbills, loggerheads, and Kemp's ridleys have extra thickly keratinized scutes in keels (ridges) along their shell—three **keels** along the carapace and two along the plastron.

Prominent spines of a juvenile ridley's central carapace keel

The center carapace keel is most pronounced and is made of sharp, finlike spines similar to the lateral projections from the posterior marginal scutes. To a shark, the spines may make a little turtle harder to swallow.

A male loggerhead with a soft, thinly keratinized center plastron

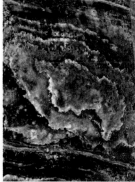

Loggerhead carapace with growth bands (L), shedding scutes (R)

This juvenile green turtle has extra (supernumerary) scutes

A young loggerhead beginning to lose its central keel spines

Head scales (color coded) of a loggerhead sea turtle

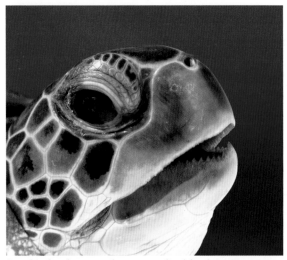

Jaw sheaths of green turtles are specialized for clipping seagrass

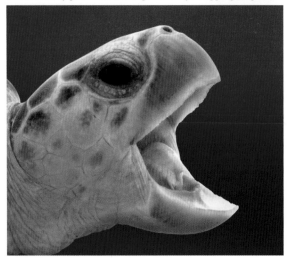

A loggerhead beak can both cut and crush

Head Scales

Each of the hard-shelled sea turtles has keratinous scales in distinctive positions covering the head. These scales have names and are helpful as anatomical landmarks.

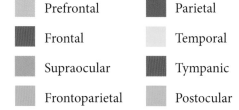

Prefrontal	Parietal
Frontal	Temporal
Supraocular	Tympanic
Frontoparietal	Postocular

Although most of the named head scales occupy a predictable position, extra scales and seams (lines between scales) do occur. These unique patterns stay with a turtle for life and can be used for individual identification.

Sea Turtle Beaks

A turtle's beak is made of keratinous jaw sheaths called rhamphothecae (or singular, rhamphotheca). The sheaths cover the jaws and serve as the operative tools used by a turtle to acquire and preprocess its food.

Green turtles have jaw sheaths that facilitate grazing—snipping marine algae and seagrasses off at the base. The upper sheath is rounded and delicate with serrations along the cutting edge (tomium). The lower sheath is serrated with sharp toothlike cusps. A particularly sharp point at the front of the lower jaw fits into a conical pocket inside the upper jaw sheath. Serrations also mark corresponding sets of interior ridges in the upper and lower sheaths.

The jaw sheaths of a **loggerhead** are thick and strong with features for both cutting and crushing. The lower sheath has a broad depression that fits up against a thick crushing surface on the palate of the upper sheath. The tomium of the upper sheath is sharply serrated in some young loggerheads but is often worn blunt in older turtles, especially those that favor eating hard-shelled mollusks.

Hawksbills have narrow, moderately thickened jaw sheaths that aid in accessing tight reef crevices. The cutting tomium and inner surface of the upper sheath are smooth. The lower cutting edge is also smooth, but the inside has a slightly raised triangular surface.

Kemp's ridleys have thick jaw sheaths able to cut and crush. Features include a pronounced cusp in the forward cutting edge of both the upper and lower jaw. The interior of the lower sheath has grooves that accept crushing ridges in the palate of the upper sheath.

Although a **leatherback's** beak is only thinly keratinized and has no true rhamphothecae, it still proves effective in seizing and snipping apart soft-bodied prey. The jaw's cutting edges close tightly together like scissors, and the lower tomium fits snugly into a slot inside the upper jaw once the mouth is closed. The leading upper jaw has two sharp cusps that point slightly rearward. The forward lower jaw has a single sharp medial cusp that fits neatly into a conical pit inside the upper jaw.

Hatchling Caruncle (Egg Tooth)

Sea turtle hatchlings of all species have a sharp, keratinized projection in their upper jaw sheath called a caruncle or egg tooth.

Egg tooth

Head of a loggerhead hatchling showing its egg tooth (caruncle)

The only function of the egg tooth seems to be to pierce the eggshell, which begins the process of pipping (escape from the egg). As the hatchling grows, the caruncle blunts and becomes an increasingly smaller part of the turtle's beak.

The beak of a hawksbill is slender and birdlike

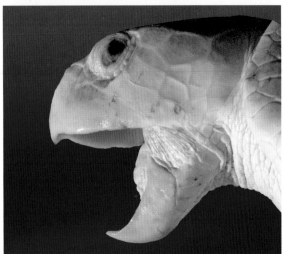

Kemp's ridleys have cusped upper and lower jaws

A leatherback's beak cuts like scissors

This hawksbill's front-flipper scales are sharper at the trailing tip

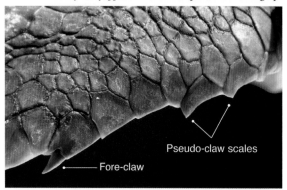

Pseudo-claw scales

Fore-claw

A juvenile loggerhead's front flipper with "pseudo-claw" scales

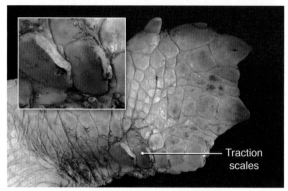

Traction scales

A loggerhead's rear-flipper traction scales help them get a grip

This shallow-water juvenile green turtle has a dark suntan

Flipper Scales

A sea turtle's front flippers are stroking hydrofoils, with a rounded leading edge and a sharp trailing edge. In the hard-shelled sea turtles, the trailing fringe comprises growing scale margins and is stiffer and sharper toward the flipper tip. In young turtles, the trailing flipper tip can slice skin. But rather than a defense feature, this cutting sharpness is likely favored by natural selection for its low-drag hydrodynamics.

Pseudo-claws and Traction Scales

Sea turtle flippers are not just for swimming. The appendages are also used to manipulate food and crawl on the sea bottom. In addition to their front-flipper claws, juvenile ridleys, hawksbills, and loggerheads have protruding, leading-edge, front-flipper scales that are used to grip food and tear off bites. These **pseudo-claws** are most pronounced in young loggerheads. Larger loggerheads lose their clawlike scales but develop thick **traction scales** beneath their rear flippers. These help a foraging loggerhead to crawl along the sea bottom.

Skin

Sea turtles are not completely covered by scales. The neck, shoulders, and inguinal surfaces are covered by supple skin interspersed with thin oval scales. It's the same in leatherbacks,

A blushing leatherback

although their remaining areas of flipper and shell are mostly covered with smooth skin, sans scales. A sea turtle's skin does not always match its scale colors. Turtles that spend their time in deep or turbid waters have pale skin, and turtles in clear, shallow waters get darker, **sun-exposed skin**. A turtle that has spent time in captivity away from natural light becomes pale around the shoulders, cheeks, and scute seams, although thicker scales and scutes remain normally pigmented. This gives most aquarium sea turtles a distinctive look.

The less pigmented skin areas of a leatherback can reveal the turtle's physiology. Leatherbacks often blush. The pinkness is likely a sign of higher blood pressure and warmth rather than embarrassment. The flushed look is especially visible in nesting females exerting themselves on a warm beach.

A loggerhead's yellow neck skin and head scute seams

The recurved "thumb" claw of an adult male loggerhead

Claws

Sea turtles have toenails, which have a definitive set of uses. Hard-shelled sea turtles use their **fore-claws** to tear away the remainder of prey items they've bitten. An adult male's first digit (thumb) claws are extra strong and recurved, allowing him to grip the front carapace of the female he is mounting. A male's primary **rear-flipper claw** is also curved, giving males a five-point hold (prehensile tail included) on their mate.

Rear-flipper claws seem to aid the low-energy locomotion of bottom-crawling. Although most sea turtles without a voluminous breath of air naturally sink, their negative buoyancy is only slight, making bottom traction difficult. Rear claws act like baseball cleats to pierce and grip the sea bottom substrate.

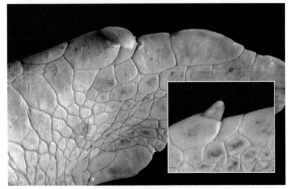

Male loggerhead's front-flipper claw, compared to female's (inset)

The distinct rear-flipper claws of a juvenile Kemp's ridley

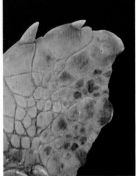

Male (L) and female (R) loggerhead rear flippers, underside

The Skeleton

A turtle's skeleton provides shape and strength. This framework is composed of bone and cartilage. Bone is strong but rigid, and cartilage is flexible. Important cartilaginous parts of a sea turtle's skeleton, like the bridge between the upper and lower shell, do not persist well enough to be represented in assembled skeletons.

The general parts of a sea turtle's skeleton include the axial skeleton (skull, spinal column, and carapace), and the appendicular skeleton (flippers with their supporting bony girdles, both pectoral and pelvic). The plastron bones have elements from both the axial and appendicular skeletons. The bones are joined (articulated) in at least three ways. 1) carapace and skull bones are joined along jagged sutures; 2) some pectoral and pelvic girdle bones articulate with connections made by stiff cartilage; and 3) the limbs articulate at moveable joints, such as the hinge joints and ball-and-socket joints of the larger flipper bones. Various composites of cartilage compose ligaments that bind bones together and make up important skeletal elements like the plastron.

Some bones are tiny, but perform important functions. These include the bones of a sea turtle's inner ear (see page 93), which transmit sound vibrations. Sea turtles also have a small ring of bones, called scleral ossicles, within their eyes to support the eyeball's spherical shape.

In addition to providing support, a sea turtle's skeleton is a storehouse for calcium. Adult females draw on these stores to produce the hundreds of shelled eggs they will lay during a nesting season. Because sea turtles have little or no opportunity to feed during this reproductive period, getting calcium from their diet is not an option. To make calcium carbonate eggshell, females metabolize their skeleton, undergoing significant bone resorption (bone breakdown and transfer of calcium to the blood).

Carapace and Plastron Bones

Because of their protective shell, turtles have more bone than most other animals. But in comparison to the other turtles, sea turtles have a much lighter

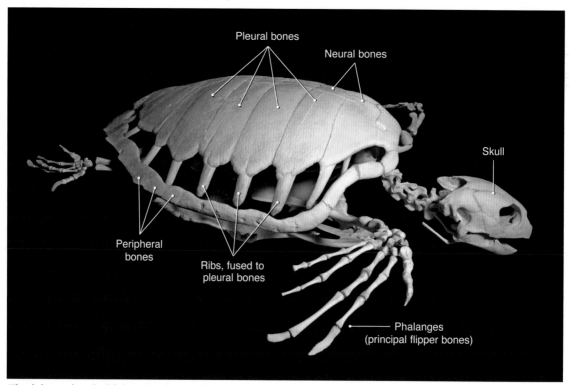

The skeleton of a subadult loggerhead sea turtle

and more flexible set of shell bones. Sea turtles are most flexible as hatchlings. Their **carapace bones** begin as separate ribs, and their nine plastron bones are initially thin, independent elements imbedded in connective tissue. As a sea turtle grows, flat, membrane (dermal) bone fuses the turtle's spine and ribs together. The fusion includes neural bones that fuse with vertebrae, and pleural bones that fuse with neural bones and ribs, expanding outward toward the rib tips as the turtle matures. Growth slows at adulthood when the pleural bones meet the peripheral (marginal) bones lining the edge of the carapace. This fusion occurs at the front of the carapace, leaving fontanelles without bone at the widest part. Meanwhile, **plastron bones** have also been growing outward. The three largest on each side eventually fuse together front to back, leaving an open center and lateral edges filled with cartilage and spiked projections from the joined bones.

The arrangement of shell bones is vastly reduced in leatherbacks, which have no neural, pleural, or peripheral bones in their carapace, and have only a reduced set of sinuous plastron bones joined into a large oval. Some skeletal support of the leatherback's carapace comes from a forward nuchal bone and from hundreds of thin, coin-size dermal ossicles. These tiny bones form an articulated honeycomb-patterned jigsaw puzzle of bone embedded under thick skin throughout the entire leatherback carapace.

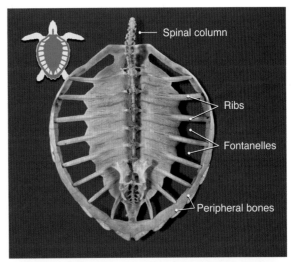

The underside of carapace bones from a juvenile green turtle

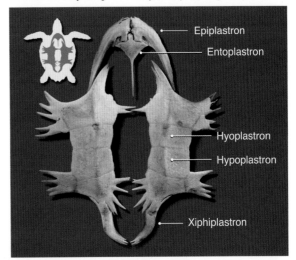

Plastron bones from a juvenile green turtle

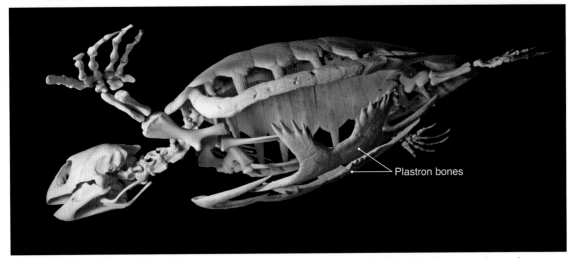

The plastron and carapace bones do not connect, which leaves sea turtles with more shell flexibility than most other turtles

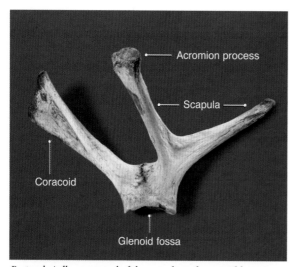

Pectoral girdle, composed of the scapula and coracoid bones

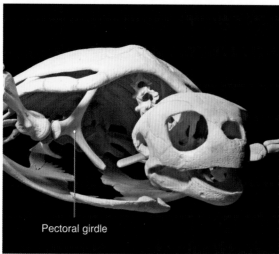

Arrangement of a loggerhead's pectoral girdles

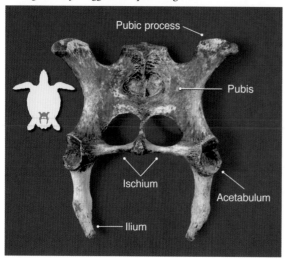

Ventral view of an adult loggerhead's pelvic girdle

Pectoral and Pelvic Girdle Bones

Having a shell has had profound evolutionary consequences for the turtle skeleton. For one, the girdles that support limb movement are inside the rib cage. In this trick of contortion, it is as if a broad thoracic umbrella swallowed up the shoulders and hips, which are outside the ribs in other vertebrates. The **pectoral (shoulder) girdles** are strong, with pronounced processes (projections of bone) that connect to the plastron and provide attachment surfaces for swimming muscles. Left and right girdles each comprise two joined bones, the scapula and the coracoid, which together have three processes. The scapula attaches with ligaments to the front of the carapace and to the plastron by the bone's acromion process. In the image of a loggerhead's articulated pectoral girdles (left middle), the scapula can be seen spanning the carapace and plastron. Scapula and coracoid bones join at a shoulder socket, called the glenoid fossa, which connects to the humerus. The coracoid bone extends back within the turtle's chest and has a flared out coracoid process, which is the main attachment surface for the turtle's powerful pectoral muscles.

The **pelvic girdle** is a set of three bone-pairs, the pubis, ischium, and ilium. These bones are completely fused together in the hard-shelled sea turtles, and are connected only by cartilage in the leatherback. Each ilium connects the pelvis by ligaments to the carapace at the sacral vertebrae, which are extra wide. On each side, the three bones converge to form a hip socket (acetabulum), which accepts the head of the femur. In the image of a loggerhead's pelvis (lower left), you see the underside as if you were looking through the turtle's plastron, with the rear of the turtle pointed down. The projection of each ilium would have connected to the carapace, and the pubic processes would have pointed forward and down toward the turtle's plastron.

Flipper Bones

Inside a sea turtle's **front flipper** are the standard limb bones most vertebrates share, but with important modifications. The upper arm bone (humerus) is thick and short—only about twice as long as it is wide. Near the head of the humerus where it connects to the pectoral girdle, the bone's medial process provides an attachment surface for muscles that extend the flipper up and forward. About midway down the bone, the protruding lateral process multiplies the attachment area for strong pectoral muscles, which thrust the flipper downward and back. These bony features allow for powerful swimming strokes. At the end of the stocky upper arm extends an even shorter set of forearm bones—the radius and ulna. These bones are fused together by fibrous connective tissue. This same tough connective tissue binds the wrist and hand bones—carpals, metacarpals, and phalanges. The widest part of the flipper blade represents the turtle's wrist and palm, with the digits (five of them, just like us) extending outward within the tough webbing. In the hard-shelled sea turtles, the turtle's first (thumb) digit ends in a claw that pokes out at the flipper's leading edge. In loggerheads and hawksbills, the second digit has a smaller protruding claw.

A sea turtle's **rear flipper** is roughly half the length of the front flipper but just as wide. Within the rear flipper, the upper limb bone (femur) bears an offset head that articulates with the pelvis at the acetabulum socket. The femur is about as long as the two shin bones (tibia and fibula) it connects to. Next, a short, broad set of ankle bones spread five digits into the rear flipper's rudder shape.

In leatherbacks, the large bones of the flippers and their support girdles have a different makeup that indicates rapid bone-growth potential. These leatherback bones have extensive vascularized cartilage and relatively little cortical (outer) bone layers like the hard-shelled sea turtles show. The vascular features of a leatherback's limb bones allow the turtle to grow rapidly and reach its massive size.

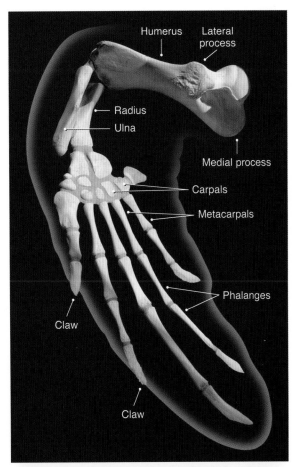

Ventral view of bones within a loggerhead's right front flipper

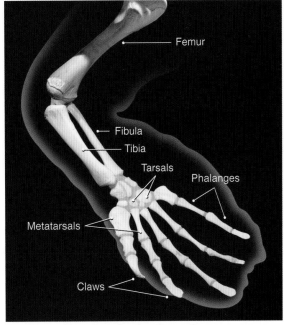

The bones within a loggerhead's right rear flipper

81

Skull, Hyoid, and Spine

Elements of a sea turtle's **axial skeleton** support feeding, critical senses, and the turtle's command and control center—its brain. A sea turtle's skull is roofed over with dense bone, and an inner braincase (neurocranium) holds the brain. The outer bony superstructure includes the upper and lower jaw bones, support for jaw and neck muscles, and housing for salt glands, ears, eyes, and nose. The bones that make up the external skull are mostly the same in all sea turtles, although how they fit together varies among species. Upper and lower jaws are each composed of mul-

tiple strongly articulated bones. The large muscles that close the lower jaw are inside the skull at its widest point behind the eyes. Below the skull, a free-floating apparatus of cartilage and bones called the hyoid supports the turtle's tongue and throat muscles. Large orbits surround each eye, containing a ring of bones known as scleral ossicles. The rear of the braincase connects to the first cervical (neck) vertebra (atlas) of the spine. Sea turtles have sliding joints between their neck vertebrae that allow vertical and horizontal movement, but no twisting.

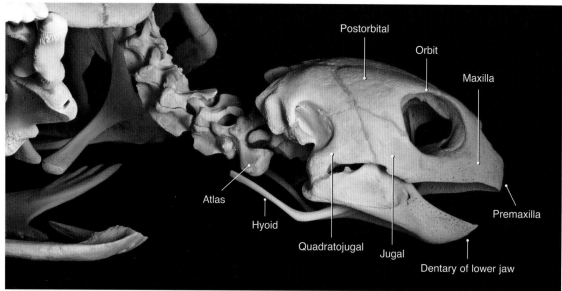

Lateral view of a loggerhead's skull, hyoid, and cervical spine

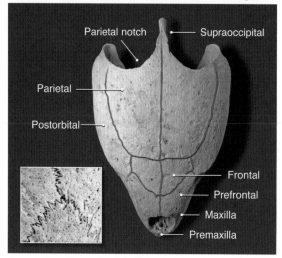

Dorsal view of loggerhead skull. Bone sutures inset and in red

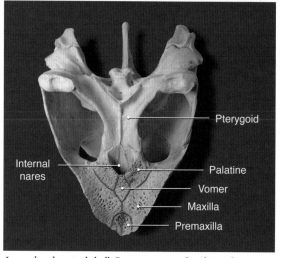

Loggerhead ventral skull. Bone sutures outlined in red

Green Turtle Skull

Green turtle skulls are bullet-shaped with a rounded snout and shallow parietal notches. These notches are the are the indentations on either side of the rearward projecting supraoccipital bone. The palate, which is the roof of the upper jaw ahead of the internal nares, has a distinctive pair of ridges running parallel to the outer jaw edge. Similar ridges in the lower jaw join at a short ridge along the center.

Loggerhead Skull

A loggerhead's skull bulges widely behind the orbits and tapers into a blunt angle in front. Loggerheads have a palate without any ridges. The two maxillary bones, which make up most of the palate and upper jaw, connect behind the set of premaxillary bones (lower images on the facing page). This condition separates loggerheads from ridleys and hawksbills. When in doubt of a skull's identity, turn it over and examine the upper jaw roof.

Hawksbill Skull

The skull of a hawksbill has a distinctive narrow shape and a birdlike set of jaws. The skull is less narrow in hatchlings and small juveniles, but elongates into the familiar hawksbill profile before a turtle reaches dinner-plate size. For larger juveniles and adults, the skull length is about twice the width. As in loggerheads, hawksbill skulls have deep parietal notches. Unlike loggerheads, the two maxillary bones in the roof of the jaw are separated by the vomer bone, which extends forward to connect with the set of premaxillary bones that lead the upper jaw.

Green turtle skull

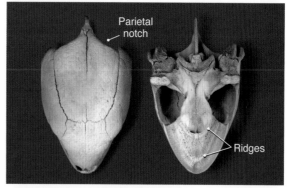

Green turtle skull dorsal (L) and ventral (R)

Loggerhead skull

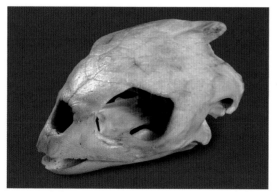

Hawksbill skull

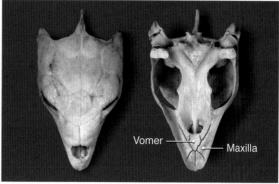

Hawksbill skull dorsal (L) and ventral (R). Sutures in red.

83

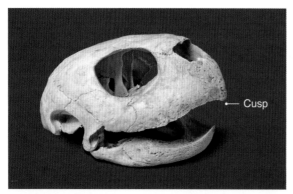

Kemp's ridley skull

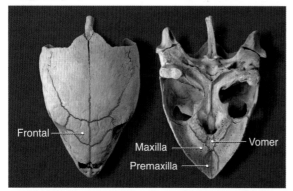

Kemp's ridley skull dorsal (L) and ventral (R). Sutures in red

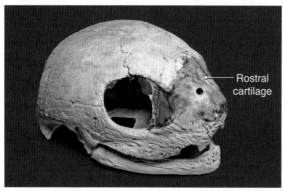

Leatherback skull

Leatherback skull dorsal (L) and ventral (R)

Kemp's Ridley Skull

The profile of a ridley skull is similar to but more narrow than a loggerhead skull. As in loggerheads and hawksbills, ridley skulls have deep parietal notches. One conspicuous difference is the presence of a cusp at the leading edge of the upper jaw. The lower jaw cusp is also conspicuous, more so than in loggerheads. But ridley skulls are easily distinguished from loggerhead skulls by the features of the upper jaw palate. Unlike loggerheads, Kemp's ridleys have distinct ridges along their palate and have their maxillary bones separated by a vomer, which extends forward to contact the premaxillary bones. Another difference is that a ridley's frontal bones take part in the skull's orbit (eye socket), unlike the frontal bones of a loggerhead (see page 82). The olive ridley has a similar skull to Kemp's ridley, but is extremely rare in our region. To separate the two ridleys, note that olive ridleys have no palatal ridges and an extremely wide set of pterygoid bones, which form the shelf behind the palate.

Leatherback Skull

Leatherback skulls are very different from the skulls of other sea turtles. The skull is wide and rounded at the rear with large orbits. There are no parietal notches because the supraoccipital bones are so short. The skull also has a vastly reduced palate. The upper jaw has sharp cusps in the front, and the lower jaw points upward at the tip, just as the beak does in the living turtle. Because a leatherback's skull bones fit together so loosely with intervening cartilage, specimens tend to disarticulate (fall apart) if not treated carefully. This loosely assembled condition is similar to the way that skull bones are joined in very young sea turtles of other species. Such a loose articulation may facilitate rapid growth. Some bones are missing in a leatherback's skull. For example, the nasal bones are completely replaced with rostral cartilage, which is a soft extension of the nasal septum.

Muscles and Tendons

Sea turtles don't seem like muscular animals because much of their musculature is hidden within their shell. But swimming, crawling, feeding, and breathing require coordinated power applied by muscle groups that are very similar to other vertebrate animals.

The Swimming Muscles

These are the largest sea turtle muscles. Those that power the front flippers include the pectoralis major, a fan-shaped muscle that takes up most of a sea turtle's chest and attaches to the plastron and humerus. These muscles power flippers down, back, and together (retraction and adduction). The corresponding front-flipper motion up and forward (protraction and abduction) is powered by the deltoideus and the supracoracoideus muscles. The principal muscles of a sea turtle's hind end include a pair of pelvic stabilizers, the rectus abdominis set. These muscles connect the plastron to the pubis. All of the pectoral and pelvic muscles described here function in both swimming and in respiration, which requires forcible movement of shoulders, plastron, and pelvic region. Unlike us, turtles have no diaphragm.

The muscles a sea turtle uses to crawl on land include many of the muscles used for swimming. Major rear-flipper muscles are in the puboischiofemoralis complex, which attaches pelvis to femur, and can either protract or retract the leg. These muscles are strong in the hard-shelled sea turtles.

Muscles of the Head and Neck

Just as the swimming muscles are hidden in a sea turtle's shell, the turtle's strong jaw muscles are hidden within the head. The largest jaw muscle, the adductor mandibulae, originates from several points inside the skull, from the parietal to the supraoccipital projection, and connects to the dentary bone of the lower jaw. Internal muscles in the neck serve to extend the neck and retract it into the shell. The most visible neck muscles are the **biventer cervical muscles**, which flex to raise the head.

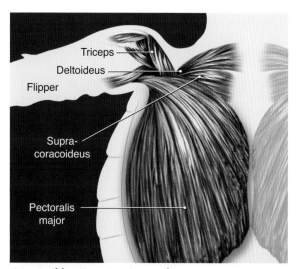

A sea turtle's major swimming muscles

A nesting loggerhead throws sand using her swimming muscles

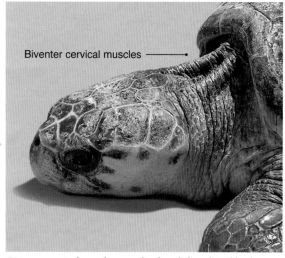

Biventer cervical muscles are a landmark for taking blood

Circulation

The **circulatory system** of a sea turtle includes the heart, arteries, veins, and the vessels that carry lymph. The heart is the main pump for the system. It is four chambered, with a sinus venosus, two atria, and a ventricle. The muscular ventricle is incompletely divided into three compartments, which separately handle blood entering from the two atria and exiting to the lungs. This separates pulmonary (to/from lungs) and systemic (to/from body) blood flows so that the turtle can adapt to periods when the lungs deliver no oxygen, like during a long dive. This trick keeps the lungs from "stealing" blood oxygen after the lungs' oxygen is depleted. Leatherbacks have almost completely separate pulmonary and systemic circuits, and hard-shelled sea turtles have slightly less separation.

Arteries

Arteries carry blood away from the heart. They have muscular elastic walls, typically lie deep within tissues, and have a relatively high blood pressure. The main arteries leaving the heart are the pulmonary artery supplying the lungs, the right aorta supplying the head and limbs, and the left aorta supplying the internal organs.

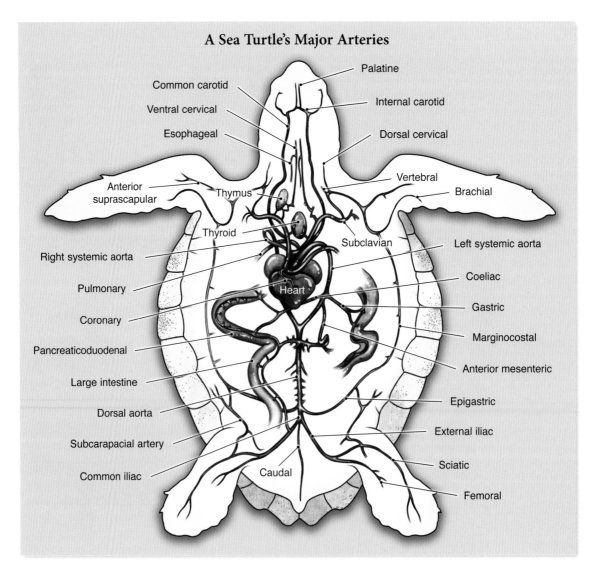

A Sea Turtle's Major Arteries

Veins

Veins carry blood to the heart. These vessels have relatively thin walls, are elastic, and can collapse. Because veinal blood pressure is low, many veins have valves that keep blood flowing in the right direction.

What is Blood?

Sea turtle blood contains cells (red and white cells, and platelets) suspended in plasma. **Centrifuged blood** separates with the cells on the bottom. Plasma is about 90% water, with dissolved proteins, glucose, electrolytes, hormones and clotting factors. Blood serum is plasma without clotting factors.

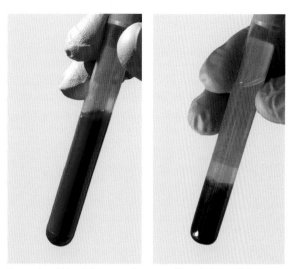

Loggerhead blood (L), spun down to cells and plasma (R)

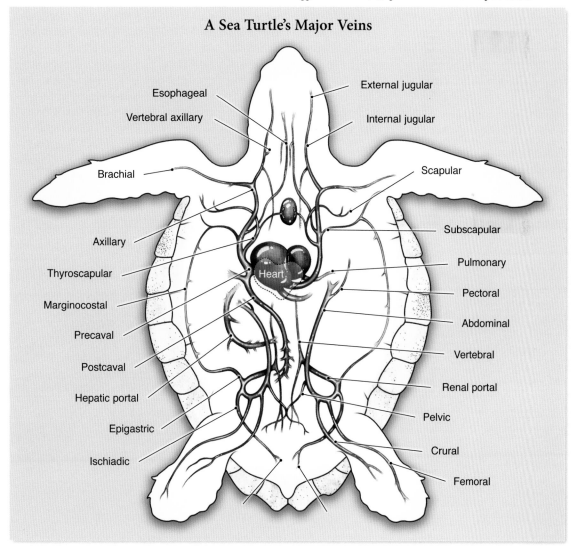

A Sea Turtle's Major Veins

Esophageal, Vertebral axillary, External jugular, Internal jugular, Brachial, Scapular, Axillary, Subscapular, Thyroscapular, Pulmonary, Marginocostal, Pectoral, Precaval, Abdominal, Postcaval, Vertebral, Hepatic portal, Renal portal, Epigastric, Pelvic, Ischiadic, Crural, Femoral, Heart

Digestion and Excretion

Sea turtles eat food to get energy and materials for activity, growth, and reproduction. Those building blocks and energy have to be extracted and absorbed, and their wastes excreted. Let's see how all this takes place as a green turtle consumes seagrass and eventually turns it into turtle.

The process begins with a bite. Green turtles snip off the marine plants they eat, so bites they get are mostly seagrass with very little bottom sediment. Once in the mouth, the grass blades may be further clipped into pieces by the cutting ridges of the turtle's palate and lower jaw. After a few bites to acquire a bolus (wad) of food, the tongue pushes it into the esophagus. The muscular esophagus squeezes the bolus to push out saltwater and complete the swallowing process. Sea turtles keep down the food they squeeze because their esophagus is lined with stiff, pointed **papillae** that point backward all the way to the stomach. These projections grip even the slipperiest food, like the jellyfish that green turtles sometimes eat. As the seagrass bolus goes down, it makes a sharp left turn just before entering the stomach.

Once in the stomach, chemical and physical digestive processes begin. These processes include stomach contractions that stir the swallowed meal within a soup of enzymes at an acidic pH of 1–2. Mucous coating the smooth walls of the turtle's stomach prevents it from digesting itself. The prepared blob of food then passes the stomach's muscular pyloric sphincter and enters the duodenum, the first section of the small intestine. Breakdown of proteins and complex carbohydrates continues with enzymes squirted into the mix by the pancreas and liver. Here, the acids of the stomach are neutralized so that digestion takes place at a pH of about 7.

Movement through the gut is by peristalsis, which describes the waves of gut-wall constrictions that push a bolus along and mix the surrounding juices. This push is toward the next sections in the small intestine called the jejunum, then the ileum. These small-intestine specializations are not visually obvious in the green turtle, although they mark a transition to a different set of digestive functions. Rather than continuing food breakdown, these latter sections specialize in absorption of the amino acids, carbohydrates, sugars, fatty acids, and minerals that digestion has freed. For this absorption, the walls of the

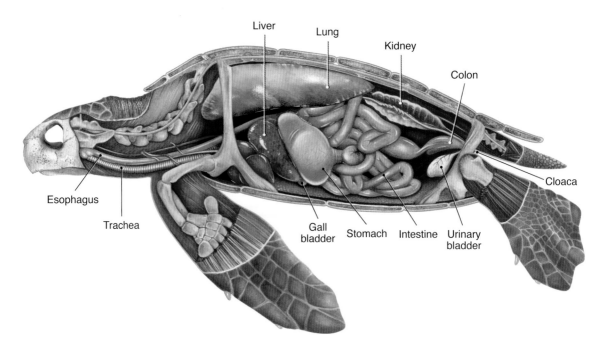

Some principal features of a loggerhead sea turtle's digestive and excretory systems, with other organs noted for reference

lower small intestine have a vast surface area compounded by tight folds covered with villi (tiny projections), which are themselves covered by smaller microvilli. The nutrients absorbed through the gut walls are taken up by a busy network of blood vessels that transport the bounty throughout the turtle.

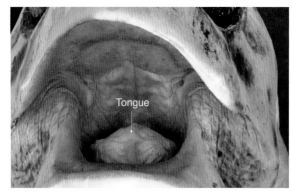

The tongue of a loggerhead sea turtle

At this stage, the food boli are still wads of firm material held together by undigested seagrass cellulose. As each bolus moves into the cecum of the large intestine, anaerobic fermentation of this plant fiber has already begun. This is a critical step in digestion for green turtles, and it is aided by a variety of microorganisms that green turtles harbor in their hind gut. These symbiotic organisms chemically convert cellulose, and the less digestible hemicellulose, into volatile fatty acids, which are an important energy source. Fermentation is helped by hind gut mixing—both peristalsis and anti-peristalsis, or the back-and-forth sloshing of material in the large intestine. Because this process is so important, the large intestine is proportionally longer in green turtles than it is in the other hard-shelled, carnivorous sea turtles.

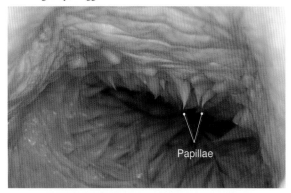

The opening of a loggerhead's esophagus, showing papillae

The mixed, digested, and fermented boli then move into the green turtle's voluminous colon where water and various electrolytes are reclaimed. The colon's fecal contents are squeezed into the rectum, and then the cloaca, which also accepts urine from the kidneys (via the urinary bladder). In the end, the cloaca empties through the **vent** underneath the turtle's tail.

The digestive efficiency of green turtles, that is, their conversion of nitrogen compounds and carbohydrates in seagrass to energy available for activity and growth, is roughly 25 to 85%. This is not bad considering the inherent indigestibility of cellulose, which is the bulk of what a green turtle takes in. The entire digestive process from bite to poop takes roughly a week at comfortable water temperatures (77° F, 25° C) and about 60% longer at temperatures that a green turtle would consider cold (59° F, 15° C).

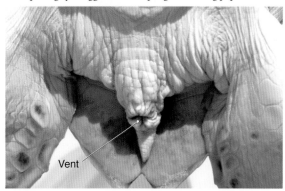

A juvenile green turtle's vent, leading to the cloaca

A fecal bolus (poop) over seagrass grazed by large green turtles

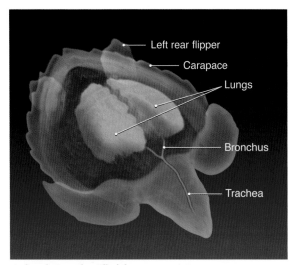

A dorsal view of a ridley's lungs

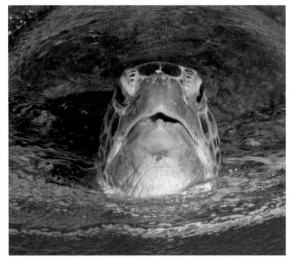

A green turtle's quick breath shows its expanded throat

Sea turtles hold their breath, even while floating at the surface

Respiration

Sea turtles breathe at the surface by rapidly drawing in air. With head up and mouth partly open, air rushes through the turtle's muscular glottis behind the tongue, into the **trachea** ringed with supporting cartilage, through the two bronchi, and into the **lungs.** As a turtle holds its breath (what they do most of the time, even on land) the glottis is shut airtight. The lungs are spongy, multilobed sacs attached to the underside of the carapace. To fill its lungs, a sea turtle uses its pectoral and pelvic muscles to depress the plastron. More air is forced in by throat muscles in a process called gular pumping. In about a second, this exchanges lung volumes as much as 10% of the turtle's total body volume. During a dive, sea turtles depend on lung oxygen (instead of blood and tissue oxygen as marine mammals do) and also use their lungs for buoyancy control. Depending on temperature and activity, a green turtle may breathe every five minutes or every five hours.

Glands

Glands are organs that synthesize substances and either release them into the bloodstream or outside the body. Substances include enzymes,

The tears of a leatherback function to excrete toxic salts

hormones, and many other compounds. One critical set of sea turtle glands is the pair of **lachrymal glands** or **salt glands**. These are found behind each eye and are the largest glands in the head. Salt glands are critical for removing excess salts from a sea turtle's blood. Although the gland's viscous tears are especially visible in nesting females, sea turtles shed these all the time.

The Nervous System

A sea turtle's nervous system coordinates both voluntary and involuntary actions and transmits this control between different areas of the body. The central nervous system (CNS) includes the turtle's **brain** and spinal cord. The peripheral nervous system (PNS) is a network of nerves that connect the CNS to the rest of the turtle and includes motor neurons (signalling voluntary movement), the autonomic nervous system (regulating involuntary functions), and the enteric nervous system (for control of the digestive system).

The controlling organ of a turtle's CNS is its multilobed brain. The forebrain includes the olfactory nerve and olfactory bulbs, cerebral hemispheres, lateral ventricles, optic nerves, and glands such as the hypothalamus, thalamus, pituitary, and pineal. The midbrain includes the optic lobes, third ventricle, and oculomotor nerves. The hindbrain features the cerebellum, fourth ventricle, cranial nerves, and medulla. The forebrain has considerable processing capacity for smell, leaving some extra room for control of complex "cerebral" behaviors. The midbrain's optic lobes seem important, based on size. The hindbrain capacity suggests important reliance on instinctive behavior, muscular movement, and on the brain stem's regulation of heart rate, respiration, and blood pressure.

How Smart are Sea Turtles?

It depends on what tests they take. Sea turtles do show a distinct capacity to learn, as concluded from experiments where they are rewarded based on their choices. These capabilities don't match the intellect of birds or mammals. But sea turtles apparently have excellent memory. They seem to recollect features of their natal coastline decades after leaving it as hatchlings. These persistent memories guide behaviors mediated by complex sensory stimuli. That is, sea turtles are able to use very old thoughts of their inception with newly acquired information to plot complex navigational courses home. If we could do that, we would be considered extraordinary savants.

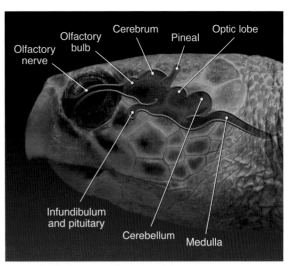

Olfactory nerve · Olfactory bulb · Cerebrum · Pineal · Optic lobe · Infundibulum and pituitary · Cerebellum · Medulla

The multilobed brain of a loggerhead sea turtle

Hatchlings have a larger brain-to-body size ratio than adults do

A loggerhead learns target choice in a hearing experiment

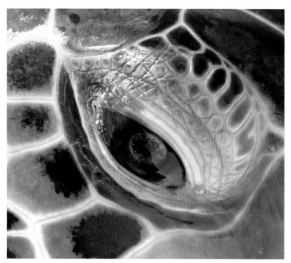

The large eye of this green turtle suggests a reliance on vision

A sea turtle's view, myopic in air, better underwater

The Senses

Sea turtles perceive their world through the classical senses of sight, hearing, taste, smell, and touch. They can also assess temperature, motion, and magnetic fields (field strength and direction, in multiple dimensions).

Vision

Sight is important to sea turtles. It's the sense they rely on most to find food. In food-choice experiments with young loggerheads, visual stimuli seem to trump olfactory (smell) stimuli. Eye size and ratios of photoreceptors (rods and cones) suggest that sea turtles sacrifice night vision for acute, color-discriminating, motion-sensitive day vision. In water, a juvenile loggerhead can resolve four to eight contrasting stripes within each degree in its visual field. This is about twice as good as human acuity underwater, but poorer than us in air. Above water, sea turtles are pretty near-sighted, but their ability to detect motion is very good. Loggerheads and green turtles can detect a flicker at 40 cycles per second, which is about twice as good as us. Like us, a sea turtle's retina has both rods and cone cells. But their three cone pigments are paired with colored oil droplets so that at least four functional photoreceptors result. Whereas our rainbow has seven colors, a sea turtle's has ten. Where we can discriminate between about a million colors, sea turtles see 100 million (potentially).

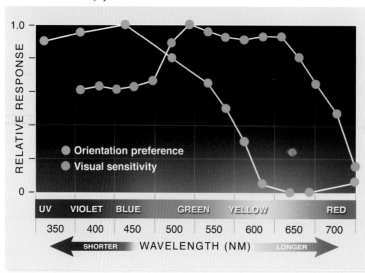

What Do Sea Turtles See?

Sea turtles see colors but are also differentially sensitive to spectral wavelengths. Dark-adapted hatchling green turtles can detect light spanning the spectrum from near ultraviolet to red-orange, with a peak in the green. But in their seafinding orientation (see page 120), the hatchlings are most strongly attracted to shorter wavelengths between the near UV and blue-green.

Hearing

Although we don't know how sea turtles use their sense of hearing, their capacity to hear is revealed by studies of their anatomy and sensory responses. Electrophysiological studies of green turtles suggest that they hear best within a range of 100 to 1000 hertz. Their greatest sensitivity is at about 300 hertz. This peak corresponds to the peak sounds of a human male with a deep voice, and to the underwater roar of breaking waves on a beach. Tone sensitivity is the same underwater as in air, although a sea turtle's hearing on land is likely to be muffled. Their capacity to collect sound is based on transmission from a dense medium (water) to an equally dense medium (the **fatty trumpet** of the middle ear). So to a sea turtle nesting on a beach, the conversations of people nearby probably sound like a muffled, high-pitched incarnation of Charlie Brown's teacher. Underwater, the deep sounds a sea turtle might be listening to carry for much greater distances than higher-frequency sounds.

A sea turtle's **inner ear** also functions to keep the turtle balanced. Within the bony otic capsule containing the cochlea are three semicircular canals. These fluid-filled tubes are positioned in three different planes. Together, they give the turtle a complete feeling of head orientation in terms of pitch (up and down), yaw (side to side), and roll (one side up and other side down).

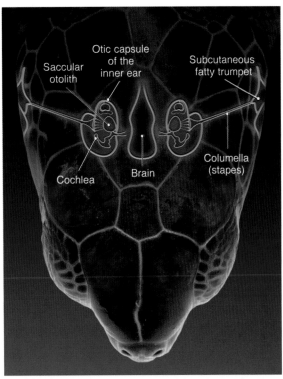

The sea turtle ear is hidden within its head. Beneath the tympanic scales, a wide cone of fat (fatty trumpet) within a bony depression either side of the skull funnels waterborne vibrations to the slender columella (stapes) bone. This sole bone of the middle ear flares into a plate that transmits to a window in the cochlea of the inner ear. When the tiny hair cells inside the cochlea vibrate, associated fibers of the cochlear nerve fire, sending a message to the brain, and the turtle hears

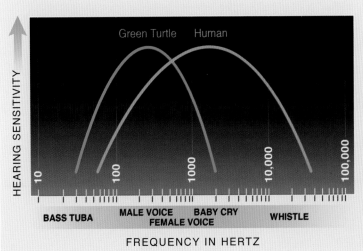

What Do Sea Turtles Hear?

Sea turtles hear deep sounds that we don't, but probably can't hear a baby crying. Equally important is what sea turtles listen to. Seagrass and jellyfish don't make much noise, and neither do potential predators like sharks. Perhaps sea turtles use the clicking cacophony of reefs and the roar of breaking surf as navigational reference points.

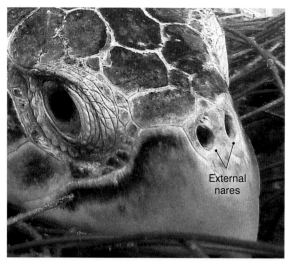

The external nares of a Kemp's ridley

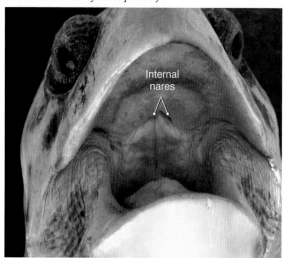

Internal nares behind the upper jaw sheath of a loggerhead

Chemical cues may guide this hatchling back to its natal beach

Taste and Smell

In matters of taste, sea turtles seem relatively unsophisticated. The taste buds they have on their tongue do not appear well developed, although little study of these taste organs has been done. The principal way that sea turtles assess chemicals in their world is through olfaction—their sense of smell. Sea turtles have two sets of nose openings, the **external** and **internal nares.** The external openings are in soft skin above the beak, and the internal openings are in the palate just behind the upper jaw sheath. Underwater, sea turtles pump water back and forth through the nasopharyngeal duct that connects these sets of nares. The ability to smell odorants in this flow comes from two sensory areas, a vomeronasal epithelium in pockets above and below the duct, and a larger nasal cavity above the duct. In both areas, odorant molecules bind to specific sites on olfactory receptors, which signal the brain. One hypothesized difference in the two olfactory areas is that while the vomeronasal epithelium floods, the nasal cavity retains an air bubble.

The ability to smell in both sea and air gives sea turtles an adaptive advantage. Young loggerheads are attracted to the airborne smell of the volatile compound dimethyl sulfide, which accumulates above productive oceanic fronts where the turtles live and feed. Sea turtles also have an excellent underwater nose. In conditioning trials where turtles were rewarded with food for making specific odor choices, researchers found that the turtles could detect a wide array of chemicals. Although an obvious use for olfaction is finding food, chemical stimuli also may be important as cues for location-imprinting and navigation. Hints that chemical cues could guide sea turtles back to their natal region come from research on loggerheads exposed to the synthetic chemical morpholine, both in their nest and as swimming hatchlings. Months later, the turtles showed that they preferred the spot in a circular tank where the chemical was concentrated. Although reliance on chemical imprinting cues to guide navigation later in life remains uncertain, it's at least possible that sea turtles can smell their way home.

Touch, Temperature, and Balance

Sea turtles are covered with scales and thick skin, but they have at least some ability to use their sense of touch. One use seems to be by nesting females in the process of digging their egg chamber. When the turtle can no longer feel sand within reach of her rear flippers at the bottom of the hole, digging stops and egg laying begins. Although it is unclear how important touch is to sea turtles in their everyday lives, they do clearly respond to tactile stimuli, sometimes in surprising ways. A researcher may observe a captured turtle to make exaggerated flinches at the slightest touch, yet no obvious response to the piercing of their flipper with a metal tag. Although it's likely that the softer areas of sea turtle's skin are the most sensitive to touch, turtles have at least some ability to detect contact even through their carapace.

A leatherback detects that her egg chamber is nearly finished

Temperature is an important assessment for sea turtles. One example of temperature sensitivity is the regulation of periodic activity by hatchlings in the nest. High temperatures instill calm in the sibling group and low temperatures prompt activity. This regulation ensures coordinated movement in digging out of the nest, and it brings about **emergence** of the group at the most opportune time—at night, when diurnal predators and desiccating conditions can be avoided.

Cooling sand triggers the emergence of loggerhead hatchlings

Wave Orientation

A sense of balance, probably governed by the semicircular canals within a sea turtle's inner ear, helps hatchlings orient offshore through the surf. Hatchlings feel the roll of the waves and turn to face the orbit within the waves that moves them back, down, forward, then up. This is the feel of swimming into the waves, which is the correct initial path away from land (see page 120).

BEACH

95

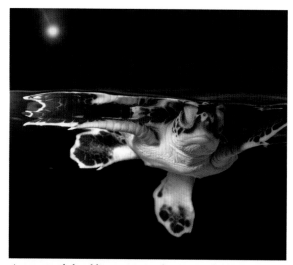
A green turtle hatchling maintains direction in the open sea

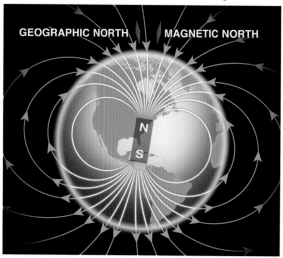
Magnetic field line angles vary with latitude

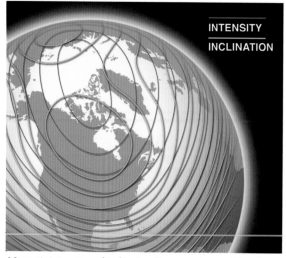
Magnetic intensity and inclination lines cross to reveal location

A Sixth Sense

Perhaps the most intriguing sensation felt by sea turtles is one we can only imagine—a sensation of Earth's magnetic field. Although many animals show some magnetic sense, sea turtles are one of few animal groups for which a highly developed geomagnetic skill has been thoroughly described. As hatchling sea turtles crawl to sea and swim into the waves, they are apparently calibrating the magnetic compass they'll use to maintain a swimming orientation away from land. But this geomagnetic aptitude rises to levels beyond simply determining a compass direction. In its early sensations of the world, a hatchling may not only learn the magnetic feel of movement out to sea, but may also acquire a magnetic awareness of location applicable to a lifetime of journeys.

Only with instruments can we sense, as sea turtles do, the details in the magnetic envelope surrounding our planet. In this field are lines curving from magnetic pole to pole, lines that are horizontal near the equator and that incline more vertically north and south. In a reading of tilt in these magnetic field lines, a hatchling assesses not only which way a pole is, but also how distant it is. In addition to this sensation of direction and latitude, hatchlings show an ability to detect varying intensities in the local magnetic field. These strengths vary over the earth along gradients, and although field intensity is greatest at the poles, many areas of the globe have **lines of equal field strength** that cross the lines of equal field inclination. So, with a reference for constant direction, with an ability to sense position on a magnetic grid, and with a magnetic memory for the places they've been, a sea turtle has the essential tools of a navigator—a compass, a global positioning system (GPS), and a map.

How sea turtles detect magnetic subtleties is largely unknown. Suspect sensors include tiny chains of an iron oxide (magnetite) in the turtle's head (its brain or maybe its nose). These miniature compass needles may shift orientation to stimulate a sense of magnetic location.

Reproduction

Right up to the age when a sea turtle starts to mature, males and females look the same on the outside. In juveniles, even an endoscopic examination of the genitalia (genital papilla) within the cloaca won't differentiate boys from girls. But as males near adult size, their tail lengthens and thickens over the span of just a few years, and they develop the recurved claws and soft, flattened plastron characteristic of adult males. Because sea turtles mature at different sizes, a short-tailed turtle just reaching the adult size range may be a female, but could also be a late-blooming male.

On the inside, developing males and females have distinct differences. Females have an **ovary** underneath each kidney, forward of the pelvis. Even in immature turtles, the ovary appears granular with the many tiny follicles that will supply a lifetime of egg laying. An oviduct runs lateral to each ovary. It begins with a funnel-shaped ostium, which receives mature follicles from the ovary, and ends with the cloaca, where shelled eggs exit. The ovaries of a female ready to breed will have varied sizes of maturing, orange-yolked follicles. If she's bred before, the ovary will also show tiny white scars (corpora albicans) where previous follicles ovulated. In males, two **testes**, each with an associated epididymis, lie beneath the kidneys and connect to the penis, which stays within the cloaca unless the turtle is mating or stressed. The testes are smooth and easily distinguished from ovaries. In adult males, the testes become large, and in breeding males, each epididymis swells with sperm. To mate, a male mounting a female wraps his **prehensile tail** under the female and inserts an erect penis into the female's cloaca. Sperm and fluids enter the penis at the base; travel down a urethral groove enclosed by engorged corpora cavernosa; and enter the female's cloaca.

A female does not need a male throughout her breeding season. Because she can store viable sperm for months, one mating is enough to fertilize the eggs in several clutches. Sperm storage apparently occurs within numerous albumen-secreting glands in the upper oviduct.

Immature turtles (A) have thin gonads, with a texture that is more granular in females. Adult females (B) have ovaries with distinct, orange follicles that enlarge prior to reproduction. Adult males (C) have smooth, elongate, pinkish testes.

Internal view of gonads in immature and mature sea turtles

A male green turtle shows his tail length

The strong, prehensile tail of an adult male loggerhead

Sex Hormones

Hormones guide sea turtle reproduction, from preparation to completion. Female preparation (see page 100) includes weight gain and vitellogenesis, which is the buildup of protein and lipid within the yolk of growing egg follicles. Adult females feed and gain weight on their foraging grounds. They may respond to their own plumpness by recognizing leptin, a hormone produced by fat cells. Estrogen production by ovarian follicles seems to stimulate plump females to secrete vitellogenin, an egg yolk precursor synthesized in the liver and carried by the bloodstream to the ovaries. Thus begins vitellogenesis, which takes place before and during migration to the nesting beach. At mating time, the egg follicles are at maximum size, estrogen wanes, and there are elevations in testosterone and corticosterone. Weeks after mating, a female ovulates her clutch of eggs, prompted by peaks in a variety of gonadotropic hormones and a decrease in testosterone.

Females emerging onto the beach to nest proceed through nesting stages that are marked by the differential rise and fall of arginine vasotocin and two prostaglandins, which are hormonelike lipids in the blood that may mediate the contractions that accompany egg laying. These prostaglandin levels fall when the turtle completes the final throwing of sand over her nest, and drop near baseline levels as she returns to the sea.

Mature males go through annual cycles in testosterone, although not all turtles will migrate to breed. In robust males ready to breed, rising testosterone begins sperm production in the testes and sends males off in a restless search for mates. Males in courtship have the highest levels of this hormone, which correlates with general levels of aggression around mating time. Because females too have a peak in testosterone during courtship, they also show enhanced aggression.

Hormones drive mating behavior. This male green turtle clings to the carapace of a female just off a Florida nesting beach

Breeding Cycles

A female's reproductive cycles include her remigration interval, which is the number of years between her active reproductive seasons, and her clutch frequency, or the number of nests in an active year. The inter-nesting interval is the number of days between successive nests in a season.

The most variable measure of a sea turtle's reproductive output over time is remigration interval. A turtle's decision to leave her foraging grounds, travel hundreds of miles, and produce hundreds of eggs is a serious move. Going through all this and not making the most of it (making a full complement of nests) would be imprudent. For this reason, sea turtles respond to lean times by forgoing reproductive migrations altogether, rather than simply cutting back on clutch frequency or clutch size. However, clutch frequency has proven difficult to measure. Turtles seen making just one nest for the season are represented in many estimates of clutch frequency, even though they may have made additional nests where they weren't observed.

A female that migrates and prepares yolked follicles has at least some recourse should she not be able to lay all her eggs. Follicles not ovulated may undergo atresia, wherein the yolk is resorbed and used for other metabolic needs—like getting home.

This green turtle will return to nest again in about two weeks

After her last nest, a green turtle returns to distant foraging grounds

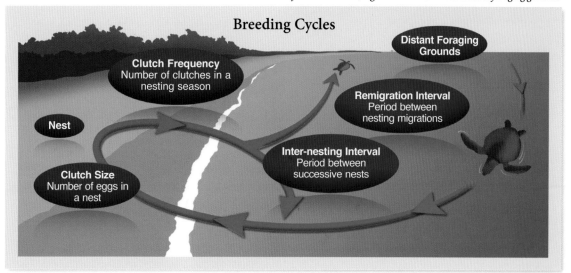

Breeding Cycles

Distant Foraging Grounds

Clutch Frequency
Number of clutches in a nesting season

Remigration Interval
Period between nesting migrations

Nest

Inter-nesting Interval
Period between successive nests

Clutch Size
Number of eggs in a nest

A loggerhead's contractions raise her flippers during egg laying

Newly laid loggerhead eggs within the nest's egg chamber

How an Egg is Made

A female sea turtle begins egg production by gathering energy on her foraging grounds. Her fat will be converted into egg yolk during vitellogenesis, roughly eight months before her eggs are laid. During or after her breeding migration, she will mate and acquire all the sperm needed to fertilize a season of eggs. Ovulation occurs when mature follicles in the ovary shed their eggs, packaged with spheres of yolk, which enter the ostium of the oviduct. Eggs are fertilized by sperm (perhaps by multiple males) stored in the upper oviduct. They then move through a region where glands coat them with albumen, which contains a little protein and a lot of water. Lower in the oviduct is the shell gland region. There, a shell membrane envelops the albumen and becomes crisscrossed by protein fibers on which aragonite calcium carbonate crystallizes. The embryo reaches the gastrula stage, stops developing, and will not resume until it is dropped into the nest. Once laid, the albumen will absorb water to fill out a small dimple in the papery eggshell.

Egg Production in a Female Loggerhead

1 **Weight gain**

2 **Vitellogenesis**
Eight months before nesting

3 **Breeding migration**

4 **Mating**
About one month before nesting

5 **Ovulation of clutch**
13 days before nesting

6 **Eggs fertilized**
13 days before nesting

7 **Albumen added**
Three to ten days before nesting

8 **Membranes and shell added**
Three days before nesting

9 **Embryos develop to gastrula**
One or more days before nesting

10 **Oviposition (egg laying)**

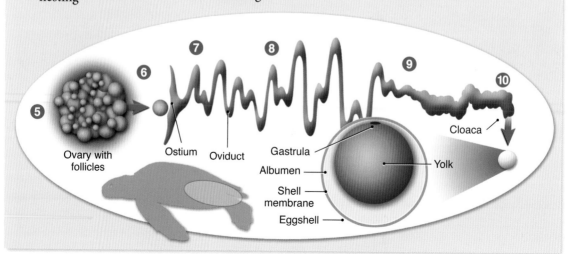

What's Inside an Egg?

Sea turtles have an **amniotic egg**. It is a survival capsule that allows an embryo to develop outside the mother and on land. Features of a sea turtle egg include a papery eggshell that protects but is porous (to air and water vapor), and an allantois, which facilitates respiration and is a reservoir for wastes. A yolk sac supplies nutrition for the developing embryo and shrinks as the turtle grows. An amnion, filled with amniotic fluid, surrounds the embryo and provides it a stable environment.

The amniotic sac is equivalent to the same structure in placental mammals (like us). Surrounding the allantoic, vitelline (yolk sac), and amniotic membranes is the chorion, which encloses the embryo. Albumen surrounds the chorion and serves as a water supply without preventing exchange of oxygen and carbon dioxide. These gasses, and water vapor, pass through the porous eggshell, allowing the egg to "breathe" and "drink."

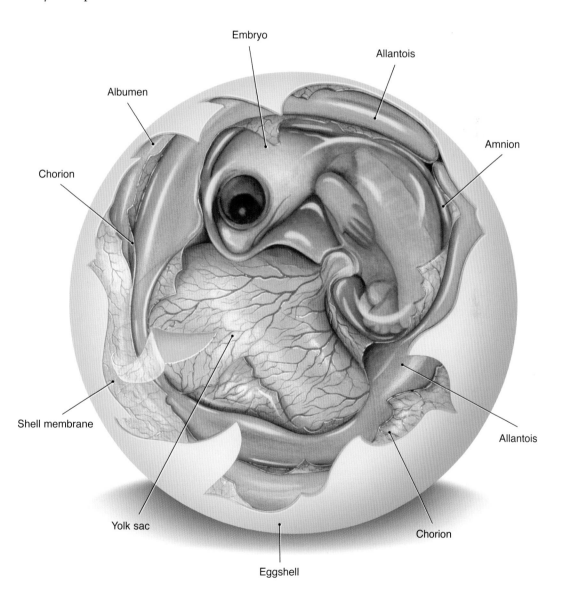

The amniotic egg of a loggerhead sea turtle, with a developing embryo about four weeks old

Pelagic green turtles are often warmer than 100° F (38° C)

A basking loggerhead floats high and raises its flippers to the sun

A nesting green turtle returns past dawn during an upwelling

In 2010, thousands of green turtles were stunned by an early chill

Thermal Biology

A sea turtle's body temperature is balanced between heat soaked up from or lost to the environment, and heat generated by metabolism. Sea turtles are big (with a large thermal inertia), move into temperatures they like, and have physiological mechanisms to manage their body temperature. As a result, they are able to avoid getting too hot or too cold—most of the time.

Basking

One way to warm up is to **bask** in the sun. Sea turtles do this by inflating their lungs and raising their flippers out of the water. On a calm, sunny day, even the submerged parts of a turtle gain heat in the warm sea-surface layer. Small juveniles live in this zone and may benefit from the high activity and enhanced growth rates that a warm body allows.

Cold-water Upwelling

Sea turtles make seasonal migrations to avoid cold water, but chills sometimes develop even in summer. Breeding loggerheads and green turtles off the southeastern US occasionally experience cold during upwellings. These occur when winds drive surface water offshore, to be replaced by cold water upwelling from the depths. An upwelling can lower sea temperature 18° F (10° C) or more. When this happens, turtles slow down. The number of nesting turtles each night drops, which could be due to the additional time required for a cold turtle (with a lower metabolic rate) to produce shelled eggs. Turtles that do emerge onto the beach take longer to nest and often linger past sunrise.

Cold Stuns

Severe, winter cold snaps can suddenly lower water temperature and stun turtles. At about 50° F (10° C), green turtles have difficulty swimming, and at 43° F (6° C), they become torpid and wash ashore. Lower temperatures can kill. Loggerheads, Kemp's ridleys, and hawksbills can also be stunned. Turtles caught out in the cold are often from bays with no southern exit, like Cape Cod Bay, MA, Long Island Sound, NY, and coastal lagoons in Florida and Texas.

Counter-current Heat Exchange

Sea turtles can conserve core body heat by warming the blood returning from a cold flipper.

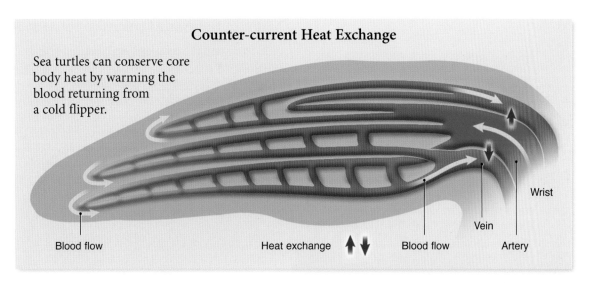

Blood flow   Heat exchange ⬆⬇   Blood flow   Artery

Wrist

Vein

Counter-current Blood Flow

Sea turtles use the constriction at the wrist of each flipper to bundle the veins draining the flipper with the arteries that supply it. This allows arteries from the warm body-core to elevate the temperature of veins from the cold flipper. As a result, core warmth is not lost from the flipper's large surface area. This system is best developed in leatherbacks, which come closest to being endotherms and can keep their core body as much as 32° F (18° C) warmer than the water around them. A leatherback that is too warm is able to send higher volumes of blood through its large flippers in order to dissipate heat over a much larger surface area than its body, relative to volume.

In warm water, a leatherback's front flipper is flushed pink

Sex and Incubation Temperature

The sex of a sea turtle hatchling is determined by the temperature it experienced within the egg during the middle third of its incubation. Warm eggs produce females, and cool eggs make males (think of hot chicks and cool dudes). In the middle is a Goldilocks zone (a **pivotal temperature**) that produces a clutch of half males and half females. This temperature varies by species and location. For loggerheads in the southeastern US, the pivotal temperature is 84° F (29° C). The difference between all males and all females spans only 4.5° F (2.5° C). Our populations seem to have a female bias that could be heading to extremes.

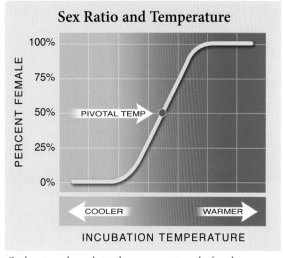

Sex Ratio and Temperature

PERCENT FEMALE

100%
75%
50% — PIVOTAL TEMP
25%
0%

← COOLER   WARMER →

INCUBATION TEMPERATURE

Cool nests make male turtles; warm nests make females

Timing of Hatchling Emergence

NUMBER OF EMERGENCES

SUNSET · SUNRISE

← WARMER · COOLER →

SAND-SURFACE TEMPERATURE

Peak time of hatchling emergence is about midnight

Green turtle hatchlings emerge the morning following a hot day

A nesting green turtle—not sad, just salty

Time of Hatchling Emergence

Environmental conditions and reduced risk of predation favor hatchlings that emerge from their nests at night. This timing is brought about by a group response to lowering temperature. Within the nest, the hatchling group goes through periodic bouts of unified thrashing that move sand from ceiling to floor and raise the group toward the sand surface. If the group reaches the surface layer during the day, the upper hatchlings are quieted by the warm conditions and this tranquility spreads. After nightfall, hatchlings at the top of the bunch sense the sand cooling and begin squirming again. Their siblings down below can't sense the surface temperature but become active when jostled by those above. As activity peaks in the boiling mass of little turtles, the sand covering them sinks below and hatchlings start spilling out of the nest. The cooling trend that starts it all occurs mostly at night, but a rain shower can bring about similar temperature conditions. When the preceding day is sunny and hot, surface sands cool later, and hatchlings **emerge** later, meaning that some events will occur near sunrise.

Water Balance

Extracting usable water from the sea is a challenge. About 3.5% of seawater is salt, and these concentrations are toxic to cellular functions. Sea turtles are no saltier on the inside than most other vertebrates. To stay this way, they must deal with a constant invasion of toxic salts from the sea they swim in. Their methods to limit salt uptake include wringing the saltwater out of the food they eat (see page 88). But some ingestion of salt is inevitable, and to cope with this a sea turtle acts as its own desalinization plant. Sea turtles incessantly purge their blood of salt with specialized lachrymal (tear) glands behind each of their eyes. The critical function of these salt glands is indicated by their size, which is much larger than the brain. The glands continually excrete a viscous fluid twice as salty as seawater. Although the tears are most obvious due to the dangling cakes of sand beneath the eyes of nesting females, sea turtles actually cry all the time.

Energetics

Compared to most reptiles, sea turtles have a high capacity for aerobic activity. Two of the most energetic things a sea turtle does are to swim at a frenzied pace away from land (as a hatchling) and throw beach sand (as a nesting female). Metabolic rates for these activities, in terms of oxygen used, approach ten times the turtle's resting rate. This scope is lowest for leatherbacks, which have a high resting metabolism to begin with, three times the green turtle resting rate and a little over half the rate of a mammal of equal size. During vigorous swimming and deep dives, sea turtles go into anaerobic metabolism. This gives them an oxygen debt they must repay by catch-up breathing during an inactive recovery period. Sea turtles often linger at the surface taking several breaths after a deep dive. Their high capacity for tolerating lactic acidosis during activity underwater allows sea turtles a "good credit rating" to temporarily incur oxygen debt.

A nesting green turtle gasps after a bout of sand throwing

Dive Patterns

Cycles of breathing and activity underwater vary widely in sea turtles. Two common patterns characterize the typical dives of turtles foraging on the bottom and those living at the surface. Pelagic juveniles forage at the surface but make occasional deep dives for additional feeding opportunities. Larger turtles in coastal waters spend most of their time submerged.

Coastal loggerheads spend about 3% of their time at the surface

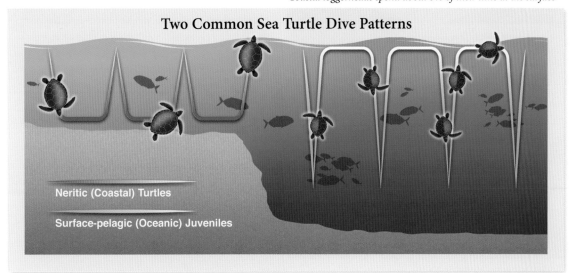

Two Common Sea Turtle Dive Patterns

Neritic (Coastal) Turtles

Surface-pelagic (Oceanic) Juveniles

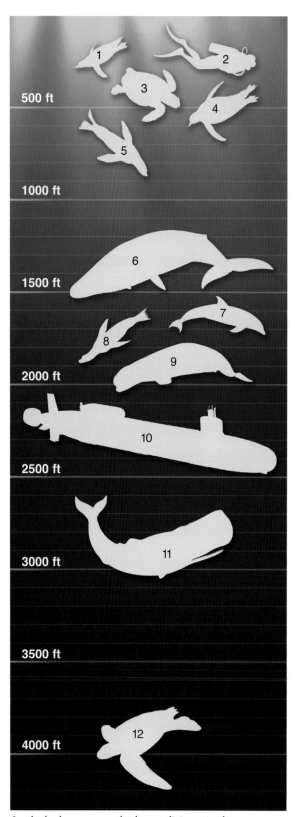

500 ft

1000 ft

1500 ft

2000 ft

2500 ft

3000 ft

3500 ft

4000 ft

Leatherbacks are among the deepest-diving animals

The Dive of the Leatherback

Leatherbacks are champion divers. Here is a comparison of how they rate:

1 Humboldt penguin, 130 ft (40 m)
2 SCUBA diver, recreational limit, 130 ft (40 m)
3 Loggerhead sea turtle, 550 ft (168 m)
4 Emperor penguin, 565 ft (172 m)
5 New Zealand fur seal, 780 ft (238 m)
6 Blue whale, 1600 ft (488 m)
7 Bottlenose dolphin 1750 ft (533 m)
8 New Zealand sea lion 1800 ft (549 m)
9 Beluga whale, 2120 ft (646 m)
10 American nuclear submarine, collapse depth, 2400 ft (732 m)
11 Sperm whale, typical dive, 3200 ft (975 m)
12 Leatherback turtle, 4200 ft (1280 m)

A leatherback's deep dive begins with a forceful exhale and a rapid rush of air into the lungs. Lowering her head into a dive, a leatherback makes deliberate strokes with her broad flippers, plunging down toward indigo depths, beyond the dimmest flicker of penetrating sunbeams. Her heart rate descends as well, to less than one beat per minute, only 5% of her resting rate at the surface. The reduced metabolism corresponds to a miserly use of oxygen stored in her blood and tissues. Air in the lungs, which began with the volume of a two-liter beverage bottle, is compressed to the capacity of a ping-pong ball. The leatherback submits to tons of hydraulic force by allowing both her lungs and trachea to collapse. With this collapse comes a controlled crushing of her body allowed by the flexible cartilage connecting her bony plastron. Upon reaching depths approaching a mile deep, there is work to do. As she searches for the faintest signs of prey sluggishly undulating in the stunningly cold darkness, we can only imagine the difficulty of her task, performed with a heartbeat and metabolic rate only slightly higher than death, and with her minimal blood flow shunted from her extremities to the brain. Then, sensing the need, the leatherback serenely makes the long return to the atmosphere where restoring breaths await.

How Sea Turtles Swim

Sea turtles use their front flippers as both wings and paddles. At modest swimming speeds, front flippers stroke in synchrony, with each flipper tip tracing a forward-leaning oval. As the flipper rises up the back of the oval, its foil shape produces lift that contributes to propulsion. As the flipper powers down the front of the oval, it pushes the turtle forward like a paddle. A typical stroke for a turtle descending into a dive is about one beat per second. When cruising, flippers may beat at half this rate, and the turtle will occasionally glide. At their most vigorous swimming, the flipper tips make more complex traces with small loops at the top and bottom. As a sea turtle swims forward, its body pivots up and down with an average angle slightly downward. In these patterns of **powerstroking**, the rear flippers act as rudders to steer the turtle. The front flippers also steer, such that injured turtles with no rear flippers are still able to swim a course. Remarkably, sea turtles with only one front flipper are also able to maintain a straight path.

Buoyancy Regulation

Sea turtles naturally sink, although they are able to float by filling their lungs. The hard-shelled sea turtles often relax on the bottom by releasing just enough air to be negatively buoyant. Because they use their lungs as both a buoyancy compensator and a store of oxygen, sea turtles must balance these two needs. A relaxed turtle in shallow water does not require as much oxygen and can carry less air to allow it to sink. A turtle on a deeper dive can take along lots of air without uncomfortable buoyancy because the air will compress and contribute less to buoyancy as the turtle descends. But this means that a turtle returning from a deep dive will have to work to return to the surface. Sea turtles with lung infections often develop buoyancy problems that keep them from diving. Various other injuries can also affect buoyancy. Scar tissue can hold gasses, and paralysis of intestinal sections can prevent turtles from efficiently passing waste material and accumulated gas.

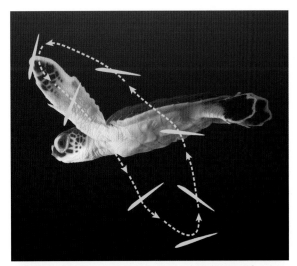

Flipper angle and tip-trace in a powerstroking green turtle

A green turtle strokes with front flippers and steers with rear

A green turtle rests on seagrass in shallow water

Life Cycle and
Life History

A sea turtle life cycle chronicles the recurring stages of life—adult, egg, hatchling, juvenile, adult. Each life stage is different based on a turtle's size and form, but also its behavior and distribution. The latter two features are described within a sea turtle's life history (or life story). This story traces important milestones of sea turtle life and details their schedule, where they occur, what habitats they occupy, and how much happens. The "how much" aspect of sea turtle life history is important. These are the measures that tell us about sea turtle populations and how they are doing. Measures include number of eggs laid, the ratio of males to females, survivorship at each life stage, body growth and stage duration, age at first reproduction, and reproductive lifespan. In population biology, these numbers plug into numerical models that tell us how our sea turtles are faring.

Natural selection has acted on sea turtle life-history traits to maximize each turtle's odds of having its genes persist. There is a consensus among sea turtles on the best way to play this game of life. The strategy is a mix of game plans from the playbooks of other organisms. Sea turtles have a lot of young that fend for themselves and incur high mortality, a strategy shared among animals that live in expansive, variable habitats. Yet sea turtles mature late and live a long time, which makes them similar to other large animals that invest greatly in their offspring to ensure high survivorship. These sea turtle population characteristics bring about vastly different "reproductive values" between life stages. Whereas a hatchling has a low expected contribution to the population based on slim odds it will survive to reproduce, an adolescent turtle just about to breed for the first time is likely to contribute a lot.

Above: A yearling loggerhead must survive for 30 years before it is able to contribute reproductively to the population

Left: An encounter between loggerhead generations on a Florida nesting beach

109

A male green turtle hangs on even as his mate crawls landward

This male loggerhead has a tail scarred by bites from rivals

The male that guarded this green turtle left a mating scar (oval)

Courtship and Mating

A life cycle has no beginning, but we'll start our description at the point where males and females get together to begin the process of making little sea turtles. This may seem straightforward, but as it turns out, males and females play a very different game of life.

The Mating Game

Sea turtles mate under the rules of "scramble polygamy." Like females, males want as many copies of their genes as possible living within the next generation. This means fathering lots of hatchlings. Males scramble for multiple mating opportunities, because one way to father more hatchlings is to hook up with lots of potential mothers. But every potential mother could have multiple suitors that would dilute a male's contribution to the paternity of each clutch of eggs. To defend against this dilution, males guard their mates by tenaciously hanging on (using their curved claws, see page 77) to block attempts from interlopers. However, males can't guard and search for new mates at the same time, so they must determine which move is best based on what other players are doing. If there are few or widely spaced females, a male might best stay with a mate to fend off rivals. If there are lots of females and few male competitors, a male might best spend his time speed dating. As long as a female turtle finds a mate, she is guaranteed motherhood, but with multiple suitors, she could refuse some males and opportunistically shop around.

The cost of losing at the mating game is in squandered opportunity and spent energy. Males use considerable energy while searching, and also may be subject to bites in sensitive areas from their rivals. Females spend a great deal on migration, nesting, and eggs, and want to insure their offspring get the best genes.

Operational Sex Ratios

This is the ratio of breeding males and females. In sea turtles, males often migrate to breeding areas more frequently than females, which means that even if a population has more females, the ratio at breeding could be even.

What Sex Ratio Do We Start With?

Because the ratio of male to female turtles has important implications for population change, you'd think that biologists would know more about it. Our information on existing ratios is a rough estimate, and we don't understand why these ratios are what they are. But we do know some things. We know that a nesting female can determine the sex of her hatchlings by putting her nest in either a cool place (producing males) or a warm place (producing females) (see page 103). We also know that future population growth is most sensitive to the number of breeding females. This is because females determine how many viable eggs are laid, not the males (as long as there are just enough males to fertilize those eggs). Theoretically, long-term sea turtle sex ratios should be about 50:50. Yet from what little we know of hatchling sex ratios in all species, most beaches produce significantly more females than males. As nesting beaches get warmer, will sea turtle populations have enough males?

Green turtle hatchlings. Odds are, most will be females

About 80–90% of our regional loggerhead hatchlings are female. As hatchlings, the sexes look identical on the outside

Development

A green turtle pips and takes its first breath

A sea turtle egg begins development within the oviduct. At the gastrula stage (a tiny cup with three germ layers), development stops until a few hours after the egg is laid. Within a week, a neural groove and head fold form, somites that will become muscle and other tissues increase in number, a V-shaped mouth forms, blood islands develop around the yolk sac, and an S-shaped heart begins beating. In the second week, limb buds form and eyes become visible. At three weeks, a carapace identifies the embryo as a turtle. Up until this middle incubation stage, rotation or jarring of the egg can tear delicate membranes and kill the embryo. Over the next three weeks, yolk diminishes, the embryo darkens and grows, and an egg tooth and fore-claws develop. At about seven weeks, the egg tooth slices the eggshell, fluids drain, and the embryo takes its first breath. Within two days after it pips, the hatchling will internalize its remnant yolk, straighten, and escape its eggshell. Cooler nests can take much longer to complete this incubation period.

A Nest and Its Developing Eggs

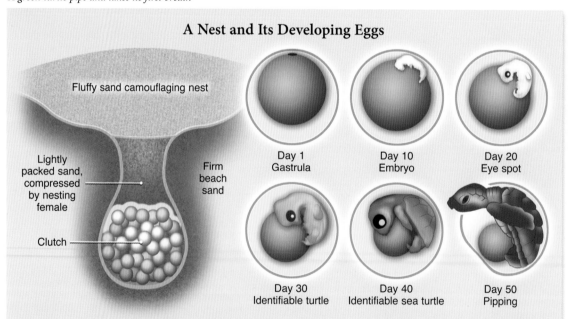

As they are laid in the nest, sea turtle eggs are developmentally paused at the tiny "gastrula" stage. Hours after exposure to oxygen outside the female, development resumes. The nest "breathes" as tides raise and lower groundwater, pumping atmosphere through the sand. Oxygen demand peaks as turtles pip and begin thrashing within the nest.

Hatchling Emergence

Emergence of hatchlings marks the end of the incubation period, but actual hatching occurs several days before this. A week before hatchlings emerge, the first eggs are pipped. At pipping, a turgid egg bursts as the embryo's egg tooth pierces the eggshell. Allantoic and amniotic fluids drain, nest contents collapse, and an air space opens above the pipped eggs. Still within their eggshells, turtles internalize their remaining yolk, straighten, and thrash free of their eggshells. About three days before emergence, most hatchlings are out of their shells. They squirm in unison, then rest, then squirm, in periodic bouts. They work within the air space to whittle away the ceiling. Sand sprinkles down through the mass of hatchlings, and the group is elevated. Hours before emergence, the sand ceiling collapses. Warm sand near the surface arrests activity, but as the top hatchlings sense cooling conditions, they resume thrashing, stimulate their siblings below, and the "boil" of little turtles pours from the nest.

Newly emerged loggerhead hatchlings

What Happens Inside a Nest?

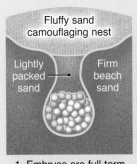

Fluffy sand camouflaging nest

Lightly packed sand — Firm beach sand

1. Embryos are full term

Air space

2. Pipping

Eggshells

3. Eggshell escape

Hatchling mass

4. Group thrashing

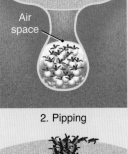

Sand depression

Ceiling collapses

5. Ceiling collapse

Second emergence

6. Emergence

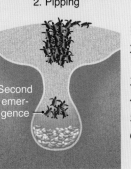

1. Embryos reach full term within turgid eggs
2. Embryos pip, fluids drain from eggs, air space develops
3. Hatchlings straighten and escape from eggs
4. Socially facilitated ascent begins
5. Ceiling collapses, nest depression forms
6. Surface sand cools, first emergence occurs. Over one to three nights, additional groups emerge

Developmental Graduation

On its first day, a sea turtle faces one of its biggest challenges. Having never experienced the sea, a hatchling must dash toward it, enter the surf, and swim away from land as quickly as it can. Failing this challenge means feeding a predator, exhausting limited energy, or dehydrating in the morning sun. This sprightly run and plunge begins a period of frantic activity called the **hatchling frenzy**. As a frenzied hatchling reaches the hard, wet sand of the swash zone, it nears the rush of frothy water from exhausted breakers. To a walnut-size little turtle, the waves are mountains. Entering the rushing sheets of water often takes several attempts as each foamy collision tumbles the tiny turtle back up the beach. A hatchling spit forth by the sea rights itself with wide rotations of the head, blinks to reacquire its target, and continues seaward undaunted. Eventually, a hatchling enters the rush of water at the apex of

its upward movement, becomes enveloped, and shoots down the beach with the seaward slide of the returning flow. Once suspended by water, hatchlings immediately swim. A two-second breath while dogpaddling precedes a dive into rapid front-flipper powerstroking. Still among breaking waves, a hatchling will dive just before the arrival of each looming crest. The dive takes the hatchling beneath the crash of the wave and puts the turtle in position to be pulled out with the undertow. Dive by dive, a hatchling makes its way out beyond the surf, where it will continue swimming for the next 36 hours. Many miles from its natal beach, this swimming tapers off, and powerstroking is replaced by bouts of rear-flipper kicks (see page 225) and resting. After a few days at sea, the hatchling's residual yolk is exhausted, and it must feed. At this point the turtle is considered to be a post-hatchling.

On its first big swim, a powerstroking loggerhead hatchling competes to finish a 36-hour biathlon. Winners get to live

Post-hatchling Stage

A hatchling's frenzied offshore swimming ensures that it will begin its post-hatchling stage away from coastal waters where predatory fishes abound. Post-hatchlings have begun the surface-pelagic chapter in their lives, but have yet to travel very far from their natal beach. Their first bites of food are likely to be found within oceanic convergence zones where the sea concentrates a smörgåsbord of floating food along with the floating algae, pelagic sargassum. These zones are common off gulf and Atlantic beaches where eddies and major currents form oceanic fronts.

Information from post-hatchling loggerheads shows that a little turtle's open-sea lifestyle is one of floating and waiting. Although they may actively swim and dive on occasion, too much of this activity wastes energy that could be channeled into growth. Within a convergence, a young turtle may not need to exert itself to find food. The swirls of currents in which turtles drift can be expected to eventually drag a variety of bite-size surface organisms by the nose of a quietly floating, patient spectator.

Surface-pelagic (Oceanic) Juveniles

Growth leads to safety. A sea turtle's risk of death decreases dramatically as it graduates from a hand-size post-hatchling to a football-size juvenile. Still living within open-sea surface habitats, these turtles have outgrown the mouths of most fishes. Sharks remain as a significant predator, in that many of these small juveniles show the telltale bites and tooth-scratches of lucky escapes. With size also comes the ability to dive deeper for food. Green turtles, ridleys, and hawksbills probably make occasional dives for jelly animals, although they will spend most of their time within surface sargassum mats until their third year or so, when they will move into coastal waters. Loggerheads occupy oceanic habitats much longer (a decade), rely less and less on sargassum habitat, and swim to stay within productive surface fronts. Leatherbacks never really end their deep-water, open-ocean phase and are likely to spend the majority of their lives far from land.

A green turtle hatchling nears the end of its frenzied swimming

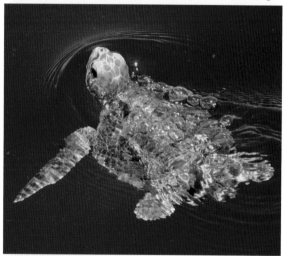

Young loggerheads spend their first decade on the open sea

A surface-pelagic (oceanic) Kemp's ridley searches sargassum

Neritic-stage juvenile green turtles frequent turtle grass pastures

A subadult loggerhead in shallow waters of the Florida Keys

A hawksbill settles into neritic reef habitat

Neritic (Benthic) Stage

A turtle's decision to leave the open sea and make a living in shallow coastal waters marks a dramatic shift in lifestyle. These coastal waters are termed "neritic" (shallower than 200 m, 656 ft), and offer "benthic" (sea-bottom) foraging opportunities. For a small turtle bobbing at the surface, a mile or more above a cold dark sea bottom, finding food anywhere but near the surface is not an option. Yet for most sea turtles, to complete their development into an adult, they must shift their feeding to organisms that thrive on the bottom of sunlit seas. This requirement for habitat change comes when turtles outgrow their diet in the open sea. At this point in their development, sea turtles become too big to grow quickly on the things that fed them during their early years. To keep growing at an optimum rate, larger juveniles must graduate to feeding on larger, more nutritious food items found in productive coastal waters.

The first juvenile green turtles to arrive in shallow coastal waters are the size of dinner plates. At this size, they become able to derive nutrition from their new diet of macroalgae or seagrasses. Hawksbills and ridleys also enter coastal waters as plate-size turtles but seek a different category of benthic victuals. Hawksbills settle onto tropical reefs where their diet shifts to sponges, and Kemp's ridleys enter shallow habitats in pursuit of crabs and tunicates. Loggerheads postpone their entry into the shallows until they are roughly the size of a large serving platter, at about a third of their weight as an adult. All of these hard-shelled sea turtles mature to adulthood in coastal waters, although they may make a few significant habitat shifts as they develop. Larger loggerheads may also make forays back into the oceanic realm, especially to avoid cold shelf waters in winter.

Of all the sea turtles, the leatherback is least likely to forage in shallow coastal waters. Perhaps by specializing on large gelatinous invertebrates that concentrate mostly in the open ocean, and because they are able to descend to tremendous depths in order to access this abundance, leatherbacks can attain adult size without ever giving up their oceanic lifestyle.

Population Changes

Sea turtle populations grow and decline, but important changes are not always reflected in numbers of turtles. Two critical measures of a population are stage duration and survivorship. Stage duration is the time it takes for sea turtles to grow into the next life stage. Survivorship describes the probability of making it to the next stage. Lucky turtles are graduated through multiple stages, all the way to maturity.

Growth and Maturity—AJ's Story

The size of a sea turtle determines its progression to the next stage in life. Until adulthood, size is a rough approximation of age, and duration of life stages can be revealed by how fast sea turtles grow. These growth rates are variable among species, among sizes of turtles, and among individuals. To demonstrate how growth rates are measured, we introduce you to a loggerhead named **AJ**.

AJ spends a lot of time on nearshore hardbottom habitat near the intake pipe for the St. Lucie Power Plant in Florida. The Inwater Research Group knows this because over a span of 24 years, they have removed AJ 42 times from the canal that draws cooling water in from the Atlantic. Each time, AJ was identified by his tags (metal flipper tags and a tiny, passive radio tag inserted in his flipper), had his carapace measured, and was weighed. One lesson from AJ's growth chart is that sea turtle measurements are not perfect. The length of the turtle's carapace increases over time, but appears to shrink on a few occasions. These are probably small errors having to do with interfering barnacles or differences between measuring calipers over the years. Another lesson is that growth is not steady. There was an eight-year period when AJ didn't grow, a time during which his weight declined. But following what was likely a period of poor nutrition, he rebounded, put on a growth spurt, and gained weight even faster than he gained size. By the way, for 20 years, AJ had a short tail like other immature loggerheads and his sex was unknown. Only in the last few years did his tail grow dramatically, indicating that AJ was ready for his Bar Mitzvah.

Part of a population of green turtles grazing a Florida reef

AJ the loggerhead has shared a quarter-century of growth data

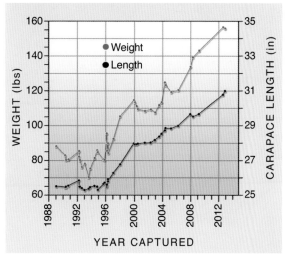

AJ's growth chart

117

Hatchling loggerheads have low survival odds

An adult loggerhead represents more than 30 years of good luck

Survivorship

Not every little sea turtle grows up. In fact, the odds of a hatchling reaching adulthood are pretty slim. Most of what we know of survival rates comes from population models that use the most readily available information on sea turtles we have—how many eggs are laid, how many females do the laying, and how many of those females disappear over time. We can also estimate other important factors like age at maturity, population sex ratio, and whether the population is declining, stable, or increasing. Only rarely do we have empirical information on survivorship of immature turtles. We infer what those rates must be, and we assume a lot.

It's a rough, scientific guess that a female loggerhead must lay at least 1150 eggs over her lifetime in order to replace herself (and for the population to remain stable). Because later life stages must have high survival to lay all those eggs, human-induced mortality in late life stages can be disastrous.

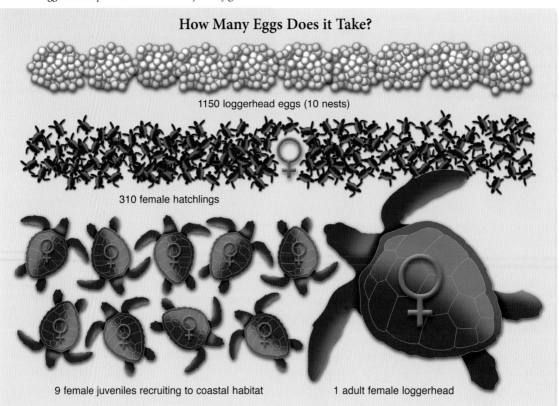

How Many Eggs Does it Take?

1150 loggerhead eggs (10 nests)

310 female hatchlings

9 female juveniles recruiting to coastal habitat   1 adult female loggerhead

Population Biology—A Game of Life and Death

Sea turtle population biology is informed by vital rates. These are the values that describe how many live, how many die, and how many there might be in the future. Here are some vital rates for our region's loggerhead sea turtles.

Survival in the nest: Highly variable, but on average, about 52% of eggs result in hatchlings that escape the nest. Tropical cyclones and high raccoon predation are negative factors.

Sex ratio of hatchlings: We may assume that this is 1:1, but we are often wrong. Most nests have more females than males, which positively affects future population growth, as long as there are enough males to fertilize the eggs.

Survival during frenzy: Largely unknown. Disorienting lights (see pages 192, 193) and fish predation are negative factors.

Survival at sea, surface-pelagic juveniles: Largely unknown, but estimates are that only 3% survive this stage. Shark predation and longline fisheries (see page 231) are negative factors.

Duration of surface-pelagic juvenile stage: About ten years on average. Changes in food can reduce growth, multiply risk by prolonging the stage, and lower stage survivorship.

Survival at sea, neritic subadults: Largely unknown, but estimates are that about 11% survive this stage. Disease and trawl fisheries (see page 231) are negative factors.

Duration of neritic subadult stage: About 20 years. Changes in food can reduce growth, multiply risk by prolonging the stage, and lower stage survivorship.

Survival at sea, adults: Unclear. Estimates range 80–95% annual survival. Artificial reductions in this rate can be important negative factors.

Seasonal fecundity: Average is 213 eggs per year, including skipped seasons. Poor nutrition lengthens remigration interval and lowers this rate.

Age at sexual maturity: Approximately 31 years

Reproductive lifespan: Over 30 years is possible

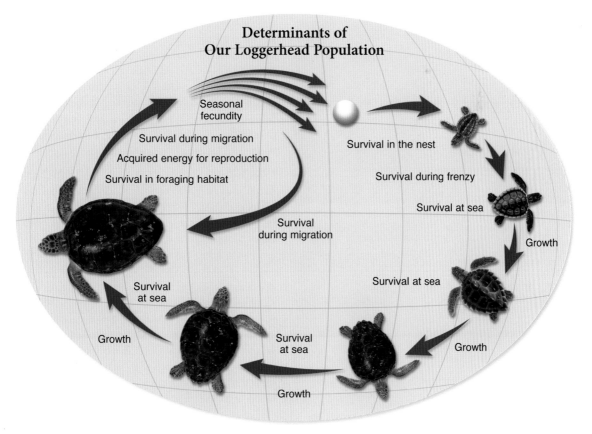

Determinants of
Our Loggerhead Population

Seasonal fecundity

Survival during migration
Acquired energy for reproduction
Survival in foraging habitat

Survival in the nest

Survival during frenzy

Survival at sea

Survival during migration

Growth

Survival at sea

Growth

Survival at sea

Growth

Survival at sea

Growth

Growth

A green turtle hatchling orients seaward from its nest

Hatchlings measure brightness across a broad, flat cone

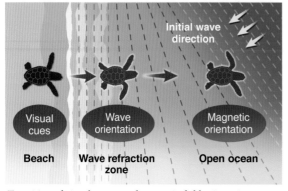

A Kemp's ridley hatchling swims away from its natal beach

Movements and Migration

Sea turtles undergo extensive movements punctuated by periodic confinement to a home range. They are both restless gadabouts and habitual homebodies. Some movements are migrations—movements with a return trip, or that reflect a pronounced change in living area. Some migrations occur daily, between feeding and resting areas. Other migrations take place on multi-year cycles, as when females commit to the lengthy voyage required to reach their nesting beaches. For sea turtles, "life's a journey" is not just a metaphor. Their journey begins the moment they first see their world.

Hatchling Dispersal

Hatchlings orient to the sea by locating the center of a bright, broad, unobstructed horizon. These characteristics typically match the open view of the night sky over a glittering ocean. The "cone of acceptance" over which hatchlings integrate their measurement of light (left image) has a vertical angle (**V**) of about 30° and a horizontal angle (**H**) of about 180°. A celestial bright spot like the moon does not contribute to the brightest direction (**D**) if it is high in the sky. Even a low moon is just one bright area over a broad seaward horizon, the remainder of which it also brightens. On a naturally lighted beach, the contrasting direction is the dark silhouette of the dune. Under natural conditions, a hatchling's trip from nest to sea takes a direct route and lasts only a few minutes.

Within and just outside the turmoil of the surf, hatchlings begin to ignore brightness cues and instead direct themselves into oncoming swells (see page 95). Their faith is in the physics of wave motion. As swells generated at sea approach land, part of the wave is slowed by the shallows off the beach. Thus, waves approaching the beach pivot on the end first reaching the shallow water. This refracts the wave, bending it, so that its travel is steered directly toward the shore. During their nearshore experience with waves, hatchlings calibrate their magnetic compass (see page 96) with the correct offshore direction. This reference guides their swimming over the next few days.

Transition of visual, wave, and magnetic-field orientation cues

Juvenile Open-sea Travel

As hatching sea turtles slow their frenzied swimming, they become post-hatchlings and are transported more by oceanic **currents** than by their own activity. It's difficult to say whether drifting is a desired outcome or simply a consequence of life for a floating turtle on the open sea. For their first couple of years, loggerheads, green turtles, hawksbills, and ridleys periodically cover distances by swimming, but are also carried by **surface currents**. This may send them out of the Caribbean, around the Gulf of Mexico, or up the Eastern seaboard, but they are unlikely to circle the North Atlantic in this time. Loggerheads have a much longer open-sea phase. They remain at sea for several more years, which gives loggerheads a lot of travel experience. Their transport is by the Gulf Stream, which swirls away from our continent and becomes the northern leg of the North Atlantic Gyre. But loggerheads at the northern fringe of this current run the risk of exiting the gyre on a path to Icelandic waters. Apparently, young loggerheads keep track of their latitude based on cues they identify in the geomagnetic field (see page 96), and swim toward the center of the gyre to stay within it.

Loggerheads roughly one to a dozen years old are found at sea around the Azores and Madeira, three-fourths of the way to Europe. These islands are surrounded by seamounts that divert the far eastern Gulf Stream waters into turbulent upwellings and create productive foraging areas for juvenile loggerheads. At this stage in their development, the turtles are large enough to maintain themselves in these abundant waters by swimming against currents.

Developmental Migrations

Several times during a sea turtle's life, it opts for a complete change of scenery. These movements are termed developmental migrations because they often trace a turtle's graduation from one life stage to the next. One of the most profound scenery changes occurs when juvenile sea turtles leave the oceanic realm and recruit to shallow coastal waters. Green turtles, hawksbills, and Kemp's ridleys take part in this habi-

Post-hatchlings and young juveniles drift within surface currents

A post-hatchling loggerhead within drifting sargassum seaweed

Most Kemp's ridleys recruit into coastal waters within the gulf

121

Small subadult loggerheads often live separately from adults

Green turtles commute between feeding and sleeping areas

A hawksbill on its daily feeding commute

tat shift when they are just a little larger than a dinner plate. For loggerheads, this migration occurs over a wide range of sizes from about 20–30 in (50–75 cm) in carapace length. These habitat shifts constitute a radical transformation in diet and behavior. Turtles used to floating over deep water and feeding on jelly plankton must get good at finding their food on the bottom. For green turtles, this shift means a transition from carnivore to herbivore.

After a sea turtle settles into shallow coastal (neritic) waters, it may make several more shifts in habitat. There is a general trend for these neritic turtles to occupy progressively deeper waters as they grow. In the Florida Keys, seagrass pastures hold green turtles ranging from four-pound post-pelagic turtles to adults a hundred times that weight. But a clear division exists between size classes. Smaller green turtles graze in the shallows, and larger green turtles feed in deeper, less confined waters. This size segregation occurs with loggerheads too, and is based on both water depth and latitude. Most of the largest immature loggerheads and adults forage in the southern part of the range. There is no strict size threshold at which a turtle decides to move on to the next coastal habitat, but sooner or later, a developing turtle will outgrow its neighborhood. Many foraging habitats contain only smaller immature turtles with few large subadults and no adults.

Daily Migrations

Many sea turtles seem to maintain a daily commuting schedule. Green turtles that graze seagrass or algal pastures during the day return each night to deeper waters where their dive pattern suggests minimal movement. In the waters off Nicaragua, green turtles do their nocturnal resting near well-known "sleeping rocks," miles away from the places they forage during the day. Hawksbills may move into shallower sections of reef at night, where they can wedge themselves in away from the biggest sharks. One theme among the sea turtle species (except the leatherback) is that a turtle's sleeping spot is likely to provide some feature that would anchor a resting turtle to the bottom, such as muddy sediment or a rocky ledge.

Reproductive Migrations

The most pronounced regular movements that sea turtles make are the periodic reproductive migrations of adult females. Two examples below describe the travels of a female logger-head named **Shiver** and a female leatherback named **China Girl**.

Shiver the loggerhead was found by researchers from Florida FWC (Fish and Wildlife Conservation Commission), NOAA (National Oceanic and Atmospheric Administration), and the University of Charleston, who captured her in early March from the shallow waters of Florida Bay at the southern tip of Florida. The researchers used ultrasound imaging to identify Shiver as a loggerhead female with mature egg follicles. She was ready to breed. To track her movements over her upcoming nesting season, the researchers attached a **satellite transmitter** to Shiver's carapace. Her broadcasts indicated that she left Florida Bay to enter the Atlantic in mid April and moved along the Florida coast to the Archie Carr National Wildlife Refuge, covering the roughly 250-mile (400 km) trip in about two weeks. Shiver lingered off the refuge and deposited several clutches over an 11-week period. Not long after her last nest, Shiver set off for home, nearly reaching her home waters of Florida Bay after a three-week swim.

China Girl was first discovered by researchers from the University of Central Florida in 1994 as she nested on the beach at the Archie Carr Refuge. This leatherback has been a regular visitor to the Refuge over a 20-year period, typically returning over two- to three-year intervals. In 2000, China Girl was fitted with a harness that carried a satellite transmitter to track her movements. The track showed her leaving the waters off her nesting beach and wandering over the continental shelf northward to New Jersey. After transmitting several months of tracking data, China Girl was west of the Gulf Stream and heading south, perhaps toward warmer waters or more productive blooms of jellyfish (see page 66). The transmitter attachment was designed with a corrosible link that would eventually allow China Girl to shed her harness and transmitter.

Shiver, after nesting. Her transmitter's blue paint is visible

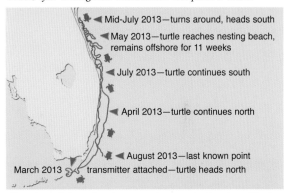

Mid-July 2013—turns around, heads south

May 2013—turtle reaches nesting beach, remains offshore for 11 weeks

July 2013—turtle continues south

April 2013—turtle continues north

August 2013—last known point

March 2013 transmitter attached—turtle heads north

Shiver's track from foraging grounds to nesting beach and back

China Girl's harness carried her tracking satellite transmitter

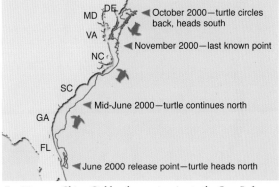

MD
VA
NC
SC
GA
FL

October 2000—turtle circles back, heads south

November 2000—last known point

Mid-June 2000—turtle continues north

June 2000 release point—turtle heads north

For 20 years, China Girl has been returning to the Carr Refuge

123

Good foraging tempts loggerheads to move north in summer

Seasonal Migrations

Like birds, sea turtles often make extensive seasonal migrations so they can feed in productive northern foraging areas without having to suffer through the cold of northern winters. However, some individual sea turtles move little with the seasons, preferring to maintain a residence in waters where both foraging opportunities and temperatures are comfortable year-round (some birds do this too). Most of our sea turtles that make regular north-south seasonal migrations are coastal, neritic-stage turtles that have not yet reached adulthood. Green turtles in this stage may move along the coastline between their summer northern range and their winter range in southern Florida or Texas. Immature loggerheads show at least three distinct seasonal movement patterns. One pattern is to move along the US Atlantic coast between bays and nearshore waters roughly north (summer range) and south (winter range) of Cape Hatteras, NC. Another pattern is to move out of coastal waters in fall and into offshore waters influenced by the warm Gulf Stream. Some of

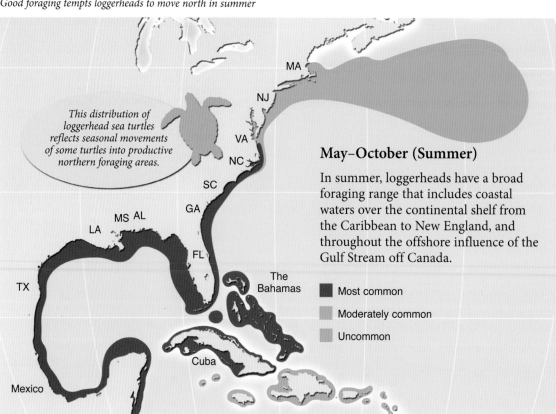

This distribution of loggerhead sea turtles reflects seasonal movements of some turtles into productive northern foraging areas.

May–October (Summer)

In summer, loggerheads have a broad foraging range that includes coastal waters over the continental shelf from the Caribbean to New England, and throughout the offshore influence of the Gulf Stream off Canada.

- Most common
- Moderately common
- Uncommon

these immature loggerheads may remain foraging in offshore waters for multiple winters before returning to coastal waters. A third option chosen by many immature loggerheads is to stay put. These loggerheads typically occupy coastal waters of southern Florida or deeper offshore reefs where the water never gets very cold. These latter two tactics are also used by most adult loggerheads. Immature Kemp's ridleys in the Atlantic respond to winter's arrival by moving out of northeastern bays and south along the coast. Ridleys in coastal waters of the northern gulf seem to simply move out into waters just a little deeper in order to avoid the chill of shallow nearshore waters. Most of our neritic-stage hawksbills forage in southern Florida where there may be little requirement for seasonal movement.

Leatherbacks make the longest seasonal movements of all the sea turtles. Although many take part in sojourns that loop around the entire North Atlantic, some turtles make the productive waters off the northeastern US and southern Canada their regular summer destination.

Green turtles make modest north-south seasonal movements

Leatherbacks feast on jellyfish off southern Canada each summer

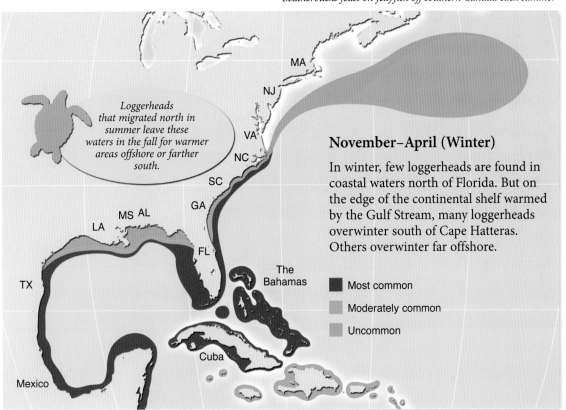

MA

NJ

Loggerheads that migrated north in summer leave these waters in the fall for warmer areas offshore or farther south.

VA

NC

SC

GA

MS AL

LA

FL

TX

The Bahamas

Cuba

Mexico

November–April (Winter)

In winter, few loggerheads are found in coastal waters north of Florida. But on the edge of the continental shelf warmed by the Gulf Stream, many loggerheads overwinter south of Cape Hatteras. Others overwinter far offshore.

■ Most common

■ Moderately common

■ Uncommon

Ecology

The role that sea turtles play in running the world—their ecology—seems to be the part of their lives most difficult for us to comprehend. Sea turtles live on a grand scale of time and geography, which greatly limits our ability to observe and measure their effect on the equally vast ecosystems they occupy. These marine systems are often remote to us, and they are generally more poorly known than systems on land.

The ecology of sea turtles describes how they interact with their fellow organisms and with their environment. These interactions take place with the plants and animals that sea turtles eat, with the predators that eat sea turtles, with competitors for food and living space, and with a host of organisms that simply hang out with sea turtles and might not exist without them. Some of these hangers-on are parasitic, others pose no harm or benefit, and some offer reciprocity within a mutualistic relationship. Sea turtles are not alone. They live within communities of fellow organisms with intertwined fates and shared processes. Some of the important ecosystem processes that sea turtles influence include primary production (plant photosynthesis), energy and nutrient cycling, and the creation of opportunities for other organisms (niche construction). In this way, sea turtles contribute to our variety of life, a concept we call biodiversity.

The ecological role of sea turtles is determined not only by their presence but also by their abundance. So in a world where we have only shadows of historical numbers, some of the influence of sea turtles has dwindled. As sea turtles have declined, many aspects of the world we know have changed.

Above: A loggerhead is swarmed by a "bait ball" of small fish trying to escape being eaten by a school of tuna

Left: The bridled tern atop this basking loggerhead benefits from having an open-sea resting station

Loggerheads are often covered by a variety of epibiont species

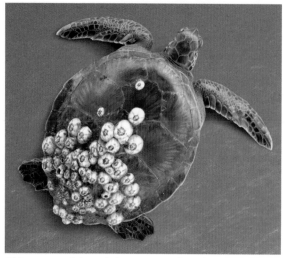
A Kemp's ridley says aaaah, showing its pharyngeal barnacles

Sea Turtle Tagalongs

Sea turtle don't just live within habitats, they *are* habitats. Hundreds of species of plants and animals are willing to call a sea turtle their home. These are **epibionts**—life that lives upon life. Some of these organisms are parasitic, but most are commensal—animals and plants that gain by living on a turtle but have little effect upon their host. Loggerhead sea turtles are exceptional for their diversity of clinging commensal creatures. On the carapace of a loggerhead, one might find dozens of hitchhiking species, including macro- and single-celled algae, sponges, tufts of colonial hydroids, anemones, soft and hard corals, moss animals (bryozoans), marine snails, clam and oyster species, flatworms, tube-dwelling and free-living polychaete worms, shrimps, crabs, amphipods, and a wide variety of barnacle types. For some barnacle species, sea turtles are the only real estate they know. This includes the **turtle barnacle**, *Chelonibia testudinaria*. All sea turtle species are known to sport these sessile crustaceans, which are seldom found anyplace else.

A turtle barnacle on the carapace of a juvenile green turtle

Chelonibia barnacles adhere almost exclusively to a turtle's carapace and head. As far as we can tell, they have very little negative effect on a turtle's lifestyle. But another family of barnacles, the platylepadid barnacles, are probably more irritating. One species, *Stomatolepas praegustator*, grows on the tongue and **pharyngeal area** inside a turtle's mouth. They also lightly embed themselves in the skin of the neck and flippers. Another *Stomatolepas (S. elegans)* embeds deeply, especially between scale seams

This green turtle juvenile has an unusual number of Chelonibia on the leading edges of flippers. They also abrade their way between head and shell scutes, occasionally reaching skull and carapace bone where they erode conspicuous **pits.**

A healthy sea turtle might be expected to have a fair number of barnacles. Loggerheads have the most, followed by hawksbills. The densest accumulation of turtle barnacles on a turtle's carapace is typically along the vertebral scutes (on the midline) and in each rear quarter. It may be that these zones of turbulence favor settlement by the barnacle's cup-shaped cyprid larvae and give them the benefit of enhanced encounters with prey particles. As a turtle barnacle grows, it is not completely stuck with the settlement choice it made as a larva. Astonishingly, they move. Over a period of weeks, a *Chelonibia* barnacle may move across an entire carapace scute or two, mostly forward, leaving a faint gray trail of barnacle adhesive.

Heavily fouled turtles are often in trouble, especially those turtles that begin to acquire thickly encrusting *Stomatolepas* barnacles, or *Balanus* barnacles, which are shaped like tiny volcanoes. Turtles that strand on shore fouled like this are called "Barnacle Bill" turtles and are suffering from any one of a number of ailments.

Some loggerheads have a lush growth of macroalgae, hydroid colonies, tunicates, and sponge, but are perfectly healthy turtles. Such impressive dreadlocks are much more common in large subadult and adult loggerheads that live in clear, shallow waters. This added drag would probably matter most for small turtles that have yet to outgrow the mouths of potential predators. Because the smallest turtles are also the fastest growing, frequent shedding of their shell scutes may help keep their backs clean of acquired hangers-on. Another way to keep one's back scrubbed is to rely on a friend. This mutualistic relationship comes in the form of the **Columbus crab** *(Planes minutus)*, a thumb knuckle–size passenger often found clinging to the tail region of pelagic juvenile loggerheads. The crabs feed on settled, cyprid barnacle larvae before they get a chance to grow. The crabs also remove many other accumulating guests. Unlike pelagic-stage logger-

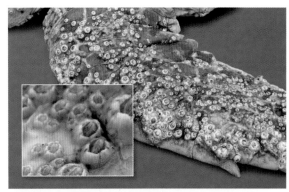

Stomatolepas *barnacles on the flipper of a sick loggerhead*

Barnacles eroded pits (arrows) in this loggerhead carapace bone

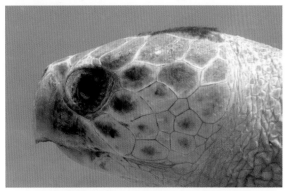

A subadult loggerhead sports a buzz-cut algal hairdo

For a loggerhead, having crabs is not that bad

129

A loggerhead sea turtle wears a cloak of adult sharksuckers

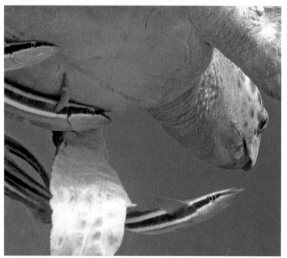

Juvenile sharksuckers accompany a subadult loggerhead

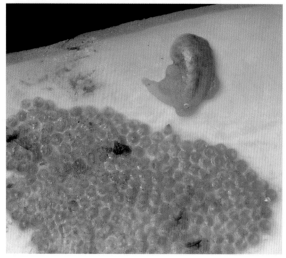

An Ozobranchus *leech (top) and leech cocoons (bottom)*

heads, larger, neritic-stage loggerheads live where there is access to the bottom and have an additional hygienic practice available. SCUBA divers have observed stations beneath ledges where loggerheads make regular visits to scrape barnacles off their backs.

Sea turtles also have relationships with fishes, especially a particular suckerfish (remora) called the **slender sharksucker** *(Echeneis naucrates)*. The fish reaches 3 ft in length (90 cm) and has an oval sucker (a modified fin) atop its head. Pelagic juvenile sea turtles are ridden by small juvenile sharksuckers, and larger turtles are accompanied by larger fish, including adults. Slatlike structures in the fish's sucker open and close to allow attachment or free swimming around a turtle. No doubt the fish benefit from a free ride, but they may also get an occasional free meal. Sharksuckers are known to feed on a turtle's feces.

Acquired parasites take from a sea turtle but do not give back. Although some cause serious diseases, others do not. Some parasite species unique to sea turtles are as rare as their hosts. The most common internal parasites are flukes (trematode worms) and nematodes. Most of the various fluke species live in a turtle's digestive system and cause little pathology. But one fluke family, the spirorchid trematodes, live in the circulatory system and can debilitate or kill the host turtle. These parasites depend on an intermediate host, commonly a snail, for their life cycle. Spirorchids leave their host snail as larvae (cercariae) and penetrate the skin of a host turtle directly.

Sea turtles also host their own species of bloodsucking **leeches.** Two species of the genus *Ozobranchus* live mostly on tender skin, like around a turtle's cloaca. The leeches reproduce by depositing **cocoons** on a turtle's plastron. Most adults that hatch from these cocoons stay with their host turtle. One location where turtle leeches are common is on fibropapilloma skin tumors (see pages 186, 241). The tumors' tender skin and numerous crevices are an ideal habitat. There, leeches cling using suckers, insert their sharp proboscis, and keep blood flowing by injecting anticoagulant saliva.

Sea Turtle Predators

Eggs and hatchlings fit into the diet of a hundred or more species of predators. In our region, the most important egg predators are mammals, especially the **northern raccoon** *(Procyon lotor)*. On some beaches, raccoons have been known to eat almost every egg that sea turtles lay. Such a high rate of predation is probably new. Raccoons drink the fresh water we make available near beaches and eat from our leftovers where we live on the coast. This subsidizes an egg predator outside the nesting season. Coyotes have a similar relationship with humans. Other predators, such as feral pigs (wild boar), did not exist in North America until we introduced them.

A raccoon in a loggerhead nest, in flagrante delicto

On most beaches, the principal nocturnal predator of hatchlings is the **ghost crab** *(Ocypode quadrata)*. These swift-running crabs are mostly scavengers, but will occasionally drag a live hatchling back to their burrow. This predation is low on most beaches, as long as emerging hatchlings are not delayed by lights, which disrupt the ability of hatchlings to find the sea. One insect species that both scavenges and preys on hatchlings is the red imported **fire ant** *(Solenopsis invicta),* which has invaded our region from central Brazil. Because sea turtle hatchlings emerge from nests mostly at night, and because most avian predators are diurnal, birds are only occasional predators of hatchlings on the beach. Yet fish crows, black vultures, and **gull** species are well known to nab hatchlings out in daylight.

A ghost crab seizes an unlucky loggerhead hatchling

Hatchlings on their frenzied swim away from land are bite-size morsels for numerous predatory fishes. These predators are most numerous near shore and include the voracious crevalle jack *(Caranx hippos)*. Farther offshore, predator densities are lower, and although floating sargassum offers some protection, many hatchlings and post-hatchlings fall prey to weedline predators like the dolphinfish *(Coryphaena hippurus)*. As a little turtle grows, fewer and fewer predators at sea are able to eat them. Juvenile turtles in the open sea often show teeth marks and crescent-shaped bites from encounters with sharks, which may be the only pelagic predators able to swallow a football-size or larger sea

Fire ants swarm a loggerhead hatchling

A laughing gull keeps a green turtle hatchling out of the surf

131

turtle. But smaller fish sometimes take bites too. The oceanic triggerfish *(Canthidermis maculata)*, nips at the flippers of pelagic turtles, leaving **U- or V-shaped marks**. The nips can take an entire flipper off a post-hatchling. It's possible that some large turtles with missing flippers sustained their injuries from triggerfish bites long ago.

One of the most important ecological attributes of sea turtles is that they quickly outgrow the mouths of potential predators, except for a few. These few include the large sharks, like the **tiger shark** *(Galeocerdo cuvier)*. These grand fish have the gape, jaw strength, and robust tooth shape that make them a specialist in

A pelagic green turtle flipper with a likely bite from a triggerfish

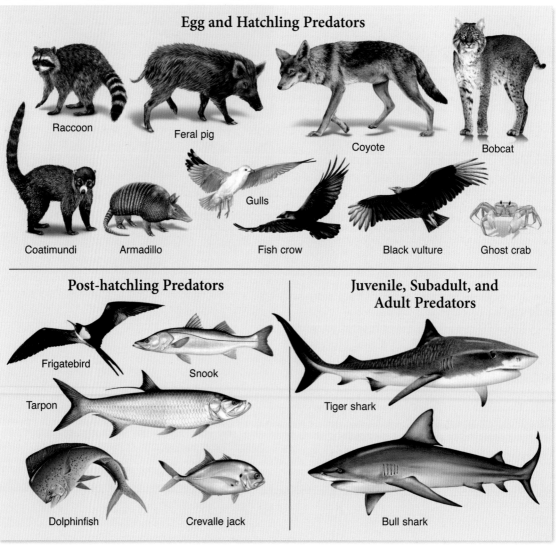

Egg and Hatchling Predators

Raccoon

Feral pig

Coyote

Bobcat

Coatimundi

Armadillo

Gulls

Fish crow

Black vulture

Ghost crab

Post-hatchling Predators

Frigatebird

Snook

Tarpon

Dolphinfish

Crevalle jack

Juvenile, Subadult, and Adult Predators

Tiger shark

Bull shark

chewing large chunks off big tough animals, including sea turtles. A tiger shark's teeth have a thick broad base and a laterally directed point that creates a notched, serrate cutting edge. The teeth allow the shark to saw off a flipper or a mouthful of bony carapace by shaking a turtle side to side. It is not uncommon for a living adult sea turtle to have a broad crescent-shaped piece missing from the edge of their shell, or to have a missing chunk of carapace correspond with a flipper amputation. But actual rates of predation by sharks and mortality from their attacks are largely unknown. Of the vast majority of sea turtles that achieve adult size, shark predation may be rare, or it may be the largest natural hazard for sea turtles in this life stage. We just don't know. Large sea turtles may both avoid shark encounters and live through them. At first thought, survival following the shock and blood loss of a ragged limb amputation is astounding, a feat seemingly at the pinnacle of toughness in the animal world. Then again, the turtles that don't survive, those that sink or are eaten completely, remain unseen.

A juvenile Kemp's ridley with a healed wound from a shark bite

A juvenile green turtle avoids the path of a lemon shark in a shallow seagrass pasture off Florida's gulf coast

133

Turtle grass and manatee grass in a green turtle grazing plot

Hawksbills eat sponges that would overgrow coral reefs

This green turtle nest will contribute nutrients to dune plants

Burrowing four-o-clock cascades into pits left by Florida sea turtles

Sea Turtles Change the World

Sea turtles have the potential to affect our marine environment in important ways. As grazers on seagrass pastures, green turtles drive functions within an ecosystem on which thousands of organisms depend. Before the European colonization of the Caribbean, this basin likely supported over 30 million adult green turtles. Such a figure is comparable to the abundance of American bison that once grazed the tall-grass prairies of North America. Like the great herds of bison, Caribbean green turtles must have been integral to the functioning of the marine meadows they foraged in. Seagrass pastures of today are grazed by green turtles at only about 5% of their historical abundance. Yet the close-cropped **grazing plots** kept by green turtles continue to enhance local productivity. This grazing short-circuits the seagrass detritus cycle, turning growing seagrass into turtle dung, with nutrients that are more accessible to plants than those locked within uncropped blades and accumulating detritus.

Similar to green turtle grazing, sponge feeding by hawksbills may have an important role in **coral reef ecosystems**. Without sponge-munching hawksbills, some sponges grow to out-compete corals for space. Reefs with hawksbills enjoy more coral living space and greater overall diversity of life.

Sea turtles of all species contribute marine nutrients to beach/dune ecosystems by laying eggs in upper beach sands. Not all sea turtle eggs hatch, and this unintentional contribution is a major source of nitrogen and phosphorus. The organic residue of reproductive failure amounts to tons of fertilizer each year for densely nested beaches, greatly benefitting the plants that struggle to grow on the nutrient-starved dunes.

The way sea turtles excavate sand during nesting can also be influential. On the dune face, many **pioneering plant species** benefit from the open space created by a turtle blasting out a nest pit. This allows established plants to be replaced by other quickly growing species.

A Sea Turtle's Changing World

Our sea turtles have dealt with millions of years of change. Throughout their life on Earth, seas have risen and fallen many times, climate has shifted, and a turtle's parasites, predators, and prey have changed as well. But lately, changes brought on by our own industrial endeavors are occurring alarmingly fast.

Not all the changes we prompt are bad for sea turtles, at least in the short term. Overfishing and eutrophication (nutrient pollution) of the seas have brought increasing **blooms of jellyfish**. These blooms cause tourist beaches to close, clog cooling intakes at power plants, and burst our trawl nets, but leatherbacks are loving it. This sea turtle specializes in eating jellies, including the nastier stinging ones. It is unclear how this unintentional ecological boost has influenced leatherback numbers.

Other sea turtle food items have begun to disappear. Loggerheads that migrate into Chesapeake Bay to forage each summer once feasted on the bay's abundance of **horseshoe crabs** (*Limulus polyphemus*). Then, this primitive arthropod with no food appeal to humans suddenly became commercially valuable as bait for eel and whelk traps. As the harvest of horseshoe crabs increased, their abundance declined, and loggerheads were left with more difficult to catch blue crabs (*Callinectes sapidus*). Loggerheads were forced into another diet shift when over-harvest in the Chesapeake blue crab fishery reduced this prey item as well. Loggerheads in the bay came to rely more and more on scavenging for **fish bycatch**—the dead remnants of fish discarded by net fishers.

Perhaps the biggest ecological challenge to sea turtles in a changing world is where to nest. Our seas are rising, and many of the beaches our sea turtles nest on will go away. An important consideration for the future is what the carrying capacity of remaining beaches will be. This ecological capacity is the number of nests a beach can support given density-dependent factors like fungal pathogens from too many rotting eggs, and turtles that can't help but dig up the eggs of others as they bury their own.

A bloom of hydromedusae (jellyfish)

Horseshoe crabs are a rare loggerhead treat these days

Herring are a common discarded bycatch of various fisheries

Sea rise and coastal buildings have squeezed out nesting turtles

135

PART TWO

Experiencing Our Sea Turtles

Above: After scrambling down the beach, a hatchling loggerhead meets the swash from a spent wave. Although most hatchlings begin their journey under cover of darkness, groups emerging at dawn and dusk are not uncommon. These daylight encounters provide a thrill to lucky spectators

Left: A loggerhead sea turtle camouflages her nest by casting sand with her flippers. These nesting events are the focus of guided turtle walks (watches), which offer a unique, up-close wildlife experience

The Sea Turtle Experience

Sea turtles lend themselves well to the human experience. They are ambassadors for the wildest places on our planet, yet they continue to intrigue us with their mystery. Rather conveniently for us, sea turtles crawl into our terrestrial world to reproduce. On sandy beaches that we can access with ease and comfort, sea turtles go about the ancient rite of burying their eggs. If we are careful, we can watch. Few of the truly wild and majestic animals would allow such an intimate encounter. Attempts to get up-close and personal with most large animals would likely end with the animal running away, which limits the experience to seeing a set of hind quarters disappearing into the distance. At worst, an intrepid wildlife observer might get trampled, bitten, gored, mauled, clawed, or eaten. Even in the water, sea turtles are relatively accessible.

Divers and snorkelers know sea turtles well and are able to watch turtles go about their business, as long as a respectable distance is kept.

Experiencing Our Sea Turtles is an important part of this book. As you'll see, we broadly interpret "experiencing" to include all our intersections with sea turtles, both good and bad. The good experiences make special contributions to our happiness. But much of what we do can threaten sea turtles. Although our intentional actions most often reflect a reverence for sea turtles, our unintentional actions can impose severe threats. These are also part of the broader experience humans have with sea turtles.

It is illegal to disturb sea turtles, their eggs, or their nests, so care should be taken during any opportunity for an experience. The safest way to

A loggerhead sea turtle offers a fleeting glimpse of its mysterious life

Most loggerheads nest at night. This nesting female on the beach past dawn offers a rare glimpse in daylight

encounter a sea turtle is to follow a permitted guide. The most common of these ecotourism opportunities facilitate direct experiences with nesting turtles on beaches at night. But because sea turtles leave so much of their story behind after they've visited a beach, there are many additional opportunities for an indirect experience during daylight strolls down a beach. Aficionados of marine wildlife are also thrilled by wild turtles seen at sea, and by sea turtles visited at zoos, aquaria, and marine rehabilitation facilities.

In this part of the book, we interpret experiences with sea turtles on land, in the water, and at captive facilities. On land, experiences include those with nesting turtles, nests, tracks, eggs, and hatchlings. But turtles may also reach land at the end of their lives. In these strandings, a death can help us understand a sea turtle's life. Next, we offer interpretation for experiences with sea turtles in the water. From our above-water perspective in boats, or from our underwater perspective while diving or snorkeling, sea turtles show us the most beautiful part of their lives as marine

creatures. Lastly, we reveal experiences with sea turtles in captivity. Whether recuperating from injury or on exhibit, sea turtles in tanks act as compelling ambassadors to link our world with theirs. This connection with sea turtles manifests in many ways. Our human experience benefits from sea turtles, but can also threaten them. To fully explore our relationship with sea turtles, we interpret ways they can affect our lives along with the ways that we affect theirs.

Sea turtles evoke positive emotions in people. We perceive them as cute, graceful, majestic, and as arousing our sense of wonder. But our experiences with sea turtles can leave us with more questions than answers. The turtles present themselves briefly, only to slip beneath the sea and glide away, living most of their enigmatic lives far from view. Sea turtles tease us with accessibility, yet they retain their mystery. Bringing their lives into our own is a gratifying addition to the human experience. Given this value, it's hard to imagine not working to keep sea turtles around.

Our Sea Turtles
on Land

What Makes a Nesting Beach?

Sea turtles are discriminating beach connoisseurs. Although many beaches seem alike to us, sea turtles see something different. Some beaches that look like delightful places for us to visit may be only marginally attractive to a nesting turtle.

It's important to understand what a nesting female wants in a beach. Her goal is to select a location that will produce the most hatchlings from her eggs, hatchlings that survive their dispersal from land and that will one day grow up to breed successfully. Of additional importance is the nesting female's own survival. We assume these needs given the way natural selection works. How beaches fulfill these needs is largely a guess. But based on how sea turtles vote with their flippers (crawl onto beaches to nest) we have a pretty good idea of what a turtle wants.

Season is important. Beaches are ephemeral deposits of drifting sand, and sea turtles seem to recognize this. To a sea turtle, a beach is just a temporary incubator. The safest incubation time is spring and summer when the beach is least dynamic. This is when sea turtles choose to nest.

Latitude determines a good nesting beach, probably by determining water temperature (high latitudes are too cold). But within a range of latitudes, there are definitive nesting hotspots that stand out. For loggerheads, green turtles, and leatherbacks, the most popular beaches are narrow, with coarse sands and a steep slope. On barrier islands, turtles favor the stretches farthest from any inlet or pass. Our hawksbills nest on tropical beaches with minimal tidal range, and our ridleys mostly like just one beach in northeastern Mexico.

Above: Tracks from green turtles and loggerheads on a popular, steeply sloped southeast Florida beach

Left: A female green turtle registers her vote for a nesting beach by leaving a conspicuous track

141

Peak nesting by loggerheads is between 10 P.M. and 3 A.M.

Kemp's ridleys come ashore to nest in broad daylight

Nesting green turtles occasionally linger past dawn

When Do Sea Turtles Nest?

The seasonal distribution of nesting is detailed in Part One of this book. Most nesting takes place in spring and summer, with leatherbacks pushing the definition of "spring" by nesting as early as Valentine's Day.

Nesting Time of Day

Hawksbills (rare in our region), loggerheads, green turtles, and leatherbacks nest mostly at night. Typically, females begin emerging onto the beach about an hour after sundown, and the last turtle is off the beach before any glow of dawn shows in the eastern sky. The busiest time for turtles taking part in the one- to two-hour nesting process is a little after midnight. However, an early high tide may prompt an earlier peak in nesting, and vice versa, especially where tidal ranges are large. A cold-water upwelling off the beach can slow turtles down and extend the nesting process, leaving some females on the beach past dawn. Most leatherback nesting is at night, but some of these turtles surprise us by emerging in the middle of the day. Several daytime leatherback nesting events occur each year in our region, and they often make the news.

Kemp's ridleys are different, being the only sea turtle species that nests predominantly during the day. Either within the *arribadas* (mass arrivals) that occur in northeastern Mexico, or as solitary females emerging to nest, Kemp's ridleys choose the most blustery days to lay their eggs. The conditions may help to conceal a ridley's nest. Because they are light on their feet for a sea turtle, and because sunshine-dried sands blow away during the windy days chosen for nesting, the place where a ridley has nested can quickly become unrecognizable.

Guided turtle watches (turtle walks, see pages 204–207) time their tours around the turtles, which are principally loggerheads. Most programs begin at 9 P.M., providing time for an introduction before significant numbers of turtles begin emerging. Groups are often able to watch a turtle lay eggs before midnight.

Where Do Sea Turtles Nest?

In the species accounts of Part One, we map the geographic nesting range of our five sea turtles. On a finer scale within this range, nesting females reveal a stable pattern of discriminating beach choices. For example, a look at a plot of loggerhead nesting densities along beaches of the southeastern US shows distinct peaks and valleys that are consistent over many years. The largest nesting density peaks for loggerheads are on the central Atlantic coast of Florida, but significant elevations also occur along southwestern Florida's gulf coast, and in central South Carolina near Cape Romain. These beaches share a common profile—a beach shape that is more **reflective** to waves than **dissipative** (wave absorbing).

The reflective beaches favored by loggerheads have several features in common. Each has relatively coarse sands and a steeply sloped foreshore (the area swept by tides). These beaches are fairly narrow and tend to form cusps, which are regularly spaced mounds and dips in foreshore sands. The good loggerhead nesting beaches of southwestern Florida have characters that are intermediate between reflective and dissipative, but they are more reflective than other beaches of the eastern gulf.

Nesting green turtles and leatherbacks prefer the most reflective beaches of southeastern Florida, and are more limited by latitude than loggerheads are. For some reason, there is little nesting by green turtles and leatherbacks on eastern gulf beaches. For each of these three species, nesting females are least likely to choose nesting locations near ocean inlets through or between barrier islands. These are the most dynamic beaches, both in terms of erosion and accretion of sand.

Other factors not clearly understood may drive the nesting beach choices that sea turtles make. Proximity to major offshore currents may promote hatchling survival, and reduced upland habitat for egg predators may lower nest mortality. We also play a role. Nesting females tend to shy away from beaches with extensive lighting and human disturbance.

Jupiter Island, Florida   Melbourne Bch., Florida   Cape Romain, South Carolina

Sands from beaches with localized peaks in loggerhead nesting

Outer Banks, North Carolina   Cumberland Is., Georgia   Alligator Point, Florida

Sands from beaches with only moderate loggerhead nesting

A steep, narrow, reflective beach at Cape Romain, SC

A flat, wide, dissipative beach on North Carolina's Outer Banks

143

The Nesting Process

To the uninitiated, it may seem that sea turtles don't put much effort into caring for their eggs. Like most reptiles, sea turtles don't guard their nests and they are unlikely to ever see their hatchlings. But leading up to the moment when a female turns back to the sea to leave her eggs for-ever, a lot of choreographed care takes place. This nesting ritual is highly conserved (similar among species), indicating that its details have a critical influence on egg and hatchling survival. Because the loggerhead is our region's most common nesting sea turtle, we'll allow this species to illus-trate the process of nesting.

How and when a loggerhead female identifies the place she'll emerge from the sea is unclear, but the decision is made mostly while the female is still in the water. The nesting process begins with a female's emergence from the sea. During her crawl out of the wave wash, a loggerhead will stop during each breath, at which time she may lift and turn her head as if making a visual appraisal. On resum-ing her crawl, a loggerhead will often plow her nose through the sand in front of her. Once she has ascended the foreshore slope onto the upper-beach berm, she will begin nest-site preparation. She begins this by parting the sand in front of her with

A Loggerhead's Seven Stages of Nesting

The stages of nesting are remarkably similar among sea turtle species. Like the other species, a loggerhead may abandon her nesting attempt before laying eggs (**4**), but seldom after.

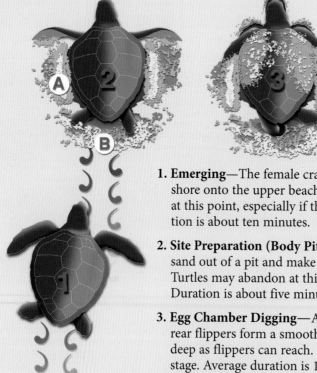

1. **Emerging**—The female crawls out of the surf and up the fore-shore onto the upper beach berm. Attempts are often abandoned at this point, especially if the turtle is disturbed. Average dura-tion is about ten minutes.

2. **Site Preparation (Body Pitting)**—Front and rear flippers move sand out of a pit and make mounds to the side (**A**) and rear (**B**). Turtles may abandon at this point, especially if disturbed. Duration is about five minutes, longer if multiple pits are tried.

3. **Egg Chamber Digging**—Alternating flick and dig strokes from rear flippers form a smooth hole, wider at the bottom and as deep as flippers can reach. Disturbed turtles abandon at this stage. Average duration is 18 minutes.

4. **Egg Laying**—The female is motionless between contractions that raise rear flippers and precede each drop of one to four eggs. Average duration is 18 minutes. Large egg clutches take longer.

her front flippers. The sluggish strokes create mounds of sand beside her and a depression in front of her that she will incrementally scoot into. As she scoots, she will deepen the rear of the depression by making alternating sweeps with her rear flippers that push back sand into a mound behind her. With the deepest portion of the depression under her rear, she becomes slightly inclined within the body pit she's excavated. So nestled within moist, subsurface sand, the loggerhead is better able to begin digging an egg chamber that will not immediately cave in. This hole is dug with alternating strokes from her rear flippers. Each stroke starts with a kick forward to flick sand out of the way. Then the flipper scoops sand from the deepening hole, draws the sand upward and pats it to the side. After a hundred or so strokes, the urn-shaped chamber (see page 112) is ready to be filled. Rear flippers aside the egg chamber curl upward with each contraction, preceding eggs in drops of one to four. After the last egg, the turtle will use her rear flippers to draw sand from the side and cover her eggs. Then, she will press down on this sand to compact it. Camouflaging begins when the turtle uses all four flippers to throw sand behind her over a broad mound. She creeps forward during this extensive sand displacement, and eventually her strokes evolve into a crawling gait. Her return to the sea is typically direct with only a few stops to catch her breath

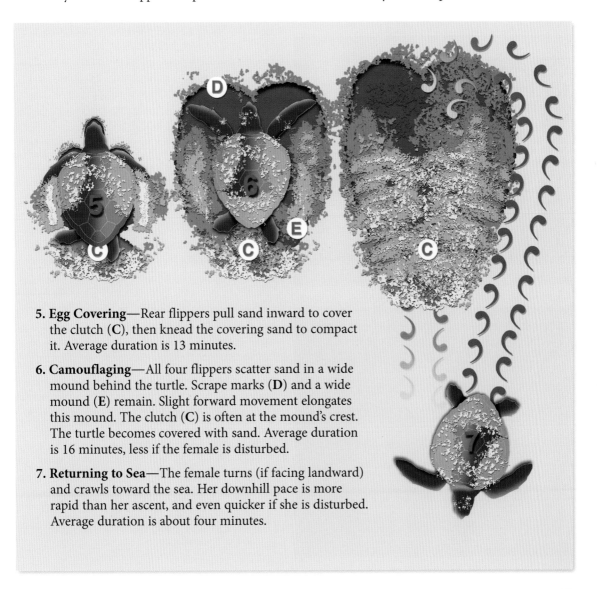

5. **Egg Covering**—Rear flippers pull sand inward to cover the clutch (**C**), then knead the covering sand to compact it. Average duration is 13 minutes.

6. **Camouflaging**—All four flippers scatter sand in a wide mound behind the turtle. Scrape marks (**D**) and a wide mound (**E**) remain. Slight forward movement elongates this mound. The clutch (**C**) is often at the mound's crest. The turtle becomes covered with sand. Average duration is 16 minutes, less if the female is disturbed.

7. **Returning to Sea**—The female turns (if facing landward) and crawls toward the sea. Her downhill pace is more rapid than her ascent, and even quicker if she is disturbed. Average duration is about four minutes.

An emerging green turtle reaches the base of the dune

Loggerheads ascend the beach with alternating flipper strokes

A leatherback crawls out of the sea with simultaneous strokes

Emerging From the Sea

Our three most common nesting species emerge from the sea to nest at night. At this stage, loggerheads and green turtles that detect an approaching observer will abandon their attempt. Depending on beach width, this ascent to the nest site takes about ten minutes.

Green turtles begin crawling with a distinctive gait as soon as the backwash of spent waves leaves the female without water to support her weight. She crawls with simultaneous movement of all her flippers. With each stroke, four flippers swing forward, dig in, and heave the turtle up the beach about 6 in (15 cm) or so. The strokes, though forceful, are not enough to keep the turtle's lower shell from dragging. She'll make several of these synchronized strokes before lifting her head to take a breath. During this rest, she may move her head as if surveying the beach. Her path typically takes her perpendicular to shore, up the beach slope, and past the highest tide mark.

Loggerheads assume an alternating gait as the retreat of water forces them to crawl. Left-rear and right-front flippers move forward as right-rear and left-front flippers push the turtle up the beach. Then, this step is mirrored. A female will make several steps before raising her head and taking a breath. As in green turtles, a loggerhead may take this opportunity between crawling steps to crane her neck in an apparent beach inspection. Upon resuming her straight path up the beach, a loggerhead will drop her head, allowing her nose to push through the sand, sometimes plowing a furrow deep enough not to be smoothed by her dragging plastron.

Leatherbacks crawl out of the ocean using a butterfly stroke that is similar to the green turtle's gait. And like a green turtle, a leatherback female requires a breath and a brief rest after each bout of several simultaneous strokes. Between bouts, she may make subtle course changes that result in a wavy, sinusoidal path up the beach. Leatherbacks are not as skittish as loggerheads and green turtles are. They will typically continue up the beach even when confronted by onlookers.

Preparing the Nest Site

This stage includes the testing of a potential nest site and site preparation (body pitting) prior to digging a chamber for the eggs. In each of these three species, females may wander the beach before beginning this stage, and may initiate site preparation only to abandon the attempt, move, and try again elsewhere. Green turtles and loggerheads are highly susceptible to human disturbance during this stage of nesting.

Green turtles begin nest-site preparation with vigorous, front-flipper swimming strokes that gather the sand ahead of them and blast it across a broad area behind. Alternating rear-flipper sweeps follow simultaneous front-flipper strokes in a repeated sequence that eventually results in excavation of a circular body pit as deep as the turtle's shell height. Although trial "body-pitting" strokes may occur just landward of the high tide line, body pits that eventually become nest sites are more likely to be located closer to the base of the dune. A green turtle will spend about 25 minutes at this vigorous activity, with short rests following sets of front-flipper and rear-flipper stroke combinations.

Loggerheads crawling up the beach show a smooth transition to nest-site preparation by slowing their forward movement while continuing their flipper movements. With their nose plowed into the sand, a female will shift front-flipper movements to slow, simultaneous strokes that scrape out a pit ahead of the turtle and pile sand along her sides. She slides into this pit while pivoting back and forth. During these pivots, her rear flippers alternate with sweeps that excavate the rear of the pit and pile a mound behind her. After about five minutes, the female is slightly inclined, tail down, within a body pit about half her body height deep.

Leatherbacks begin body pitting as green turtles do, with blasts from front flippers followed by sweeps from rear flippers. But leatherbacks differ by making wide pivots during their front-flipper strokes, which result in a lumpy, less organized body pit. The excavation lasts about ten minutes and is only occasionally abandoned, even with human observers in view.

A body-pitting green turtle excavates with all four flippers

Rear-flipper sweeps dig the back of a loggerhead's body pit

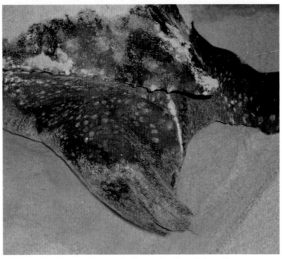

A leatherback has a messy body pit dug by all four flippers

147

A green turtle inserts a rear flipper into a deepening egg chamber

This loggerhead's left flipper flicks sand before its digging stroke

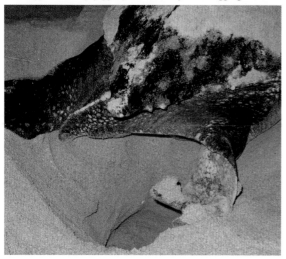

A leatherback ladles sand out of her egg chamber

Digging the Egg Chamber

All sea turtles make their egg chamber in similar ways, dug with alternating rear-flipper strokes at the lowest point in the body pit. Excavation requires dexterity in rear-flipper movements one might consider impossible for a turtle. Foam casts of egg chambers reveal their architecture—slightly wider at the bottom than at the neck. The eggs will occupy the bottom of the chamber, which is a squarish space circumscribed by the extent of the rear flippers' reach. The entirety of the chamber has smooth walls, except where the rear-flipper claws have gouged creases during the final few digging strokes. Because leatherbacks have no claws, their egg chambers are completely smooth.

Green turtles make their first digging stroke as an evolution of the rear-flipper sweeps used in bodypitting. Instead of sweeping palm down, the rear flipper supinates (rotates palm up) with a handful of sand, then quickly moves laterally and rotates to pat the sand down. Immediately, the opposite rear flipper kicks forward, throwing any sand atop it in a forward spray. This flipper recoils from the kick, supinates, swings beneath the tail, and repeats the scooping pattern of the alternate flipper. The female's front flippers are anchored in the sand and don't move, but they do force movement in the turtle, whose rear rotates to accommodate each scoop of sand. After several strokes, the rear-flipper rotation is down within a deepening hole, with cupped flippers withdrawing sand as a ladle would. At maximum depth (as far as flippers can reach), each flipper may rotate through multiple wide arcs to scrape away the lower chamber. After about 20 minutes of work, the last few strokes cannot reach deeply enough to extract more sand.

Loggerheads dig the same way green turtles do, but within a shallower body pit and with shorter rear flippers. Average digging time is about 18 minutes.

Leatherbacks mirror the digging style of the other sea turtle species, but are able to excavate a much deeper egg chamber equivalent to the size of their rear flippers. Digging lasts about 20 minutes.

Laying Eggs

Up until the first egg is laid, a female making a nesting attempt could abandon her effort and return to the sea with few consequences. But eggs are valuable, and represent an energy expense worth further investment. The additional investment made by a nesting female is to ensure that the eggs she lays are adequately covered and camouflaged from predators. So it's not surprising that turtles reaching the laying stage do not abandon their attempt and leave eggs in an incomplete nest. This is the stage at which guided turtle watches allow participants to witness the nesting turtle up close. A laying sea turtle's tolerance of voyeurs is often attributed to a nesting "trance." This does not accurately describe a nesting female's state, in that a turtle will often flinch in response to the movements of people around her. But she will continue her task, perhaps as a result of hormonal muscular commands not unlike those compelling a human female in labor.

Green turtles make their last egg-chamber digging stroke, withdraw the flipper, and slowly bring both rear flippers together covering the open hole. A minute or so may pass before the first few eggs drop into the egg chamber. The soft eggs often bounce when they hit the bottom. Contractions preceding each egg release (one to four at a time) result in slight movements of the rear flippers. Other than this subtle motion, and breaths taken every few minutes, the female is still. Egg laying lasts about 20 minutes for an average clutch of 135 eggs.

Loggerheads begin egg laying like green turtles do, but instead of rear flippers covering the egg chamber, they straddle it. Contractions just before each release of eggs correspond with distinct upward arcing of the rear flippers. Most loggerheads complete egg laying in about 18 minutes. An average clutch has 115 eggs.

Leatherbacks complete their digging and leave one rear flipper dangling into the egg chamber. Eggs dribbling down the flipper may ease the long fall. Among the last "eggs" dropped into the hole include an average of 30 small, yolkless eggs, among an average of 80 true eggs. Egg laying is complete in about 12 minutes.

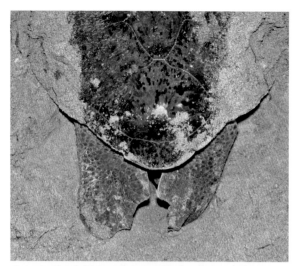

Green turtles shyly cover their egg chamber during egg laying

A loggerhead arcs her rear flippers upward during a contraction

During egg laying, leatherbacks leave one rear flipper in the hole

149

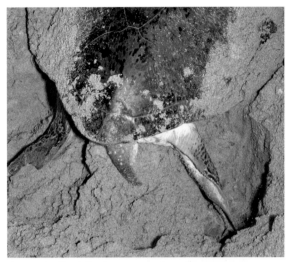

A green turtle reaches to scrape sand over her eggs

Loggerheads pile sand and knead it with rear flippers

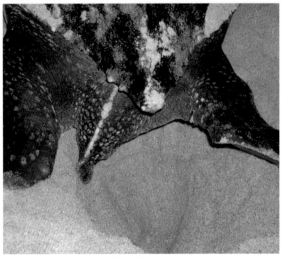

A leatherback scrapes sand over her eggs

Covering and Packing

All sea turtles spend considerable time placing sand over their eggs and packing it in.

Green turtles may show a few contractions without eggs before abruptly starting covering movements with her rear flippers. A female's first strokes are to make wide reaches to the side that scrape sand inward over the eggs. After only a few rapid strokes, alternating between flippers, the turtle's eggs are covered by several inches of sand. The rear-flipper movements become jittery, and begin to include packing movements. These include patting the sand atop the eggs with the palms of the rear flippers. Covering and packing typically last about 13 minutes in green turtles.

Loggerheads scrape sand over their eggs much like the green turtle's style but are more deliberate (less jittery). Their sand compaction is done with the leading edge of the rear flippers. The process takes about 13 minutes.

Leatherbacks cover and pack like green turtles do, but with smooth strokes and occasional pivots side to side. Stage length is ten minutes.

A dancing ridley thumps side-to-side to pack in her eggs

Kemp's ridleys cover their eggs deliberately, pack the sand with the leading edge of the rear flippers, and then they dance. The "dance" is a rapid side-to-side rocking that thumps the sand. Covering and packing last about five minutes.

Hawksbills ladle, rather than scrape, sand over their eggs before kneading sand to pack it in as loggerheads do. The stage is about 12 minutes.

Camouflaging

All sea turtles spray sand over their nest area with all four flippers. The thrown sand fills the body pit, increases egg depth, and probably serves to scatter both visual and olfactory cues that nest predators might use.

Green turtles use strong front-flipper swimming strokes with rear-flipper sweeps and spend about 30 minutes camouflaging.

Loggerheads are less vigorous than green turtles and spend less time camouflaging, about 16 minutes.

Leatherbacks make strong swimming strokes like green turtles, but have a habit of stopping, pivoting or crawling, then resuming their sand scattering. The process may take 30 to 60 minutes based on the number of these "false nests."

Kemp's ridley's have just a small body pit to fill and take only about five minutes to scatter sand during their camouflaging stage.

Hawksbills camouflage their nest as loggerheads do, and take about 18 minutes.

Camouflaging green turtles throw sand more than 20 ft (6 m)

Kemp's ridley's put in just a brief camouflaging effort

This hawksbill nest shows the turtle's penchant for tight spaces

A loggerhead throws sand during nest camouflaging

Some leatherbacks spend an hour camouflaging their nest

151

After more than two hours nesting, a green turtle returns seaward

A loggerhead's return crawl is faster than her ascent

Leatherbacks often turn an orientation circle before leaving

Returning to the Sea

In all species, the last nest-camouflaging flipper strokes often evolve into a crawling gait. Sometimes, crawling is preceded by a raised head in an inspection stance, perhaps to determine the direction of the surf. If required for correct orientation, a turtle will turn sharply before moving down the beach. Turtles that have nested will take a direct path seaward unless they are detoured by obstacles or disoriented by artificial lighting.

Green turtles must begin their return by crawling out of the deep pit they've dug during camouflaging. They reach the sea in five to ten minutes, and like all sea turtles, begin swimming away as soon as they are buoyed by water.

Loggerheads crawl seaward faster than they ascended the beach and reach the sea in five to ten minutes, depending on beach width.

Leatherbacks commonly make a complete 360-degree turn in an "orientation circle" either before or during their return to the sea. The circle's radius is typically the width of the turtle's track. Upon resuming her seaward movement, a leatherback will make slight course changes that take her along a serpentine path. A leatherback may take ten to fifteen minutes to reach the sea.

Most ridleys spends only about 45 minutes on the beach

Kemp's ridleys move down the beach quickly, have a relatively long stride, and reach the water in just a few minutes.

Hawksbills crawl quickly, like ridleys, and take little time in returning to the sea.

Signs in the Sand

Some fascinating indirect experiences with sea turtles can come from the signs they leave for us on beaches. Because sand is an excellent tracking medium, even subtle stories are recorded for us to see. Although much of the drama occurs at night, morning walks on the beach can allow us a nice appreciation of those nocturnal goings-on.

Each sea turtle species has unique physical and behavioral characteristics that influence the signs they leave in the sand. This begins with a turtle's track. Even a turtle that abandons her nesting attempt will leave all the evidence necessary to tell which species she was, how far along in the nesting process she got, and of course, where she made the attempt. We would also know which night she tried, and depending on tides, about what time of night. Given other evidence at the scene, we might also infer the reason the turtle gave up on her nesting attempt. A beach chair may have presented a barrier, or footprints may tell of more direct human interference. Some individual turtles leave a signature track. Females that have acquired flipper injuries leave distinctive flipper prints, which not only tell us about their lives but also allow us to distinguish multiple beach visits by the same turtle.

A sea turtle that makes a nest on the beach leaves abundant signs of what she did. To a savvy turtle tracker, the entire sequence of nesting behaviors is revealed in a nest site, including where the eggs are located and what obstacles were encountered.

Understanding basic sea turtle anatomy and nesting behavior, with an accounting for how these factors interact with sands of differing firmness and texture, can reveal a detailed narrative. Rule number one on reading these signs in the sand is to explore the beach early in the morning, when shadows are distinct, details are crisp, and the signs are unaltered by daytime activity.

Two loggerheads converged on a beach, and the tide revealed when each arrived

Green turtles have long front flippers that leave parallel slashes

Points in a green turtle's tail drag show rests between strokes

Making Tracks

Sea turtles crawling out of the sea leave distinctive tracks on the beach. These tracks reveal which species visited, and on occasion, tell us a little bit about the individual turtle herself. The turtle traits that separate species by their tracks include the turtle's gait, which is how the turtle uses its flippers to crawl. Sea turtles show two types of gait, simultaneous and alternating. In a simultaneous gait, all four flippers work together. This "butterfly stroke" results in incremental creeping, and leaves a set of parallel flipper prints. In an alternating gait, flipper steps (either pushing off or swinging forward) match in diagonally opposing limbs. It's how a baby crawls. This alternating gait leaves an alternating set of flipper prints in the sand.

The physical characteristics that determine a turtle's track include flipper length and tail length. Long front flippers leave slashlike marks that are not totally erased by the steps of the rear flippers. A long tail means that it reaches the sand and can make a distinct mark as the turtle crawls. Such a tail-drag mark will zigzag if the turtle has an alternating gait, and will be straight if the turtle crawls with simultaneous flipper movements. All sea turtles drag their plastron as they crawl. But this blank smoothing of sand is merely the canvas on which the turtle applies the prints from her rear flippers and tail (if long enough).

Green turtles crawl with a simultaneous gait and leave a set of parallel flipper marks. However, a disturbed green turtle on the beach may shift to alternating strokes, almost a gallop. When crawling normally, a green turtle's front flippers make close-set diagonal gouges that point the direction she traveled. These slashes remain along the margins of her track because they are long enough that they are not stepped on by the rear flippers. The tip of a green turtle's tail drags behind her, leaving a pencil-thin mark.

Loggerheads use an alternating gait. This is not often seen in the marks from a female's front flippers because they are too short to leave conspicuous marks not erased by the rear flippers. But alternating footwork is clearly evident from

The alternating gait of a loggerhead returning to the sea

the rear flippers, which leave staggered swirls that make up most of the track. A loggerhead's tail is short enough not to drag in the sand.

Leatherbacks are big, which gives sufficient distinction in the track they leave. Their gait employs simultaneous flipper movements, which seem an absolute requirement for terrestrial movement in such a large animal. All limbs dig in together to heave the turtle forward a few inches at a time. As in a green turtle, the marks left are parallel and include those left by the front flippers. But the front flippers are much longer in leatherbacks. With each stroke, the front flippers reach forward and scratch at the sand before digging in at the wrists, which support most of the turtle's weight during the heave. A leatherback's tail is longer and heavier than a green turtle's, and it leaves a deeper drag mark down the track center. If these distinctions weren't enough, leatherbacks also show us a unique choice of crawling paths. Their track both up and down the beach is typically along a wavy, sinusoidal route. And having nested, a leatherback will most often turn a complete **orientation circle** before weaving its way back to sea.

Kemp's ridleys are small and quick for a sea turtle. Because of their lightness, their alternating gait pushes them along in a fluid slide up and down the beach. With each step, a ridley is able to lift its plastron, which does not completely smooth the sand. In comparison to loggerheads, a ridley's stride is longer, which can be seen most clearly in the swirling rear flipper marks that make up most of the track. Although a nesting ridley is much smaller than a nesting loggerhead, it is almost as wide, which results in just a little overlap in track widths between the two species. A ridley's tail often leaves a zigzag drag mark.

Hawksbills are slightly smaller and narrower than loggerheads, but the two species crawl in much the same way. Hawksbills are a little quicker than loggerheads, and have a longer stride, but this does not clearly distinguish their tracks. The most reliable hawksbill track evidence may be the zigzag tail mark the turtle leaves behind.

A leatherback's large front flippers contribute to a wide track

A leatherback often turns an orientation circle over her nest

Kemp's ridleys are nimble on the beach and leave a light track

Green Turtle Tracks

Tracks are symmetrical, with parallel marks from front flippers along the margins, and from rear flippers astride the midline. The front-flipper slashes point the direction of travel. Duel ridges pushed up by the rear flippers run along the middle. At the center, a thin, straight, tail-drag mark is punctuated with tiny Vs that show where the tail pointed during rests between simultaneous flipper strokes.

- Parallel flipper marks
- Duel ridges down middle
- Slashes along margins
- Straight tail drag with intermittent V-points

39–53 in (100–135 cm)

A green turtle track—the red arrow shows direction of travel

Loggerhead Tracks

Tracks are asymmetrical, with alternating marks from rear flippers astride the midline. Comma-shaped swirls show where the rear flippers pushed against the sand, indicating the direction of travel. A flat, wavy center reveals rear-flipper steps over the area smoothed by the plastron. Front-flipper slashes are seen only occasionally, except where the turtle turned. There is no true tail-drag mark.

- Alternating comma-shaped swirls
- Flat, wavy center
- No tail drag
- No consistent slashes along margin

30–45 in (75–115 cm)

A loggerhead track—the red arrow shows direction of travel

Leatherback Tracks

Tracks are symmetrical, with parallel marks from front flippers along the margins, and from rear flippers astride the midline. The deepest front-flipper slashes point the direction of travel. Front-flipper marks make up half the track width. Dual ridges pushed up by the rear flippers run along the middle. A heavy, straight, tail-drag mark runs between center ridges. Width is greater than any from other species.

- Parallel flipper marks

- Dual ridges down middle

- Marginal slashes are half of track width

- Straight, heavy tail drag

5.9–7.5 ft (180–230 cm)

The snaking track of a leatherback

Kemp's Ridley Tracks

Tracks are asymmetrical, with alternating marks from rear flippers. These are light swirls (light gray in the track graphic) with distinct claw marks (black lines). A wavy center is often unclear in hard sand. Front-flipper slashes are seen only occasionally. The tail leaves a distinct but thin drag mark in soft sand.

- Alternating light swirls with distinct claw marks

- Flat, wavy center

- Occasional tail drag

- No consistent slashes along margin

28–31 in (70–80 cm)

Kemp's ridley tracks are faint, but for rear-flipper claw marks

157

Hawksbills often leave an irregular, zigzagging tail-drag mark

Hawksbill Tracks

These are similar to loggerhead tracks, but with a **zigzagging tail drag** down at least some of the extent (the tail can be lifted so as not to drag).

- Alternating comma-shaped swirls
- Occasional deep tail zigzags
- No consistent slashes along margin

28–33 in (70–85 cm)

Track Variation

Many sea turtle tracks show atypical variations due to the turtle's behavior, injuries it has sustained, or the nature of the sand. Some of this variation can be within a track. Always trust the story told by the clearest, least aberrant part of a track.

Nose-plow marks can confuse some into thinking they are seeing a tail drag. On their crawl up the beach, loggerheads often plow the sand ahead of them with their muzzle, leaving a furrow partially smoothed over by the plastron. These marks are typically deep and straight.

A smoothed furrow made by a loggerhead plowing with her nose

A loggerhead plows with her nose as she ascends the beach

Sometimes, a loggerhead's cloaca remains everted after nesting, leaving a **blunt zigzag** down the center of her return track away from the nest. These marks are seldom seen in a turtle's emerging track.

A blunt zigzag (arrow) made by a loggerhead's dragging cloaca

Missing Flippers

Sea turtles with flipper injuries leave unusual and sometimes confusing tracks. These injuries include paralyzed flippers, those missing various portions of their web (the broad part supported by finger and toe bones), and flippers that are completely missing. A turtle with extensive flipper injuries may leave a track that has few clues indicating which species visited the beach. Other than the track, additional evidence from a nest may not exist, in that injured turtles often abandon their attempts. Many species characteristics still come through in the track of an injured turtle, with an understanding of how her difficulty with crawling affected her stride.

Track from a loggerhead missing its right rear flipper

In the top right image, a loggerhead with a completely missing right rear flipper has made a track down the beach. With no rear flipper to erase the marks from her right front flipper, the **slashes** from the front flipper on that side remain. On the turtle's left side (right side of image), the **rear-flipper marks** are close together due to the additional difficulty the turtle had moving up the beach. But those rear-flipper marks are distinctly loggerhead-like, with no front-flipper marks on that side.

The green turtle that made the track in the middle right image had only a narrow portion of her left rear flipper remaining. The right half of the turtle made a set of typical green turtle marks (left side of image), but the left side of the turtle was clearly hampered by the missing flipper. The remnant of the left rear poked into the sand with each simultaneous push from the turtle's other flippers, but was not enough to keep the turtle from crawling askew, so that her left front flipper marks were partly smoothed by her plastron.

Track from a green turtle with a partially missing left rear flipper

A loggerhead missing the web of its right rear flipper made the track in the bottom right image. Like the green turtle shown above, this loggerhead made an off-center path. The absence of any front-flipper marks on the turtle's right side (left side of image) may mean that both flippers on that side were injured.

This loggerhead had a right rear flipper missing its web

159

A loggerhead (probably) dragged a barnacle (maybe)

A green turtle track in hard, wet sand

This green turtle left a deeper impression in soft sand

Probably a Loggerhead

Because the most common sea turtle nesting in our region is the loggerhead (except in Texas, where ridleys are most common), this species is a good guess for any track with alternating flipper prints. Hawksbills are rare, so most zigzagging marks looking like they could have been from a hawksbill's tail are likely from some oddity dragged by a loggerhead. These dragging zigzags include barnacles on the rear plastron, and even carapace injuries that leave a dangling portion that can mark the sand.

Uphill and Down, Hard Sand and Soft

The look of a sea turtle's track varies up and down the beach. Some characteristics that are invisible in firm sand come clear in the path the turtle took through softer sand. Because of sand differences, a peculiar-looking incoming track might be paired with a typical return track, or vice versa. Only the most forceful flipper strokes are recorded in hard sand. For example, the green turtle track in the middle image is made up mostly of **front-flipper slashes**, because the hard, wet sand did not allow the turtle's rear flippers and tail to make any clear marks. Another green turtle crawling in soft sand (bottom image) left a track with **distinct ridges** pinched together by the turtle's rear flippers.

Sea turtles crawling uphill face an obvious impediment in comparison to their downhill return. As a turtle ascends, its flipper strokes are close set, which may make it difficult to tell whether the turtle had an alternating or simultaneous gait. But the same turtle on its downhill slide will have a lengthened stride, leaving an overt record of how it walked. On occasion, a turtle ascending the beach will have to climb a steep, even vertical escarpment, such as what might be left following an erosion event. Loggerheads have an adaptive way to deal with these obstacles. Upon encountering a scarp, a loggerhead will bulldoze into it, hacking at the sand with regular crawling strokes until an inclined plane of sand is formed, allowing the turtle to climb. On artificial beaches, sands are often too compact for this, forcing turtles to abandon their attempt.

Other Animal Tracks

Because sand is such an excellent tracking medium, most animals can't visit the beach without leaving some sign that they were there. Ghost crabs, raccoons, dogs, and humans all inscribe characteristic tracks. But few of these could ever be confused with marks left by a nesting sea turtle.

A few beach visitors have at least some potential to leave sea-turtle-esque tracks. Among these are other turtles. Gopher tortoises, diamondback terrapins, and lost pond turtles like the **peninsula cooter** *(Pseudemys peninsularis)* all leave stubby limb pokes rather than flipper marks, and are much smaller than sea turtles (leaving tracks less than a foot wide). **Alligators** *(Alligator mississippiensis)* are much bigger reptiles, and can leave a fairly wide track, but one that is only vaguely similar to a sea turtle track. These crocodilians scoot up the beach in one of two ways, either using a walking gait or with a belly slide. In tracks from either gait, the claw marks from the limbs are easily visible, as is the sinusoidal drag from the large, thick tail.

The only bird likely to make a crawling mark in the sand is the common loon *(Gavia immer)*, which occasionally strands on beaches in the spring and fall. These aquatic birds can't walk at all and can only scoot forward by pushing with their feet, which are positioned at the extreme aft end of the bird. Any track left by these birds would be less than a foot wide.

In the northern end of our region, seals haul out onto beaches to bask. Their crawl is with vertical undulations, like a giant caterpillar. Their rear limbs drag and their forelimbs leave parallel marks with distinct claw scratches. The most common seal on northern beaches is the **gray seal** *(Halichoerus grypus)*.

The sea-turtle-track mimics that prompt the most double takes are made by people. Whether to purposefully confuse nesting beach surveyors, or to express whimsical art in imitation of nature, some of these track creations are almost convincing from a distance.

Signs that a peninsula cooter visited the beach

A walking (not sliding) track from an alligator

Tracks from a gray seal

161

Evidence of a green turtle that turned back without nesting

Two loggerhead false crawls (from the same turtle?)

A false crawl from a leatherback

Abandoned Nesting Attempts

Not every sea turtle that crawls onto a beach will lay eggs in a nest. But every turtle does leave something behind—evidence. This evidence (tracks, pits, mounds) is generally referred to as a "crawl." An abandoned nesting attempt is often called a **"false crawl."** In sea turtle vernacular, this term is occasionally used as a verb, as in, "that turtle turned around on the beach and false crawled."

Sea turtles give up during a nesting attempt for a variety of reasons, some which we don't understand. On most beaches, loggerheads and green turtles that crawl past the recent high tide line will abandon their nesting attempt about half the time. But below the tide line, these turtles may make numerous, short, arcing forays out onto wet sand before finally ascending the dry beach. Most of the tracks left by these trial efforts below the tide line are washed away by morning, but night vision observations reveal that green turtles and loggerheads commonly make nesting "attempts" that are no more than brief crawls in the wave wash. Leatherbacks are much more persistent. Only 20% of their tracks above the high tide line are without a nest.

Because sea turtles abandon their attempts at various stages in the nesting sequence, a false crawl has more than one characteristic look. Turtles that abandon nesting attempts during their emergence typically leave either an arcing track (sometimes called a half-moon) or a relatively straight hairpin. When an ascending turtle reaches a barrier like an escarpment or a wall, she may immediately turn around or she may begin to "wander." This wandering can add more than a hundred feet of length to a turtle's track as she crawls along an obstruction looking for a way around it. An escarpment in a natural (soft) beach is a minor obstruction. Nesting sea turtles can scale even a chest-high scarp by bulldozing into it and creating their own inclined plane. Harder scarps on artificial (nourished) beaches don't crumble so easily and are as insurmountable a barrier to nesting as any solid wall. Other barriers, especially hardened structures on the beach such as rock revetments, sea walls, sand fences, and sand bags, are one of the most readily identifiable reasons for abandoned nesting attempts.

Turtles that begin preparing their nest site before abandoning it leave the evidence of that behavior. It's common for turtles to leave an **abandoned body pit**. Depending on which species made the crawl and how long the turtle worked at it, this evidence ranges in extent from an abrupt sand mound bulldozed aside, to a deep pit and extensive scatter of sand. The top right image shows the crawl from a loggerhead that made only a few body-pitting strokes. This was enough to push a mound of sand over her incoming track and create ridges of sand on either side of where she sat. Because she arced to her right (arrow shows crawling direction) as she made her body-pitting strokes, the ridge on her right is less distinctive (she may have crawled over some of the ridge). The middle image shows a crawl from a loggerhead that made a small body pit near the base of the dune, then turned left and departed without nesting. In both of the preceding examples, the mound pushed back by the turtle's rear flippers covers the incoming track but is only about the width of the track. And any remaining ridges made by the front flippers as the turtle scraped sand to her sides, are separated by a span no broader than the width of the turtle, which is roughly the width of her track.

Green turtles that abandon their body pits leave more extensive evidence behind than loggerheads do. In the bottom image, a green turtle partially excavated a body pit and left. Abandoned green turtle body pits are coupled with mounds of scattered sand much wider than the turtle's track, and tend to be either circular, or with less length than width. Length of the mound would come from the turtle advancing forward as she throws sand with all four flippers. But green turtles don't do this much while body pitting. The circular mound next to an abandoned body pit differs from the larger and more elongate mound at a nest site, which comprises two overlapping mounds—from both body pitting and camouflaging.

Abandoned body pit from a loggerhead with a missing flipper

A loggerhead started a body pit but left without nesting

An abandoned body pit from a green turtle

Sign from a loggerhead that made two body pits before leaving

A loggerhead body pit and abandoned egg chamber

Abandoned egg chamber within a green turtle body pit

Sea turtles often complete a **body pit,** abandon it, and crawl to another site where they make another attempt. In the top image, the signs reveal that a loggerhead completed two body pits before crawling forward, turning, and leaving the scene (red arrow shows crawling direction). In each body pit, there is a track-width mound that was pushed over the track, and two ridges aside the pit.

Occasionally, a loggerhead will creep forward as she moves sand during body pitting. In the middle image, a loggerhead left an elongate trench of disturbed sand. Because the mound is no wider than the turtle's track, the evidence is still convincing as a body pit, even though the mound and side ridges are extensively long. But there is additional evidence showing that the turtle continued on to the next step in nesting—digging an **egg chamber.** At the deepest point in the body pit, the loggerhead began digging an egg chamber that was abandoned before completion. In the bottom image, evidence left by a green turtle shows that she completed a body pit and began digging an egg chamber before abandoning her attempt.

An abandoned egg chamber can convince some that a human dug into a nest. Sea turtles occasionally crawl away from the hole they've dug leaving it completely intact. Because the architecture of an egg chamber is unexpectedly elegant, it's hard to imagine a turtle digging it with its feet. But they do. A completed egg chamber is about a third wider at the bottom than it is at the neck and has walls smoothed by fine contouring strokes from the turtle's rear flippers. Don't assume such a neatly constructed hole was dug by a human who stole the eggs, unless there is additional evidence showing that the turtle actually nested.

Loggerheads and green turtles are just as skittish during body pitting and digging their egg chamber as they are during their emergence from the surf. Many abandoned body pits and egg chambers may be from turtles that were frightened away by people. But these trials could also be tests of beach conditions. False crawls tend to increase if the beach is extraordinarily wet, dry, compact, or wide.

Nests

Biologists count the number of sea turtle nests left on beaches to represent numbers of egg clutches produced by the population. Each nest equals one clutch. A count of nests (clutches) measures the relative abundance of the females that laid the eggs. Seasonal nest counts give us only relative abundance because their number reflects both the number of females and the number of nests per female per season (called clutch frequency). Nest counts contribute to an indirect census of the population and represent the population's reproductive output. Biologists emphasize nest counts as a way to understand how our sea turtles are faring.

A sea turtle nest is a buried clutch of eggs covered with a mound of scattered sand. This mound contains sand excavated from a secondary body pit (in addition to the first body pit) during the nesting turtle's camouflaging behavior. Unless extraordinary circumstances arise, all sea turtles that put a clutch of eggs in the beach will camouflage it by throwing sand. This sand-throwing leaves both a conspicuous sign that eggs are there, and a set of characteristics revealing which species laid the eggs. However, two turtles of the same species behaving in the same way can leave different looking nests. A turtle camouflaging her nest in dune vegetation may have difficulty gathering sand to throw behind her, and may end up producing a mound partly composed of uprooted plants. Turtles nesting in sand soaked by rain may only pile the sand up in abbreviated mounds, rather than spraying sand far behind them. Sand that is dry often makes for nests with flat mounds and no sharply defined pit edges. Like vegetation, a wide variety of obstacles can impede a nesting turtle and prevent her from fully expressing her art. Although each sea turtle species keeps to a common theme, no two nests are exactly alike, just like snowflakes.

The characteristically elongated mound and deep pit of a green turtle nest

A green turtle nest in coarse wet sand on Florida's Atlantic coast

A loggerhead nest on a South Carolina beach

A loggerhead nest where the turtle crawled over her nest mound

Green Turtle

Green turtles are vigorous in their nesting style and leave dramatic evidence behind when they lay a clutch of eggs. The female's excavation and mound-building during nest camouflaging is similar to the turtle's preceding body-pitting behavior. As a result, the nest a green turtle leaves behind is composed of two overlapping mounds (body-pit and camouflage mounds) and a single pit. The two mounds typically blend in what appears to be a single elongate mound with considerable sand spray outside the mound area. The height of the mound averages roughly the depth of the secondary body pit—about 12 in (30 cm). All of these characters are less pronounced if the turtle was amidst obstacles during her bout of camouflaging.

Loggerhead

Loggerhead nests are far less extensive than green turtle nests. The original mound from body pitting is often apparent, in that the nest mound from camouflaging does not cover it completely. Although the body-pit mound is only the width of the turtle's track, the nest mound is twice the track width or wider. This mound from nest camouflaging tends to be flat in dry sand. In wet sand, or where an obstacle has kept the turtle from creeping forward, the nest mound is short (but still wide) and crested. Especially in flat mounds, there is a gull-wing pattern to the layers of sand spread over the nest by the females flippers. Many of these subtleties can be obscured if the nesting loggerhead turns 180 degrees to depart, and crawls directly over her nest mound. Still, some signs of nesting will remain, such as the scrape marks from front-flipper strokes, and the spray of sand outside the mound, both evidence that nest camouflaging took place. If a turtle's camouflaging strokes were impeded by plants in the dune, then the subtle signs of sand spray may be the principal evidence indicating that the loggerhead female camouflaged a nest, and did not simply bulldoze her way through a body pit and leave. Often, this sand spray will stick to dewy vegetation, which provides the telltale sign that the turtle left eggs behind.

Leatherback

A leatherback's great size helps distinguish its nest from that of any other sea turtle. The breadth of **disturbed sand** left by a leatherback can be 35 ft (10.7 m) or more. This extent comes from the turtle's great flipper span, in addition to the leatherback's habit of making multiple "false nests." The female scatters sand over the general location of her eggs, but she is also likely to cease her sand throwing, move a few paces, and resume her behavior. The turtle may end up camouflaging several locations, throwing sand over much of the track and body-pit evidence a researcher would use to locate the clutch. As a result, leatherback eggs are especially difficult to find. But by leaving a conspicuously broad area of tilled beach, a nesting leatherback makes it easy to determine that there are eggs in there somewhere.

Nesting leatherbacks leave a broad area of disturbed sand

Kemp's Ridley

Because Kemp's ridleys are small sea turtles and spend little time camouflaging their nest site, their nests are easy to miss. The site is a smaller version of a loggerhead or hawksbill nest, but any similarity may become obscured by wind-blown sand. Ridley nests fade quickly because the turtle lays and covers her eggs when blustery conditions prevail and during the day when the sand is dry and easily blown. This flattens an already low mound and fills the shallow secondary body pit.

A recent Kemp's ridley nest that has not yet faded away

Hawksbill

Because hawksbill nests look so much like loggerhead nests, the track may be the best way to tell which of these two species nested (see page 156). This distinction is not important on most beaches, because the two species seldom share nesting sands in our region (one exception may be on Mexico's Caribbean beaches). The one trait that commonly separates hawksbills from the other species is the hawksbill's penchant for nesting underneath the bushes. This makes the detective work challenging. Often, a hawksbill nest is little more than a track disappearing under foliage, with some scattered sand over the leaf litter.

A hawksbill nest on an open beach. Many nest in dense vegetation

Not Every Egg Hatches

Sea turtles lay a lot of eggs, and there is a reason for that. Few of those eggs will result in a turtle that matures and makes more eggs. That's just the way it is. These are simply the given odds on a sea turtle's strategy for maximizing its genetic contribution to the next generation. Slim survival chances, times many eggs, equals reasonable prospects that some will make it.

The slim survival odds of an egg leading to an adult turtle are influenced by rates of hatching success. This rate is the percentage of eggs from which a hatchling escapes. Because some hatchlings may escape their eggshell but not emerge from the nest, an additional rate, emergence success, describes the percentage of eggs that result in a hatchling able to scamper down the beach. Given widely varying factors, hatching success on most nesting beaches averages a little over 50%, and emergence success is just a little less (most hatchlings out of the eggshell also escape the nest).

Eggs that don't hatch may be infertile, suffer embryonic death due to congenital difficulties or pathogens, fall prey to egg predators, suffocate under the sand, or be washed away by the sea. Some of these mortality factors are conspicuous. When a large predator digs into a nest to eat the eggs, it typically leaves messy evidence of its guilt. The sea also leaves clear traces. If one knows where on the beach eggs are incubating, then overwash and erosion can be linked to nest fates. But many nests that appear on the outside to be completely undisturbed have less than complete hatching success rates.

Loggerhead eggs tumble out of a nest following erosion from a tropical storm. Eggs like these seldom survive

Washed Out Nests

On most nesting beaches, the sea takes more eggs than any other egg-mortality factor. When the sand surrounding an incubating clutch **erodes away**, the eggs seldom survive. Passing storms can temporarily remove surface beach sand, leaving a conspicuous escarpment in or near the dune, which indicates how much sand was lost. This scarp height can show whether any nests (formerly about knee deep) survived. On beaches with frequent nesting, other signs of erosion-related mortality include eggs tumbling in the swash. Almost none of the eggs discovered this way are viable, having succumbed to movement-induced mortality (see page 112) and drowning (suffocation).

Loggerhead eggs in the swash zone after a storm erosion event

Overwashed Nests

The sea commonly rises up to send waves washing over the beach. These **overwash** events can occur during times of large surf, and when moderate surf coincides with high tides near the full- and new-moon periods. Some eroded beaches are susceptible to overwash even under moderate tidal and surf conditions. In most cases, seawater washing over a sea turtle nest has little negative effect, and may even be beneficial. Seawater probably reduces the number of pathogenic fungi and bacteria that can kill eggs. Overwash causes the most problems when water lingers in ponds over nests, especially when this ponding coincides with the time that hatchlings are escaping from eggshells (pipping). At this time of high oxygen demand, an overwash event can cause an entire nest of hatchlings to drown.

Wave-washed algae shows that this marked nest was overwashed

Nests Buried by Accretion

In addition to rapidly removing sand from the beach, wind and waves can add sand to the beach almost as quickly. This sand **accretion** can cover incubating sea turtle nests with significant amounts of additional sand. A little additional sand depth has little consequence, but doubling sand depth can reduce gas exchange within the nest and suffocate eggs and hatchlings.

A sign of accretion

A typical sign of raccoon predation with eggshells scattered 360°

Raccoon prints around a depredated nest

Most canine predators dig into nests from one side

Signs of Predation

Just as beach sand can faithfully record a nesting turtle's tracks, it can also record evidence of nest predators. Mammalian predators leave a pretty big mess, but footprints and styles of digging can typically separate which animal did the deed. Crows and ghost crabs also leave unique tracks, but leave less extensive traces from digging. Anytime a scatter of eggshells is seen at the surface, it's a predator that has dug them up. Hatchlings that escape from their eggs leave the eggshells under the sand. One important thing to understand about sea turtle nest predators is that most are scavengers as well. This means that a nest opened by one animal may receive visits from other species.

Raccoons

For most of our region's nesting beaches, the most destructive sea turtle nest predator is the northern raccoon *(Procyon lotor)*, a nocturnal mammal. Although some beaches have little or no raccoon predation, other beaches may have the majority of nests dug by raccoons. Raccoons typically excavate sand and eggs into a circular pile around a hole, which leads directly into the clutch. The egg contents are eaten, leaving the papery shells torn, but commonly in large pieces (or a single piece). Raccoons often dig up nests with pipped hatchlings that have not yet escaped from the egg and absorbed their yolk sac. Although it seems wasteful and mean to simply eat the yolks off these hatchlings leaving them to die, it's just the raccoons way of capitalizing only on the most energy-rich portion of its prey. Nests are most vulnerable to raccoons on the night eggs are laid and later when hatchlings start pipping. These are both times when smells give away the clutch's location under the sand. In some cases of raccoon predation, every egg is destroyed, but on average, about a quarter of the eggs in a depredated clutch survive.

Coyotes, Foxes, and Dogs

These are all canine predators that share similar styles of digging and have similar tracks. They are readily identified as a group but difficult to tell apart. The typical canine digging pattern is to excavate a hole angled about 45 degrees, piling the sand into a single mound. Like raccoons, these canines commonly dig into nests with hatchlings that are not yet ready to emerge. The hapless hatchlings are eaten whole or may be strewn about the site after having their yolk sacs eaten or heads bitten off. Coyotes *(Canis latrans)* are known to eat hatchlings whole, but are unlikely to consume an entire nest. In the disarray that ensues following a nest-predation event, it's a challenge to determine who crawled away and who got eaten. Domestic dogs *(Canis lupus familiaris)* are common on many beaches, and their "recreational" digging is common, even with mindful owners. It is possible that dogs expose far more eggs than they eat. Foxes (typically the red fox, *Vulpes vulpes*) and coyotes are more serious about their search for turtle eggs. A single coyote may be responsible for several depredated nests per night.

A loggerhead nest excavated by a fox

Bobcats

Although bobcats *(Lynx rufus)* may dig shallow holes into sea turtle nests and eat some emerging hatchlings, they are not believed to be a major egg predator. Their tracks distinguish them from other predators.

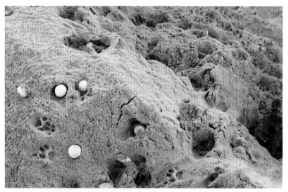

Bobcat tracks around a depredated nest

Feral Pigs

Also known as feral hogs or wild boars *(Sus scrofa),* these destructive beasts introduced from Europe can have a devastating effect on sea turtle nests. Pigs will often excavate a large pit and consume every egg in a nest. Pigs are smart, persistent, strong, and have an excellent sense of smell.

Nest destruction from a feral pig

Armadillos

Egg predation from nine-banded armadillos *(Dasypus novemcinctus)* has become common on some Florida beaches. This mammal leaves a round, inclined burrow into the nest, with prints from its clawed feet and heavy tail. This and other predators open nests to scavengers like fish crows.

Armadillo predation, with tracks from a scavenging crow

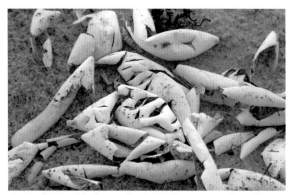

Exposed eggs with ghost crab snips and raccoon teeth marks

Egg theft at a ghost crab burrow in a loggerhead nest

Fish crows flock to nests opened by other predators

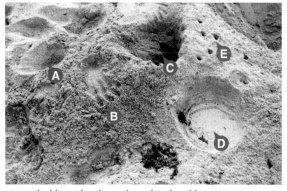

A poached loggerhead nest shows hand and knee prints

Ghost Crabs

The Atlantic ghost crab *(Ocypode quadrata)* is a common sight on our regional beaches. The adult crab excavates **burrows** roughly the diameter of a sea turtle egg. Because the crabs prefer to dig in freshly tilled sand, their burrows often begin in new sea turtle nest mounds and intersect with buried eggs. Crabs open eggs by snipping them with their claws. These **snips** may look much like the teeth marks from raccoons. Snipped eggs that were damaged underground indicate crab predation. Sometimes, ghost crabs drag eggs out of their burrow. Crabs enter many nests but on average destroy only a few eggs per nest. A small fraction of crawling hatchlings are seized by ghost crabs on the beach (see page 131) or tumble into crab-burrow pitfalls between the nest and the sea.

Birds

The most common avian predator of sea turtle eggs is the **fish crow** *(Corvus ossifragus)*. Some depredated sea turtle nests have a wide scatter of crow footprints showing graphic evidence of a murder (a group of crows is called a murder). But crows can't dig deeply, and in these cases they have probably followed an excavation from some other guilty party, such as a raccoon. At dawn, fish crows and yellow-crowned night-herons *(Nyctanassa violacea)* may eat turtles torn from their shells by a nocturnal predator, and during the day, scavengers like gulls may finish the clean-up.

Poaching

Throughout our region, a few humans still illegally take eggs from some nests. Poaching nests is rarer than it used to be, but southern Florida seems to have a regular occurrence. Some signs of poaching, or attempted poaching, include evidence of human digging: prints from knees (left image, **A**) and hands (**B**), and excavated sand (**C**). There may also be impressions from the bucket or bag the poacher used to carry the eggs (**D**). Poke marks in a fresh nest (**E**) may be from the rod (sometimes a fishing pole or car antenna) that poachers use to probe the sand in search of eggs.

Predator Tracks

The evidence of predation at a sea turtle nest is often a big mess. Many players may have taken part in a frenzy of gluttony that widely scattered sand and eggshells. The instigators are often difficult to identify, but every visitor to the feast is likely to leave their own characteristic set of prints.

Raccoons have handlike prints with distinct claw marks. The front paw length is about 2.2 in (5.6 cm) and the elongated hind paw is about 3.1 in (7.9 cm) long. On some beaches, many of these tracks may be superimposed along a raccoon highway at the base of the dune.

Bobcats leave rounded prints with no claw marks. The rear pad mark has two lobes in front and three in back (seen only in excellent prints). Both front and hind paws are about 1.9 in (4.8 cm) in length. A domestic cat has prints only 1.1 in (2.8 cm) long.

Canines of various species are difficult to tell apart. They all have four distinct claw marks and a rear pad mark with one lobe in front and two in back. A coyote leaves paw prints about 2.4 in (6.1 cm) long, in comparison to fox tracks, which are smaller at about 2.2 in (5.6 cm) long. Domestic dog tracks vary widely in size. One of the best ways to identify dog tracks is to follow them and look for signs of play. Coyote and fox tracks travel along direct routes in a more businesslike fashion.

Feral pigs leave tracks from rounded hooves. Their prints differ from deer tracks in that deer leave more pointed hoof marks. In beach sand, pig toes tend to spread apart and sink deeply so that the animal's two dewclaws leave distinct impressions behind the hoof. These dewclaw prints are spread wider than the hoof. Prints are 2–3 in (5.1–7.6 cm) long.

Armadillos leave deep, widely spread claw marks from four toes on each front foot (length 1.5 in, 3.8 cm) and five on each hind foot (length 2 in, 5.1 cm). Their thick tail typically leaves a drag mark in the sand.

Rear (upper left) and front paw prints from a raccoon

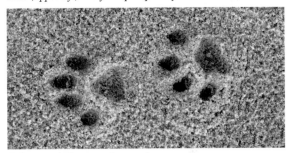

Bobcat tracks have no claw marks

Canine paw prints

Hoof prints from a feral pig showing a wide dewclaw (arrow) mark

Armadillo tracks on the upper beach. Note the tail-drag mark

173

Hatchling Emergence

The emergence of hatchling sea turtles from their nest is an exciting event. This is the distinct milestone that marks a turtle's entry into the world. A hatchling's breakout night occurs several evenings after it hatched from the egg. Although hatchling emergence events are sometimes called "hatches," they're not. Days before, unseen under the sand, a great deal of important action takes place between hatching (escape from the eggshell) and emergence (see page 113). Even though the hatchling emergence is often referred to as the end of a nest's incubation period, each egg's incubation actually ended at hatching.

Experiencing a hatchling emergence is a rare and inspiring treat. Yet our role is as a fan, not as a participant. Hatchlings scrambling down the beach don't need our help. Interfering with a little turtle's initial struggle might deprive it of a critical and informative experience. It may also be viewed as harassment, which is against the law. So enjoy these events as a spectator.

How does one witness such a commencement of sea turtle life? Other than sheer luck, many factors will adjust your chances. First, pick a busy beach. The most densely nested beaches for loggerheads (see page 26), our most common species, are a good start. There, target the busiest season for loggerhead hatchlings—late July through August. Walk the tide line either just before dawn (best when there was not rain the afternoon before) or at dusk (best when there was afternoon rain that day). These conditions bring favorable temperatures (see page 175) when there is enough light to see. Alternatively, you could camp out at nests with other hatchling groupies when your local conservation organization predicts an emergence. There are a number of groups that orchestrate these events (see page 207).

Although most hatchlings emerge from their nests at night, this group of loggerhead hatchlings scrambles into the surf at sunrise

Stages of Emergence

Like any great escape, a **hatchling emergence** is the culmination of much advance activity. This activity positions the mass of hatchlings at the surface where they wait for the cue signaling the start of the event.

The Wait

Sea turtle hatchlings emerge from their nest mostly at night. The signal that nightfall has arrived seems to be lowering temperature. High daytime temperatures subdue the squirms of little turtles as they near the surface. The top hatchlings pushed upward into warm surface sand cease their movements first, which plugs the entire mass and prevents emergence. Occasionally, the activity of cooler hatchlings down below can push inactive top hatchlings into the daylight. When this happens, motion-less heads and flippers poking through the surface sand at the bottom of a bowl-shaped depression (from the sand-ceiling collapse) reveal sure signs of an impending emergence.

The Boil

After sundown, or occasionally after a hard rain, surface sands cool. These conditions are felt first by the uppermost hatchlings in the nest, which begin to get antsy. These active hatchlings can't help but poke at their siblings. As the upper turtles step on the heads of their brothers and sisters below, a fidgeting-sibling chain-reaction begins. In short order, restless-ness in a few surface hatchlings initiates flip-pers flailing in the entire mass of squirming lit-tle turtles. This **"boil"** soon rises up (surface sand sinks through it) and begins to spill out of the emergence depression. The first hatchlings out don't wait for the others. Once they lift their heads to get a visual bearing on the sea (see page 177), they are off and running. An average mass of emerging loggerhead hatch-lings will involve about 70 turtles. Somebody has to be the last one, and this last turtle (or several last turtles) may get left behind. These stragglers may emerge later that night or the following evening.

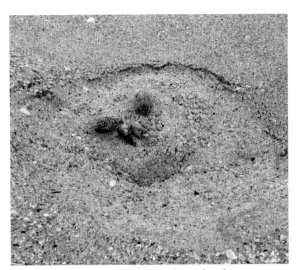

Little loggerheads begin thrashing at the sand surface

The first few hatchlings leave the nest

A boil of little loggerheads

Green turtle hatchlings spill out of their nest

Leatherback hatchlings begin their race

The Run to the Sea

The race from nest to sea is not just a test of athletics, it is an exercise in wayfinding. An energetic hatchling cannot win the race if it crawls in the wrong direction. For this reason, a hatchling punctuates its bursts of rapid crawling with brief stops during which it carefully assesses its next move. In fits and starts, an individual loggerhead hatchling can cover 100 ft (30 m) in about ten minutes. But a green turtle hatchling can sprint this distance in less than half this time. Along this run, there are many obstacles. Driftwood, seaweed wrack, nest pits, crab burrows, and man-made impediments like beach furniture and tire ruts can cause delays in a turtle's seaward trek.

From what we can tell, **seafinding** is an individual rather than a team sport. Although hatchlings may bump into one another on their way down the beach, individual paths soon fan out. The duration of a hatchling emergence event varies with the width of beach the hatchlings must cover. Most hatchlings will have left the nest in a span of a few minutes, but their crawl down the beach could take another ten minutes or so. Hatchlings that are disoriented by lights seen from the beach either crawl in circles or in the wrong direction, which adds great distances to their initial journey. This disoriented crawling may persist for hours until the turtles exhaust themselves, unable to continue.

A Kemp's ridley hatchling gets its bearings in wet sand

Active hatchlings that have had direct paths reach the hard wet sand of the swash zone with plenty of energy. This wet, firm ground with its downward slope contributes to a final burst of speed during this last leg of the terrestrial phase of a hatchling's race for survival.

Hatchling Behavior

Hatchlings show behaviors during their seaward crawl that are important for meeting the challenges of this event. During their crawl, each hatchling will make many crucial decisions about which way to go.

The narrow fan of hatchling tracks from a loggerhead nest

Proper orientation is critical to these loggerhead hatchlings

Even if you miss the event, you can still experience evidence from an emergence the next morning. The pitter-patter of little flippers will have left a distinct **fan of tracks** originating from a bowl-shaped depression. A narrow fan indicates natural lighting conditions that did not interfere with hatchling orientation. This orientation is crucial, which is why each hatchling pauses repeatedly during its crawl to reassess its route. During a pause, a hatchling raises its head in an **inspection stance**. The stance often involves a push-up that momentarily elevates the turtle's head even further. This may give a little turtle a better view amidst the lumpy landscape it must navigate. After each pause and course adjustment, a hatchling lowers its head and scrambles onward.

A hatchling that reaches the area of wave wash must deal with the sheets of water that rush up the beach. These can send a turtle tumbling and leave it **flipped** upside down. To turn upright, a hatchling immediately swings its head in wide circles, which flips the turtle back on its belly. A hatchling may get tumbled and have to flip upright a few times before it meets the slowing apex of a wave that grabs the turtle and sweeps it into the surf.

A loggerhead hatchling in an inspection stance

A tumbled loggerhead swings its head to flip upright

177

Green turtle hatchling tracks reveal their long stride

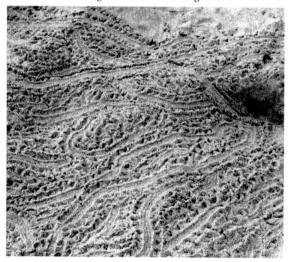

Hatchling loggerheads leave a conspicuous plastron drag

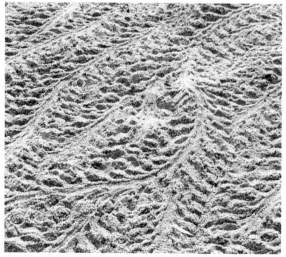

Leatherback hatchlings crawl with butterfly flipper strokes

Hatchling Tracks

Just as the tracks from nesting female green turtles and leatherbacks can identify these species on the beach, so can the tracks from their hatchlings. The hatchling tracks from loggerheads, Kemp's ridleys, and hawksbills are more difficult to separate because their pattern is so similar, but each is distinctly different from green turtles and leatherbacks. Loggerhead-looking hatchling tracks in the southeastern US are probably loggerheads, and similar tracks in Texas or northeastern Mexico are probably Kemp's ridleys. Hawksbill nests are rare in our region, so tracks from their hatchlings would be an unlikely occurrence.

Green turtle hatchlings leave tracks that reflect their bounding run down the beach. The dimples from their alternating flipper prints are separated down the length of the track almost as much as they are spread across the track's width. This long, energetic stride leaves little mark from the plastron. Green turtle hatchling tracks are typically 3.5 in (9 cm) wide.

Loggerhead hatchlings have tracks with a distinct plastron drag between alternating flipper prints. Their front flippers are shorter than those of hatchling green turtles and leatherbacks. Most of their prints are from their rear flippers, just as in their mother's track. A hatchling loggerhead's track width is about 2.9 in (7.5 cm) with a stride (distance between flipper prints) only about a third of this width.

Leatherback hatchlings are large and have long flippers. They also crawl with a different gait. Unlike the hatchlings of all the other sea turtles, leatherback hatchlings use a simultaneous push from all four flippers to move down the beach. This is evident in the tracks, which look like miniature versions of the tracks their mother left. A leatherback hatchling track is mostly front-flipper prints, which span 5.5 in (14 cm) wide and give the impression that a giant centipede crawled by.

Who Emerged?

The sea turtles in our region have hatchlings that are not just small versions of the adults. Each has a larger head and eyes in proportion to the body. Their color patterns and shells are also different, and their limbs are rounder at the ends and more paddlelike than in an adult. All hatchlings bear a conspicuous egg tooth (caruncle, not a real tooth) below their nose (see page 75).

Green turtle hatchlings have head scales outlined by gray

Green turtle hatchlings (1 oz, 25 g) are dark above contrasting with pure white below. This countershading is more pronounced in green turtle hatchlings than in the other species. Between dark scales, and on the neck and other soft upper parts, the green turtle hatchlings are blue-gray. Their carapace and flippers are rimmed with white.

Loggerhead hatchlings vary widely in body color

Loggerhead hatchlings (0.7 oz, 20 g) vary widely from pale brown or gray to dark brown or charcoal. Most are lighter below, but some are uniformly pigmented. Their carapace is lumpy with raised scutes that show no signs of overlapping.

Leatherback hatchlings (1.6 oz, 46 g) have beadlike scales covering their body, except the head, which has slightly larger and flatter scales. Their carapace has seven contrasting white lines on a black background, and their eyes are flecked with turquoise.

Leatherback hatchlings have eyes speckled with turquoise

Kemp's ridley hatchlings (0.6 oz, 17 g) vary little from a charcoal gray color pattern above and below. Like the loggerhead hatchlings, ridleys have a carapace that is lumpy with raised, non-overlapping scutes. Because there is a lot of size overlap, loggerhead and Kemp's ridley hatchlings are easy to mistake for one another. One separating trait is the ridley's cusped upper jaw.

Kemp's ridleys have a noticeable upper jaw cusp (arrow)

Hawksbill hatchlings (0.5 oz, 15 g) are a light to medium brown above and are lighter below. Like loggerhead and ridley hatchlings, hawksbill hatchlings have a lumpy carapace with raised scutes. But most hawksbills differ in having shell scutes that slightly overlap.

Hawksbill hatchlings are lighter than most loggerhead hatchlings

179

What Happened Under the Sand?

Once a nesting sea turtle buries her eggs in the sand, the contents of that nest will remain buried throughout the incubation period unless a disturbance unearths it. A successful nest will produce hatchlings that leave the sand, but the evidence of their development will stay behind. The papery shells they escape from remain as vouchers for the emergent hatchlings. Evidence of unsuccessful incubation also remains in the form of unhatched eggs—those destroyed underground, penetrated by roots, invaded by pathogens, or without a chance to develop because of infertility. Some hatchlings also get left behind. Not every turtle is fit or lucky enough to escape the nest.

About three days after the first hatchling group emerges from a nest, no additional hatchlings are likely to emerge. Such a nest can be said to have surpassed its incubation period. An unsuccessful nest (one producing no hatchlings) can be declared as such after time has passed equal to the longest incubation period of known successful nests. These determinations are important before researchers excavate a nest to conduct an inventory (see page 211). Hatchlings in a nest waiting to emerge will not be ready to scramble and swim if a researcher digs into the nest too soon. But after a nest's incubation period has passed, much can be learned from an inventory of its contents. How many eggs resulted in hatchlings? What happened to the eggs that didn't? With careful, representative choices of which nests to inventory, these questions can be answered for an entire population of sea turtles. This essential information is gathered by conservation biologists who are required to have state and federal sea turtle research permits.

This leatherback hatchling pipped its egg late and was not able to escape the nest with its siblings

The Eggs

The eggs of our five sea turtle species are similar in superficial appearance but differ in size. Leatherbacks lay the largest eggs, followed by green turtles, loggerheads, Kemp's ridleys, and hawksbills. Although their true eggs are the largest, leatherbacks also lay much smaller yolkless "eggs" (an average of 30 in a clutch of 80 yolked eggs). These spheres of albumen enclosed by shell cannot produce hatchlings and are less frequent in the other species.

A yolkless leatherback egg (aka "spacer," right) is typically much smaller than a yolked egg (left, actual size)

Although **yolkless eggs** are often termed "spacers," implying a space-filling function, no purpose for these little spheres has been clearly demonstrated. They may satiate a predator that would otherwise consume viable eggs; they may cap the clutch, preventing sand from trickling in and blocking gas exchange; they may release moisture to developing eggs; or they may simply be mistakes in egg making.

Unless an egg gets eaten or washed away by the sea, the evidence of its existence remains in the nest. Although some eggs get pretty rotten by the end of a two-month incubation period, some uncompromised but unhatched eggs appear much as they did when they were laid. Eggs that produced hatchlings typically remain as torn shells in a single piece. Even an egg that has been invaded by roots or pathogens will persist in a form that allows us to identify it at inventory time as one unhatched egg.

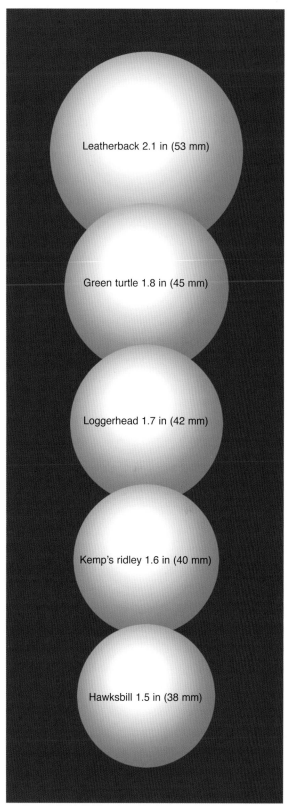

Leatherback 2.1 in (53 mm)

Green turtle 1.8 in (45 mm)

Loggerhead 1.7 in (42 mm)

Kemp's ridley 1.6 in (40 mm)

Hawksbill 1.5 in (38 mm)

Egg sizes (average diameter) of five sea turtle species

The unhatched egg on the right is misshapen

Unhatched eggs from the bottom of a loggerhead nest

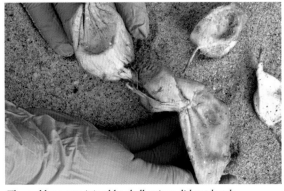

These oblong eggs joined by shell strings did not hatch

A green turtle without pigmentation and head development

Clues From Old Nests

A post-incubation inventory of nest contents is a catalog of success and failure. The unsuccessful part of incubation is often the most obvious.

Unhatched Eggs

Some unhatched eggs look like they should have hatched. Their shells are relatively white and seem not to have suffered any penetrating insult. Inside, their yolk is intact with no sign of an embryo. Although it's tempting to call these eggs infertile, they may in fact have had a developing turtle that died before it could grow beyond the microscopic stage of just a few cells. Other unhatched eggs may show clear signs that something went wrong in their production. Eggs with oblong or dumbbell shapes, and those joined by **strings of shell material,** indicate trouble in quality control. But most whole, unhatched eggs appear to have suffered their fate after the female turtle left them in the nest. For these eggs, something got to them, such as a fungal or bacterial pathogen. These unhatched eggs are typically deflated by dessication or swollen with bacterial gasses. In either case, they are just as stinky as any other rotten egg.

Embryonic Deformities

Sea turtle embryos commonly develop to the point where the hatchling would pip the egg (break out of the eggshell), but they don't. These turtles often have obvious deformities. Some hatchlings with deformities do escape from the nest, but turtles with the most serious troubles don't get out. Many, especially those with **head defects,** never hatch. Head irregularities generally stop a turtle from getting out of the egg, perhaps because proper head movement and a good egg tooth are critical for slicing open the shell. The number of abnormalities seen in the contents of inventoried sea turtle nests may be helpful for understanding elements of the environment that adversely affect animal development. Because sea turtles lay so many eggs, the rates of deformity are more evident than they would be in animals that have fewer offspring.

Pipped But Unhatched

Before pipping, an egg is turgid with fluid. This slight pressure may help rupture the shell when a little turtle pops it with its egg tooth. Pipping continues with additional slicing of the eggshell and the draining of fluids out of the egg. At this point, hatchlings must breathe air. Because the demand for oxygen becomes high during this time, some turtles can suffocate. Technically, a turtle is not hatched until it escapes from the egg. Sea turtles remain unhatched for a day or so until they internalize their yolk sac. This leaves them a distinct bellybutton (**umbilicus**). In addition to possible suffocation, the time after pipping is also dangerous because of predation. Fluids that drain from the opened eggs release odors that can lead predators to the nest. It is common for raccoons to dig into nests during this period, often scattering the bodies of pipped turtles after eating their attached yolk sacs.

Straightening Up

After a pipped turtle internalizes its yolk sac, it wriggles free of the eggshell to graduate as a hatchling. But a hatchling at this point is by no means ready to emerge. For about a day, the hatchling will remain hunched over in the fetal shape it occupied while in the egg. Until a hatchling's plastron flattens, it is not able to crawl or swim with the speed and efficiency it will need to win the survival biathlon.

Late Starters

Conservation biologists wrestle with how to treat live hatchlings they find in an inventoried nest. These are mostly turtles that would never have gotten out on their own. Some are clearly disadvantaged. Others may have simply had the misfortune of late development. Without help from its siblings, a left-behind hatchling cannot dig its way to the surface. These live hatchlings discovered during a nest inventory (see page 211) may either be released immediately or held until nightfall. Inactive hatchlings may be observed until they regain activity, but they are rarely taken into rehabilitation; there just is not enough room for little turtles with such dim prospects.

Two are not better than one. This green turtle did not survive

A late-hatching loggerhead at the bottom of a nest

This leatherback will lose its plastron crease as it straightens

A loggerhead's umbilicus (arrow) remains for weeks

Tightly curled, perforated eggshells indicate predator bites

Shells with slight or no curling suggest that the hatchling escaped

Inventoried nest contents, both unhatched (left) and hatched (right)

Old, yellowed loggerhead eggshells from a previous season

Eaten or Hatched?

Predators often leave behind the shells of eggs they eat, which are typically curled from dried residual contents and may bear bite or claw marks. Marks on buried shells are likely from ghost crabs. A sea turtle egg's papery shell often stays in a single torn piece after the hatchling leaves it. Each grayish white hatched egg indicates that its hatchling has left.

Causes of Egg Mortality

Some unhatched eggs reveal evidence of why they failed. **Roots** of dune plants occasionally penetrate eggs and leave a fibrous ball where the egg contents were. Other failed eggs bear signs of **bacterial pathogens**, which produce

Plant roots can penetrate eggs and destroy them

Eggshells with purple staining from bacteria

pink, purple, green, or yellow pigments staining the eggshells and yolks. Charcoal-like smudges that discolor eggs are often from the pathogenic fungus *Fusarium*. These pathogens may be secondary invaders following egg damage but can also kill eggs in an undamaged clutch.

Turtles in Trouble

Although some of the sea turtles we might experience on land have emerged into our world to reproduce, many that reach land are in trouble. When a sea turtle is too weak to swim, it often floats on tidal currents until onshore waves and wind drive it onto a beach or other coastline. A weakened, injured, or dead sea turtle reaching land is said to strand. It is called a stranded turtle, or a stranding. The youngest sea turtles that strand back onto the beach where they emerged from nests are referred to as wash-backs.

Sea turtles strand and wash back for many reasons. Some of these reflect natural hazards out at sea, such as shark bites, parasite infestations, and various pathogens. But most sea turtle strandings are due to threats originating from humans, including boat strikes, encounters with fishing gear, and entanglement in discarded line. Even some strandings that seem to have natural causes have us to blame. Nearly all of the young sea turtles that wash back onto the beach following storms have been weakened from ingesting plastic debris.

Only a tiny fraction of compromised sea turtles reach land where someone can record them. Dead turtles sink, and do not float as they decompose unless they are in shallow water. Floating turtles do not reach land unless they survive scavengers and are carried by landward currents.

A post-hatchling loggerhead "wash-back" that stranded on the beach following a tropical storm. This little guy survived

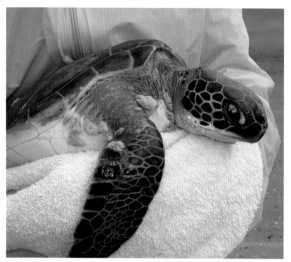

This thin, weakened green turtle has skin and eye tumors

Strandings

Both live and dead sea turtle strandings are of great interest to biologists and conservationists. Live turtles can be saved, and dead turtles tell an important story. The rescue, rehabilitation, and release of live stranded sea turtles is covered in the section on *Our Sea Turtles in Captivity* (see page 244). Although dead stranded turtles are lost to the population, the information they carry is valuable. Fresh-dead sea turtles reported to authorities can be necropsied, an inside and outside examination of the animal's body. These examinations allow samples to be taken for genetic and chemical analyses, diet analysis, sex (not externally apparent in juveniles), and disease. A necropsy can often point toward the cause of the turtle's death, but not always.

After a week on the beach, this loggerhead is just skin and bones

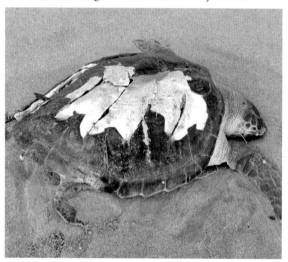

Propeller slashes mark this loggerhead's boat encounter

Even turtles that are mostly decomposed can provide critical evidence of threats where sea turtles live. A dead turtle shows that an individual of its species and life stage (e.g., juvenile or adult) recently died nearby. From this, patterns of mortality can be traced back to local activities, such as fishing, dredging, or harmful algal blooms like red tide. Managers can't always immediately stop these threats, but long-term mortality data have been instrumental in shaping policies on many of the things we do that threaten sea turtles. For example, mass sea turtle strandings following the opening of shrimp trawling season were the principal impetus behind requirements for fishers to use devices that allow turtles to escape trawl nets without drowning.

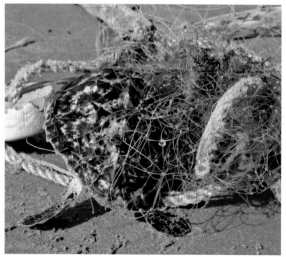

A juvenile hawksbill entangled in abandoned fishing net

Why Do Sea Turtles Strand?

Except for nesting females, a sea turtle on land is almost always in trouble. Sea turtles strand because they are unable to swim. Generally, stranded turtles are weakened from sickness, severely injured, or dead.

The fates that have befallen stranded sea turtles tell us a lot about the risks turtles face in the water. Most stranded sea turtles are young. Adults also strand, but few give any indication that they have succumbed to old age. Most often, the cause of a stranded turtle's debilitation is connected to things that humans have done, albeit accidentally.

Some hazards encountered by turtles leave conspicuous evidence. **Boat strike injuries** include parallel slashes from the boat's spinning propeller. Wounds from outboard motors may also involve an additional skeg slash cut at right angles to the prop marks. Turtles suffer even more destructive injuries from suction dredges, which can break turtles into pieces. **Entangled sea turtles** typically strand with the materials that have tangled them up. These include fishing nets, fishing line, trap rope, and a wide variety of plastics such as the infamous single-use shopping bag and six-pack rings. Many stranded turtles have suffered unlikely fates, such as underwater **entrapment** within discarded lawn furniture. Other evidence on stranded turtles includes coatings of tar, fish hooks, and wounds from bullets and spear guns. Much of the causal evidence for a turtle's troubles is only revealed from an internal examination. Many stranded sea turtles show high loads of ingested plastics (see page 233). Others may have internal fish hooks, line, or intestinal impaction from other materials. Emaciated turtles generally show evidence of disease such as tumors, parasites, and pathogens. Dead turtles that seem to be in fine physical shape may have been affected by acute effects from algal bloom toxins or from cold water. But the most common cause of acute death is drowning after being caught in trawls and other fishing nets. Most often, this cause of death leaves no evidence on a stranded turtle.

A Kemp's ridley drowned after being trapped in a lawn chair

After storms, weakened little turtles wash back onto the beach

This post-hatchling loggerhead was weakened from eating plastics

187

Dead Sea Turtles Teach Us About Their Lives

Should you encounter a stranded sea turtle, even one that has been long dead, please report it. Throughout our region, various agencies interested in the information from dead sea turtles can be found by an Internet search for: "sea turtle stranding NOAA." Most of these agencies have telephone hotlines where one could record a message. Critical elements of the message are exactly where the turtle was seen, whether it was alive or dead, and a return call number.

Dead sea turtles provide information that could help keep living turtles alive. They teach us about their genetic origins, growth, sex ratios, and diet. Dead turtles also tell us about ongoing hazards that we might be able to manage. Fresh dead turtles that get retrieved quickly by biologists provide the most information, but even a decomposed turtle can reveal important patterns of mortality. What condition is a turtle in? Live turtles may breathe infrequently, with movement detectable as a blink response to a lightly touched eye. These turtles need immediate attention (see page 247). Fresh dead turtles are generally stiff from rigor mortis, but with no bad smell or bloating. Through the **stages of decomposition**, a stranded sea turtle bloats, loses its scales and internal organs, dries in the sun, and is eventually reduced to scattered scutes and bones.

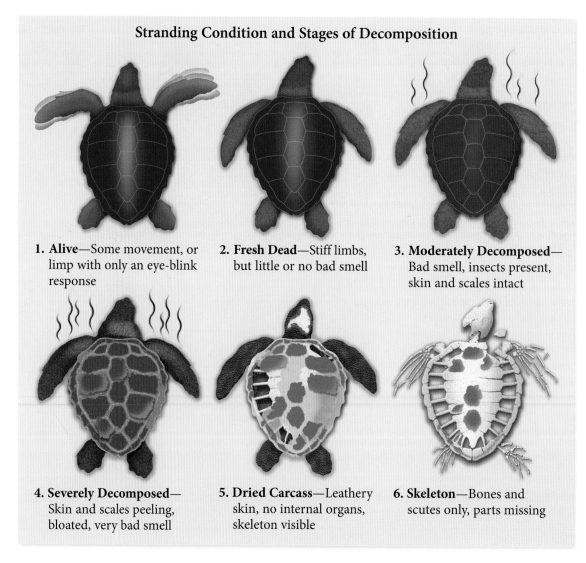

Stranding Condition and Stages of Decomposition

1. **Alive**—Some movement, or limp with only an eye-blink response

2. **Fresh Dead**—Stiff limbs, but little or no bad smell

3. **Moderately Decomposed**—Bad smell, insects present, skin and scales intact

4. **Severely Decomposed**—Skin and scales peeling, bloated, very bad smell

5. **Dried Carcass**—Leathery skin, no internal organs, skeleton visible

6. **Skeleton**—Bones and scutes only, parts missing

Sea Turtle Pieces and Parts

Even after the parts of a dead sea turtle have been scattered by scavengers, waves, and currents, they still tell a story of the turtle that owned them. Sea turtles have a similar set of bones and shell scutes, but differences between species and life stages can reveal this identity to a careful observer. For example, a long rib extending out from the pleural bone it is fused to indicates that the turtle was a juvenile. Please keep in mind that all of these sea turtle parts are illegal to keep without a permit.

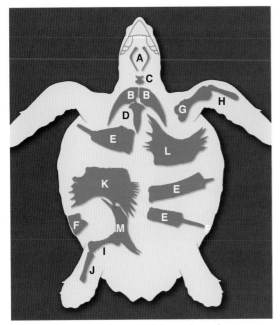

Letters indicate where bones (right) were located

A. Ceratobranchial bones (of hyoid process)

B. Epiplastron (part of the plastron)

C. Cervical vertebra

D. Entoplastron (part of the plastron)

E. Fused pleural and rib bones

F. Peripheral (marginal) bone

G. Humerus

H. Radius

I. Femur

J. Tibia

K. Hypoplastron (part of the plastron)

L. Hyoplastron (part of the plastron)

M. Xiphiplastron (part of the plastron)

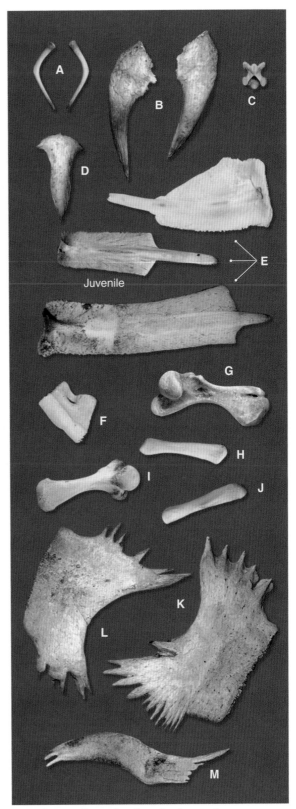

Ventral views of bones from loggerhead sea turtles

189

The jaw sheaths (rhamphothecae) of an adult loggerhead

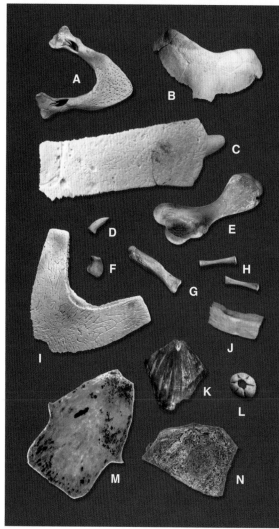

Dorsal views of sea turtle bones, scutes, and other "parts"

More Pieces and Parts

The persistent parts of a sea turtle include many things other than heavy bone. These include smaller flipper bones, the thick **jaw sheath** of a loggerhead, shell scutes, claws, and even barnacles, which could be considered to be "part" of a sea turtle.

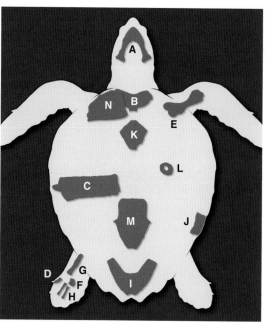

Letters indicate where bones (left) were located. Parts are from a loggerhead, unless otherwise noted below

A. **Lower jaw** (composite of six fused bones)
B. **Nuchal bone** (part of carapace)
C. **Fused pleural and rib bone** (of carapace)
D. **Claw digit**
E. **Humerus**
F. **Astragalus** (an ankle bone)
G. **Tibia**
H. **Phalanges** (part of flipper)
I. **Suprapygal** (of carapace)
J. **Peripheral (marginal) bone** (of carapace)
K. **Juvenile green turtle vertebral scute**
L. **Turtle barnacle** (see page 128)
M. **Adult green turtle vertebral scute**
N. **Subadult loggerhead lateral (costal) scute**

Threats to Nesting Beaches

Sea turtles *need* nesting beaches to accomplish their reproduction during a brief visit within their nesting season. We *want* beaches because we find them pleasant. We visit beaches, but we also stake our claim to them by building "permanent" homes and businesses at the water's edge. These superimposed wants and needs of humans and sea turtles do not make a fair competition—there is nothing a sea turtle could really do to directly affect our use of the coastline. On the other hand, we have profound effects on the use of beaches by sea turtles. Most of these effects come from coastal development that is close to the beach, often dangerously so.

Our presence near the beach used to be cautious and informal. Before the middle twentieth century, a typical beach cottage was a temporary wooden structure with a sand path through the dunes. But our modern presence has become bolder. High beachfront property values dictate development of multistory concrete buildings with elaborate boardwalks and extensive outdoor lighting. These features add luxury to beachfront living, but they can threaten nesting sea turtles and their hatchlings. As these expensive structures are inevitably threatened by erosion, they are defended with rocks, walls, and sandbags, all of which can eliminate the sandy beach required by nesting turtles. Threatened coastal properties also prompt the pumping and trucking of sand to artificially build back naturally moving beaches. These berms often function better as protective engineering structures than as functioning dunes and nesting beaches. But despite our obtrusive nature, it remains entirely possible to effectively share beaches with sea turtles. Many of the challenges we pose to nesting sea turtles have some relatively straightforward solutions.

Artificial lighting visible from nesting beaches deters nesting and leads hatchlings away from the sea

Lights from beachfront buildings deter sea turtles from nesting

Roadway lighting can lure hatchlings from the beach into traffic

On some beaches, one bright light can kill thousands of hatchlings

An exhausted loggerhead hatchling in dune vegetation

Artificial Lighting

One of the most conspicuous ways we alter the natural world is to light it up at night. This has consequences for sea turtles because their activity on beaches occurs mostly at night. Natural light at night provides critical information to nesting turtles and their hatchlings, including the cues that direct turtles to the sea.

Where lights are visible from the beach, sea turtle nesting is reduced, and the nests that are made have hatchlings that are unable to find the sea. When they emerge from their nest at night, hatchlings use the natural brightness of the open sky above the water as a signal for the seaward direction. Artificial lighting outcompetes this natural light and can lead little turtles astray. Hatchlings are **disoriented** if they circle about and cannot orient in a single direction, and they are **misoriented** if they simply head off in the wrong direction.

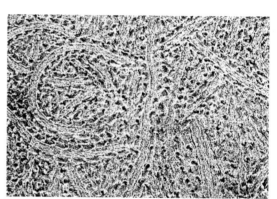

Tracks from loggerhead hatchlings disoriented by lights

Hatchlings that do not move quickly and accurately from nest to sea get in big trouble. With every misstep, the clock is ticking on their supply of available energy needed to swim offshore, and on the dehydration they incur by being out of water. Lost hatchlings also risk predation by nocturnal animals, and especially by birds once there is light in the eastern sky. Where there are **lighted roadways** near nesting beaches, hatchlings drawn away from the beach end up crushed by vehicles. Many other hazards threaten hatchlings off the beach, and once the sea is out of view, they have little chance of survival. Where there are lights near nesting beaches, hatchling sea turtles are regularly found in **dune vegetation,** storm drains, parking lots, pool filters, and the mouths of pets. Artificial lighting provides an overwhelming stimulus for hatchlings, and because of this, hatchlings will crawl great distances toward lights even when other cues would seem to indicate the hatchlings' directional choice is wrong. One extreme example of the power of light to attract sea turtle hatchlings is their tendency to crawl into the flames of **abandoned fires**.

Beach bonfires are unnatural and harmful light sources

The adult females that emerge on beaches to nest must also find their way to the sea. Although it takes more light to confuse a nesting sea turtle than it does to send a hatchling in the wrong direction, like hatchlings, adults use sky brightness to find the sea and can be led astray by lights left on during the night. Several adult female loggerheads have wandered off beaches and onto lighted roadways in Florida where they were struck and killed by cars.

Remains of green turtle hatchlings that crawled into a fire

The good news about this threat to sea turtles is that there are some relatively simple solutions. Throughout most of our region where sea turtles nest, local laws prohibit light visible from the beach during the nesting season. These laws don't keep beachfront residents from using light, they simply require that lights used on private property should not shine onto the public beach. The term for this is "light management." Managing light involves lowering light sources so they have a smaller lighted footprint, directing them downward so they shine only where needed, and shielding them so that light is hidden from the beach (see page 215). Other helpful light-management tactics include substituting red, orange, and amber (long-wavelength) light sources for whiter or bluer (broad spectrum and short-wavelength) sources. As it turns out, sea turtle hatchlings do not have their orientation disrupted as much by long-wavelength visible light, even though we can see by it at night pretty well. But reddish light is not invisible to sea turtles, so the use of this light does not alleviate the need to hide the lighting as much as possible. Although much progress has been made in the US to protect sea turtles from artificial lighting, this threat still kills tens of thousands of hatchlings each year.

A track from a loggerhead female that was confused by lights

Hidden long-wavelength light sources on a beachfront building

193

A volunteer fills a pit that could entrap nesting turtles and hatchlings

Turtles on some beaches must pass a gauntlet of furniture

Tracks from a loggerhead show her encounter with a chair

These boats prevented a green turtle from nesting

Sand fencing can block access and entangle nesting turtles

Obstructions

Nesting sea turtles face many obstacles on our beaches. On most natural beaches, females have an incline of sand providing an unfettered path to and from their nesting site. But on beaches occupied by humans, a wide variety of obstructions prevent beach access, impede a turtle's ability to scatter sand over her nest, and entrap turtles as they nest or as they attempt their return to the sea.

Holes

Many people who visit the beach like to dig holes in it. This digging provides joy to kids and therapy to adults. Most of this activity does not present extraordinary harm to sea turtles, especially if the holes are filled in when it's time to leave the beach. But some holes are large, and don't get filled in. These pits can entrap both adult females and hatchlings. Some nesting turtles that have plunged into pits have died as a result of injury or suffocation.

Beach Furniture and Beach Toys

Furniture and recreational equipment can cause problems if it remains on the beach after we are done with it. Umbrellas, chairs, picnic tables, boats, and other large items are known to present significant obstructions to nesting sea turtles. Each piece might seem to be a small barrier, but on many beaches furniture can span long stretches of shoreline, completely blocking access by turtles.

Sand Fences

Sand fences are used to keep wind-driven sand on the upper beach and to prevent human access. Nesting turtles are also blocked, although this can be reduced by placing the fencing in multiple, obliquely angled sections. Following storms, sand fencing can become tangled into masses of splintered wood and rusted wire. Dune plants gather sand without obstructing sea turtle nesting and can regenerate following modest storms.

Crossovers

Along developed stretches of beach, access by people is facilitated by (mostly) wooden boardwalks through the dunes with stairs down to the beach. These crossovers are typically supported by multiple posts and diagonal cross braces. Some crossovers end with steps directly onto the beach, but others are extensive ramps that block lengthy areas of the upper beach. The multiple posts and bracing supports are known to **entrap nesting turtles,** which cannot back up once they are wedged between posts. Monopole crossovers that would reduce sea turtle entrapment and sharing of crossovers by neighbors both remain uncommon.

A track from a loggerhead that bumped into crossover steps

Coastal Armoring

Armoring of coastlines is the practice of using physical structures (e.g., walls, rocks) to protect property landward of those structures from being eroded by the surf. Armoring takes many forms. It is a major cause of nesting beach habitat loss for sea turtles because it prevents turtles from accessing dry sand. In our most densely nested states of Florida and South Carolina, approximately 20–25% of nesting beaches are armored.

A nesting green turtle is trapped between crossover posts

Rocks and Sandbags

Throughout our region, many buildings built too close to the sea are defended by revetments of rock or sandbags. Some of these are informal piles of material, but others are extensively engineered defensive units. Sandbags are common in North Carolina, whereas harder revetment armoring is used in South Carolina through Florida and into Texas. Although sand bags may seem like a "softer" option for armoring the beach, they are no different from rocks to a nesting turtle. Some sandbag systems, called geotextile tubes, consist of long, fabric tubes packed with sand and tied together. These structures are occasionally buried within artificial dunes. Their ability to retain a covering of sand that sea turtles could nest in seems limited. Tubes that are placed at high elevations or near the water are quickly exposed by erosion from high tides.

Tracks indicate a pile of rocks prevented a loggerhead from nesting

Sandbags take up nesting beach in front of threatened homes

195

Erosion at the toe of a steel, sheet-pile seawall

A seawall with rocks effectively prevents sea turtle nesting

This loggerhead flanked a seawall and fell to her death

An inclined "waffle wall"

Seawalls

Seawalls are solid, vertical, or inclined structures on a beach or dune designed to retain sediment on the landward side. They are constructed of varied materials, including wood, concrete, aluminum, and steel. Metal walls are typically made of **sheet piles**, which are thick corrugated sheets joined together.

This type of armoring is especially controversial, not just because of its negative effects on sea turtles, but because of its adverse effects on the beach itself. Seawalls are known to exacerbate **erosion** on the beach in front of them and to have down-drift effects on adjacent beaches. The walls lock up beach sand so that waves and prevailing currents cannot bring about drift of sand to areas downstream.

Seawalls are barriers that prevent nesting sea turtles from accessing the upper dry beach. Where the walls are inclined, or are fronted by rocks, this loss of nesting habitat is even more complete. The walls are also an entrapment and fall hazard to nesting turtles. Occasionally, turtles that crawl around a wall become wedged and cannot escape. Turtles have also flanked seawalls to access the dune behind the wall, only to fall to their deaths upon returning to the sea.

Some sea turtles end up nesting in front of seawalls, which can have severe consequences for their eggs. Often, turtles stop short of the seawall and do not put their eggs into the highest and driest sand. This may be because the turtles cannot differentiate between the artificial wall and a natural dune escarpment. In comparison to nests on natural beaches, nests in front of seawalls are much more likely to wash out during high tide events.

The effects of a seawall on sea turtles and their nests seems to be a function of how close the wall is to the sea. Exposed walls are hazardous barriers, whereas walls buried in dune sands may have no effect, at least until the armoring is eventually exposed by erosion.

Groynes and Jetties

These types of coastal armoring extend out from the shore and interrupt the flow of sand within the longshore current just off the beach. Groynes (groins) extend perpendicular to a stretch of beach, and jetties extend out on either side of an inlet or pass. Both are constructed of rock, steel, wood, or sand-filled textile (geotextile) tubes. Because these structures halt longshore sand movement in the surf, they tend to build sand on their updrift side and cause erosion on their downdrift side. A groyne's dual effects of erosion and accretion can be seen in the saw-tooth pattern they leave on the shoreline. Like any pile of rocks or corroding mass of steel, groynes and jetties have the potential to entrap nesting sea turtles and their hatchlings. But the most significant effect from these structures is downdrift erosion. For many miles along the downstream flow of the longshore current, groynes and jetties contribute to net beach erosion, and an increased need for armoring and artificial placement of sediment.

Steel and concrete groynes in front of a Florida seawall

Groynes are often combinations of wood, rock, and steel

Armoring: Temporary Protection with Permanent Harm

Coastal armoring is engineered to remain solid and perform the heroic task of property protection despite repeated onslaughts from the temperamental sea. These structures all eventually fail to protect their upland property, but their solid structure ensures that they will occupy the former sand beach for decades beyond their useful lives. One example that contrasts engineering technology and environmental wisdom is the fight to save what's left of Fort Fisher in North Carolina. The fort was built of earth and sand in 1861. In the late 1800s a rock jetty built near the fort caused its shoreline to rapidly erode. To save the historic structure, a revetment was constructed in 2000. The armor was composed of granite boulders and **Sta-pods,** which look like a set of giant concrete jacks. Since then, the beach fronting the fort has disappeared, just like most of the fort, which is also underwater. Loggerheads don't nest there anymore. Sealevel models predict that the entire fort will be submerged by the end of this century.

A granite jetty engineered to block longshore sand movement

Cast concrete Sta-pods at Fort Fisher, North Carolina

Beach driving is a hazard on some sea turtle nesting beaches

A hatchling will crawl along a rut until it dies from exhaustion

Raking creates an unnaturally featureless beach

Beach raking is regulated to minimize harm to nesting sea turtles

Beach Driving

Some sea turtle nesting beaches are used as roadways and for beach-access parking. Of these, the wide, flat (dissipative, see page 143) beaches have traffic including, standard passenger vehicles, but beaches with softer sands receive use only by off-road (typically four-wheel-drive) vehicles. Nesting sea turtles and their hatchlings are occasionally run over by vehicles operating at night and can become disoriented by headlights. Restricting driving to daytime hours can reduce this threat, except in Texas, where daylight-nesting ridleys emerge to reproduce. **Shore-parallel ruts** in the sand left by driving can be an impediment to hatchlings attempting to reach the sea. The hatchlings are able to climb out of footprints equal in depth to the ruts, but once in a rut, hatchlings choose to crawl along it rather than over its edge. The reason for this reflects a hatchling's penchant for orientation toward open horizons, which in a rut are in either direction along its length.

Beach Raking

Also called beach grooming or beach cleaning, this practice mechanically flattens the beach, uproots sprouting dune plants, and removes the wrack (drift material from the sea). Beach raking on sea turtle nesting beaches is regulated by states and is most common on urban and resort beaches. In addition to diminishing the beach-building attributes supplied by the wrack, beach raking can obliterate signs of sea turtle crawls used by conservation workers to count and protect nests. Beach-cleaning regulations typically prohibit raking at night, landward of the high tide, and before nesting surveys have been conducted. Raking only the topmost layer of sand and the use of low-pressure tires can reduce some effects on nests and hatchlings.

Artificial Beaches and Dunes

Artificial beaches and dunes are the result of sediment accretion by artificial means. These means include pumping sediments from inlets or offshore shoals, trucking it from inland pits, or bulldozing sediment from any of these sources into upper beach deposits. The process is known as beach nourishment (or renourishment), beach restoration, and dredge-and-fill.

Pipes carry dredged sand and water to be spread over the beach

These projects take place on many sea turtle nesting beaches where there is an unsatisfactory sand buffer between coastal development and the sea. Artificial beaches are generally wider, flatter, and harder than beaches assembled naturally. In comparison to natural dunes, bulldozed dunes have less stratified sediments and a less diverse assemblage of dune plants. If the dune or beach sediments originate from carbonate-rich inland mines, the resulting material may form stonelike concretions.

Artificial beach filling is considered to be an environmentally acceptable alternative to armoring as a way to defend threatened beach-front properties from erosion. Beach-fill projects are often justified in part by putative benefits to sea turtles based on a notion that nesting turtles, like beach tourists, can be accommodated more by more beach. This idea has no support. As it turns out, nesting loggerheads and green turtles prefer narrow, steep beaches to the wide, flat beaches produced by artificial methods. But where artificial beach fill is the principal alternative to an upper beach completely walled off by armoring, sea turtle nesting can indeed benefit from more sand.

Artificial beaches tend to be wide and flat

Heavy equipment moves pumped sediments over the beach

Because beach-fill projects have the potential to disrupt sea turtle nesting and smother existing nests, most projects are required to take place outside the sea turtle nesting season (May–October, except March–October in southeastern Florida). Some beach-fill projects extend into the early nesting season and have intensive monitoring to discover and move nests made by turtles amidst the industrial, 24-hour, sediment-spreading operation. Because the projects place fill immediately before the height of the season, nesting must take place during the new beach's equilibrium period. Over this period,

Artificial beach-fill projects occur both day and night

199

Abandoned loggerhead egg chamber in artificial beach fill

A persistent mid-beach scarp on an equilibrating artificial beach

the beach begins to be reshaped by waves and currents. The result is a more dynamic beach than would naturally occur, with symptoms that include lower-beach erosion and mid-beach **scarp formation**. The compact sediment of an artificially filled beach can make these scarps insurmountable to nesting turtles. Compact sand also affects the ability of turtles to dig their egg chambers.

Unnaturally wide beaches seem to be one reason for high nest abandonment on new artificial beaches. Nesting turtles may assess that the beach is newly accreted, and therefore, more dynamic and susceptible to egg-threatening erosion. And they'd be right. Wide beaches also create conditions where lights behind the dune are more visible to emerging hatchlings. These conditions can increase frequency and severity of hatchling disorientation (disruption in sea-finding). Considering the many artificial attributes of fill placement, describing it as beach and dune "restoration" is as appropriate as referring to a toupee as hair restoration.

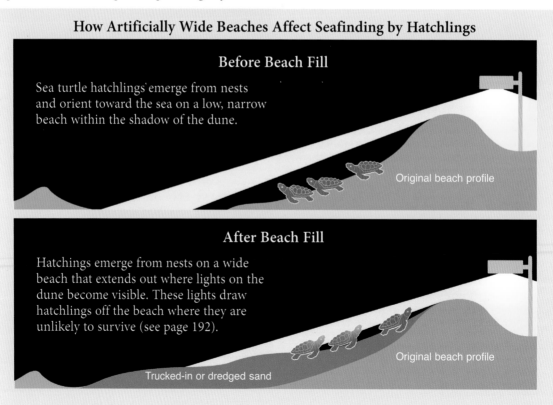

How Artificially Wide Beaches Affect Seafinding by Hatchlings

Before Beach Fill

Sea turtle hatchlings emerge from nests and orient toward the sea on a low, narrow beach within the shadow of the dune.

Original beach profile

After Beach Fill

Hatchings emerge from nests on a wide beach that extends out where lights on the dune become visible. These lights draw hatchlings off the beach where they are unlikely to survive (see page 192).

Trucked-in or dredged sand

Original beach profile

Interpretive Programs and Public Outreach

One of the best opportunities we have to experience sea turtles comes when they visit us at the beach. Because such important parts of their lives occur on beaches, these accessible sandy shores are ideal places to get to know our sea turtles.

Dozens of conservation education groups run interpretive programs featuring sea turtles on beaches. These programs include beach releases of turtles that were rescued and rehabilitated, and of hatchlings that were raised in hatcheries. Opportunities also include morning walks on the nesting beach with naturalists, who can point out the many signs that sea turtles leave behind. Some groups allow visitors to observe the marking of nests for protection and the inventory of nest contents for hatching success evaluation. And of course, the ultimate sea turtle experience on a beach is to take part in a guided turtle watch. In these programs, visitors are carefully guided at night to witness a nesting sea turtle.

No matter what kind of experience one has on a sea turtle nesting beach, a good guide can make all the difference. A skillful interpreter can convey an interesting, inspiring, evocative, yet hopeful story, which makes an ecotourism enterprise more than just entertainment. It brings about caring and becomes a driving force to save sea turtles by changing the things we do to threaten them. Some sea turtle stories told on beaches are far-reaching. They tell of extensive journeys at sea and draw in thousands of vicarious observers. These are the tales told by publicly released nesting females equipped with satellite transmitters. With the orchestrated excitement of a turtle's beach release, and with the locations of its international travel regularly updated for thousands of spectators on the Internet, this spectacle is about as public as a turtle can get. And it brings just the sort of fan base a sea turtle needs.

Johnny the loggerhead, with her newly attached tracking satellite transmitter, crawls past her fan base on her way home

A rehabilitated, Florida Keys loggerhead returns home

An early morning release of Kemp's ridley hatchlings in Texas

Public Sea Turtle Releases

Troubled sea turtles are helped by a network of caring people who rescue turtles, rehabilitate them, and release them back into the sea (see pages 247–253). The releases are often conducted on beaches. This provides a convenient access to the water and allows the public to experience a turtle's homecoming. The events have all the ingredients of a compelling conservation story. There is the tragedy of circumstances (or on occasion, villainy) that brought the turtle in, the heroism of the rescue, and an uplifting return home. With the right interpretation provided, the released turtle can become the emblem for a conservation challenge and can instill the passion needed to right wrongs. It sounds like a lot to expect from a mended turtle, but the charisma these animals have, coupled with effective storytelling, can deliver a powerful message. The best way to experience a sea turtle's return home is to contact your closest sea turtle rehabilitation facility (see page 253) and ask about upcoming releases.

Hatchling sea turtles are darn cute, and they have their own special charisma. The challenge of orchestrating public experiences with hatchlings is that the opportunity for seeing unfettered hatchlings is fleeting and occurs mostly at night. Holding back hatchlings that emerged from nests the previous night so they can be released in the morning is generally considered to be harmful to the turtles. For this reason, few groups have large-scale public hatchling release events. However, in Texas, Kemp's ridley nests are moved into hatcheries to protect the eggs from predators and beach driving. The artificial nature of the hatchery necessitates human intervention to physically transport little ridleys from their hatchery to the beach. These releases are publicly scheduled based on the due dates of hatchery nests and the public is welcome. Both the Padre Island National Seashore and Sea Turtle Inc. conduct these public releases on south Texas beaches.

Some sea turtles in rehab become famous. Their stories make compelling public interest segments in various media and the turtles grow a significant fan base. When the day comes for

Fans watch hatchlings from a nest on a North Carolina beach

the turtle to reenter the sea, an enormous crowd may show up to sneak a peek and provide a bon voyage. The same attention is generated by some turtles that offer only a brief acquaintance. Turtles in this category include subjects of scientific study that also function as ambassadors for their species. Few sea turtle studies conduct marine-life diplomacy more effectively than the Tour de Turtles.

Tour de Turtles

The Sea Turtle Conservancy, in partnership with many other conservation groups, hosts a series of annual public sea turtle releases emulating the Tour de France. Since 2008, sea turtles of five species on nesting beaches all over the wider Caribbean, including Florida, have taken part in this celebration and study of sea turtle migration. Each participating turtle is a female intercepted on her return to the sea after nesting. She is delayed just long enough to glue a path-tracking transmitter atop her shell. The device communicates the turtle's position to orbiting satellites, and subsequently, to anyone on planet Earth with an Internet connection.

At a well-advertised time in the early morning, people from all over watch the transmittered turtle reenter the sea and begin her race. The "race" is the turtle's migration back to her home foraging waters, which are often hundreds of miles away. It's not a race in the traditional sense. There is no finish line. Success is measured by the awareness and goodwill fostered by the turtles. Each competing turtle represents a cause—conservation challenges like keeping nesting beaches naturally dark at night or making ocean-friendly seafood choices.

Turtles on the tour are represented online with maps that show their travel paths (search: Tour de Turtles). The race ends after three months of travel. With only distances to compare, leatherbacks have a distinct edge on the other species. But in terms of a fan base, the loggerheads do very well. All the turtles are compelling ocean ambassadors and convey effective conservation messages. The events inspire thousands, connect nations, and allow us a unique understanding of a sea turtle's world.

A loggerhead released from the SC Aquarium, with well-wishers

Ripley the loggerhead starts her Tour de Turtles marathon

An enthusiastic crowd cheers for Elsa on her homeward trip

Night Turtle Watches

This is our best opportunity to get up close and personal with a wild sea turtle. These nighttime guided excursions onto nesting beaches are also called night walks or turtle walks. The watches typically take place on the most densely nested beaches by loggerhead sea turtles during the main part of their nesting season in June and July.

If you would like to watch a loggerhead nest (and you really should) please use a guide. Many who think they know how to approach a nesting sea turtle end up frightening the turtle away after approaching her during early nesting stages when she is sensitive to disturbance. This prevents the desired experience and is technically harassment, which is against the law. Using a guide will replace guilt with awe, and will provide interpretive narration of the event. But you will need to plan ahead by reserving a spot. These programs (see page 207) fill quickly once they are announced just before the beginning of each nesting season.

Turtle watch programs begin after sundown with an introductory presentation on sea turtles. During the show, scouts begin patrolling the beach for nesting turtles. When a loggerhead is found, scouts radio the watch leader who then guides participants onto the beach. The scouts observe the turtle from a distance until she progresses to the egg-laying stage of nesting. Then guests are brought to the turtle where they can see egg laying, egg covering, nest camouflaging, and the return to sea (see pages 149–152).

Watching a sea turtle on her nesting beach is a uniquely profound experience. Few other large wild animals would allow such an up-close appreciation of natural behavior. Nesting turtles are not only tolerant of our curiosity, they arouse it. Sitting in the dark with a big sea beast as she lays her eggs instills awe, wonder, and persistent thoughts about our relationship with the natural world.

A loggerhead sea turtle laying eggs receives respectful attention from participants on a guided turtle watch

What to Expect on a Turtle Watch

- It's at night. The experience may last until 1 A.M. Be sure you are well rested and be mindful of the endurance of little ones.

- The turtles are not paid to show up. You might not see a turtle your first night out.

- You may get wet feet. The walk to the turtle is close to the wave wash. Wear sensible shoes.

- It may be a long walk. The turtle may end up being mile or more down the beach.

- There may be **mosquitoes**. If you are sensitive to bites, bring repellent and long sleeves.

A scout's view of a body-pitting loggerhead, not ready for guests

Watch participants wait by the waterline for the scout's okay

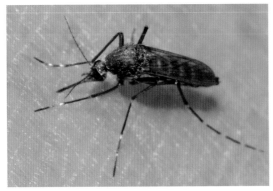

The eastern saltmarsh mosquito, Ochlerotatus sollicitans

- Keep your lights at home. Flashlights and flash photography are not allowed. Your guides will have special **red lights** or night vision goggles to help you see. But you will be surprised how well you see at night once your eyes adjust.

- Try reserving a bright night. Because there is a nice moon in the sky for the week leading up to the full moon and a couple of days after, these are the nights when everything on the beach becomes more visible.

- July is the beginning of hatching season. Reserving a watch spot in this month presents the bonus opportunity to see hatchlings emerging from other nests.

- If you are moved to do so, donate. Most groups that conduct turtle watches are not-for-profit, and they need support for their education and outreach efforts.

A red light illuminates the egg chamber of a watched turtle

Under the light of a full moon, a loggerhead returns to the sea

This loggerhead sheds tears because she's salty, not sorry

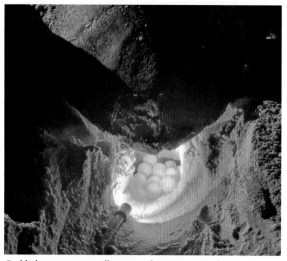

Red light we can see well appears dim to a sea turtle

Loggerhead eggs with a dimple and a glossy coating of mucus

Don't Be Afraid to Ask …

Your guide can elaborate on answers to these frequently asked questions on a turtle watch.

Does she know we are here? Yes. She continues to nest because the hormones that drive her behavior compel her. It also makes adaptive sense for her to complete the nest for her valuable eggs. However, if she is extensively harassed, she may leave early.

Why is she crying? Tears are her way to rid her body of excess salt. Sea turtles shed tears all the time, not just while nesting.

Why the red light? Because we see red light much better than the turtle can, deep red is the best color to light a nesting turtle without disturbing her.

How many eggs does she lay? An average loggerhead nest has 115 eggs. She will average five nests for about 575 eggs in a season.

What is the mucus on the eggs? It acts as a lubricant that allows the carbonate-shelled eggs to pass. It has also been shown to inhibit pathogenic fungi that could kill the eggs.

Why do the eggs have a dimple? To accommodate water they will take up within the nest. It may also allow them to bounce and not burst when they are dropped into the nest. The shells are papery rather than brittle.

Does she return to her nest? No. She will put investment into hiding her eggs within the nest, but she does not guard her eggs.

How many will survive? Roughly 52% of all eggs survive storm erosion, egg predators, and pathogens. About one in 310 hatchlings that leave the nest will make it to adulthood.

What is the glow on her shell? Bioluminescent dinoflagellates (one-celled plant-critters) that emit light when disturbed.

Do her barnacles harm her? Most don't. They are just catching a ride.

How old is she? That's a mystery. At about 30 years her growth stopped when she reached puberty. She may have aged decades beyond that. We aren't able to measure that time.

Turtle Watch and Other Public Beach Programs in Florida

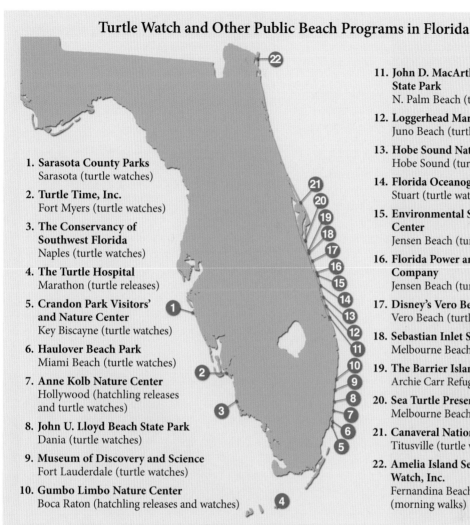

1. **Sarasota County Parks**
   Sarasota (turtle watches)

2. **Turtle Time, Inc.**
   Fort Myers (turtle watches)

3. **The Conservancy of Southwest Florida**
   Naples (turtle watches)

4. **The Turtle Hospital**
   Marathon (turtle releases)

5. **Crandon Park Visitors' and Nature Center**
   Key Biscayne (turtle watches)

6. **Haulover Beach Park**
   Miami Beach (turtle watches)

7. **Anne Kolb Nature Center**
   Hollywood (hatchling releases and turtle watches)

8. **John U. Lloyd Beach State Park**
   Dania (turtle watches)

9. **Museum of Discovery and Science**
   Fort Lauderdale (turtle watches)

10. **Gumbo Limbo Nature Center**
    Boca Raton (hatchling releases and watches)

11. **John D. MacArthur Beach State Park**
    N. Palm Beach (turtle watches)

12. **Loggerhead Marinelife Center**
    Juno Beach (turtle watches)

13. **Hobe Sound Nature Center**
    Hobe Sound (turtle watches)

14. **Florida Oceanographic Society**
    Stuart (turtle watches)

15. **Environmental Studies Center**
    Jensen Beach (turtle watches)

16. **Florida Power and Light Company**
    Jensen Beach (turtle watches)

17. **Disney's Vero Beach Resort**
    Vero Beach (turtle watches)

18. **Sebastian Inlet State Park**
    Melbourne Beach (turtle watches)

19. **The Barrier Island Center**
    Archie Carr Refuge (turtle watches)

20. **Sea Turtle Preservation Society**
    Melbourne Beach (turtle watches)

21. **Canaveral National Seashore**
    Titusville (turtle watches)

22. **Amelia Island Sea Turtle Watch, Inc.**
    Fernandina Beach (morning walks)

Other Sea Turtle Beach Programs in the US

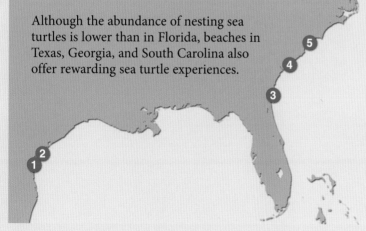

Although the abundance of nesting sea turtles is lower than in Florida, beaches in Texas, Georgia, and South Carolina also offer rewarding sea turtle experiences.

1. **Sea Turtle Inc.**
   Padre Island, TX (hatchling releases)

2. **Malaquite Beach Visitor Center**
   Padre Island, TX (hatchling releases)

3. **Georgia Sea Turtle Center**
   Jekyll Island, GA (turtle watches)

4. **South Carolina Aquarium**
   Charleston, SC (turtle releases)

5. **Sea Turtle Hospital**
   Surf City, NC (turtle releases)

Research and Conservation on the Beach

Part of our collective sea turtle experience involves studying these interesting marine creatures. Some of you reading this book have unique access to sea turtles this way. The research you do is specially permitted by federal and state agencies charged with protecting sea turtles. Measuring sea turtles, delaying them, or taking samples from them would be considered harmful if the acts were not offset by the valuable information generated by this applied science. Understanding sea turtle biology, their population changes, and threats to their survival is essential to saving these endangered animals. For the remainder of the general public who are able to look but not touch, our experience includes witnessing researchers in action and appreciating the conservation science they perform. Getting to know our sea turtles means understanding what these researchers are doing and why they do it.

Sea Turtle Science

Most of the research conducted on sea turtle nesting beaches applies directly to conservation. Tagging and resighting records, nest counts, and hatching success evaluations all measure population changes. DNA samples from blood or skin can be used to identify nesting turtles' relationships to turtles nesting elsewhere. Tissue samples can also reveal where a turtle has been, and attached satellite transmitters can reveal where a turtle will go.

Sea turtle researchers include university faculty and their students, agency biologists, biological consultants, and both non-profit and for-profit organizations doing philanthropic conservation work. In the US, sea turtle research is specially permitted by the US Fish and Wildlife Service and by state conservation agencies.

Leatherbacks occasionally nest in daylight. This turtle gets measured by university students monitoring the Archie Carr Refuge, FL

Tagging and Tracking

Nesting sea turtles crawl onto land where we can conveniently attach tags to them. Because it's easier to find sea turtles on their nesting beaches than to capture them at sea, the vast majority of what we know about these animals has come from nesting-beach research. This is great because nesting turtles are easy to mark with identification tags and see again, which helps us understand how many of them there are and how many survive each year. This is not-so-great because the abundance and survival rates we measure apply only to nesting females, which represent one sex among the oldest members of the population.

The tags applied to nesting turtles include stainless steel alloy **flipper tags** attached to the turtle in one of the large scales trailing the turtle's inside front or rear flipper. Turtles also receive tags injected just under the skin that persist much longer. These are passive integrated transponders (PIT tags), which are tiny radios encapsulated in glass (see page 242) and read by biologists using a special **scanner**. Each of these tags allows researchers to identify individual turtles. Identification is key to measuring many important elements of sea turtle population change. Abundance of turtles on the beach is measured by tagging turtles, looking for them again, and using the frequency of resighted individuals to reveal how many turtles were there but not counted. Over many successive nesting seasons, researchers can also determine the rate at which individual turtles should have been resighted, but weren't. This rate reveals mortality.

A few nesting sea turtles receive fancy tags. These are **satellite tags**—radio/computers that record the turtle's position on the globe, along with water temperature and many other variables. The tags send this information to orbiting satellites, which rebroadcast back down to recording stations. The information from a satellite-tagged turtle allows researchers to trace movements to and from the beach, revealing how many nests she makes. The tags also track migratory movements back to the turtle's home foraging waters.

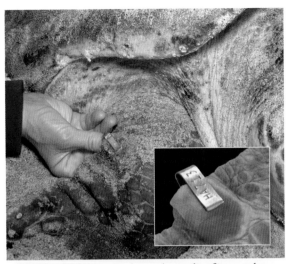

A loggerhead ID'd by a metal tag in her trailing flipper scales

Researchers identify a nesting loggerhead with a PIT tag scanner

This loggerhead's satellite tag will chronicle her travels for science

Nesting beach surveyors use ATVs to cover long beaches

ATV tire marks record this green turtle false crawl as counted

Walking nest surveyors often make a heel drag to mark crawls

A marked nest is checked for signs of hatchling emergence

210

Nest Monitoring

The most conspicuous sea turtle research and monitoring work takes place the morning after turtles have nested. These nesting surveys record the number of turtle visits to the beach. Each "crawl" (see pages 162–167) gets counted, assigned to a sea turtle species, and is appraised to be a nest or an abandoned attempt (a "false crawl"). Surveyors trained to recognize turtles by their tracks and nest appearance either walk the beach or ride it using an **all-terrain vehicle** (ATV) with low-impact, low-pressure tires. The ATV **tire imprints** provide a way to mark each track so it is not counted again the following morning. Walking surveyors make a **heel drag** through each track to achieve the same goal.

Dates and locations of nesting beach crawls reveal patterns to biologists on the seasonality and spatial distribution of nesting. Total seasonal nest counts are important because they represent an annual index of the number of nesting females. Because females seldom nest every year, two or three successive annual nest counts don't tell us much about population trends, but over many years, these assessments provide a reliable way to measure changes in adult numbers. The ratio of nests to false crawls can help to reveal whether beach conditions are deterring turtles from nesting. On average, about half of loggerhead and green turtle nesting attempts should result in a nest. Lower "nesting success" across a season may reveal problems with human disturbance, artificial beach profile, or sand compaction. But daily changes in nest site abandonment could be from temporary variations in sand that is too dry or too wet, either from heavy rains or high tides (all of which can lower nesting success).

During the late months of the nesting season, surveyors begin excavating the contents of representative marked nests in order to estimate hatching success. This additional assessment, just like nest counts, is coordinated by state conservation agencies with the goal of creating a whole greater than the sum of its parts. With input from many nesting beach locations, the production of hatchlings for an entire population management unit (see page 9) can be estimated.

Why are Nests Marked?

On some nesting beaches, every sea turtle nest is marked by stakes, ribbons, and signs. These marks might be in addition to any nest-protection installed, such as an anti-predator cage. Marking a nest serves many purposes. It may be solely as an aid to researchers so that they can re-find the exact location of the eggs when the time comes to assess hatching success (see pages 182–184). On beaches with too many nests to assess all of them, only a sample of nests are marked this way. This is the case for high-density nesting beaches in Florida, where stakes hidden in the dune are the only marks used. Researchers use measurements from multiple dune stakes to triangulate the egg clutch location at the time of hatching-success assessment (nest inventory). The standard time for this assessment for loggerhead nests is three days following the first sign of hatchling emergence, or 70 days, whichever comes first.

Marking a sea turtle nest with conspicuous signs also has a conservation benefit. The signs describe sea turtles as protected species and demonstrate the use of the beach as important nesting habitat. Cordons also deter foot and vehicle traffic over the nest.

One Needn't Be a Turtle to Judge an Egg

In addition to nest counts and estimates of hatchling production, researchers also strive to understand the genetic identity of turtles that nest across each species' range. On a long stretch of coast from South Carolina to northeastern Florida, the University of Georgia and cooperating partners have sampled egg tissue from almost every loggerhead nest. The sampling was done to genetically fingerprint each female that laid the eggs. This identification not only described how many nests each loggerhead made, it also uncovered sister/sister and mother/daughter relationships. The results reinforce the idea that females return to their natal beach (see page 9), and that loggerheads can get pretty old. The mother of an adult female is at least 62 based on an average maturation time of 31 years.

A marked loggerhead nest on a South Carolina beach

Some nests marked for research do not have signs

Some nests are re-found through measurements to dune stakes

Marked nests receive an inventory of hatching success

211

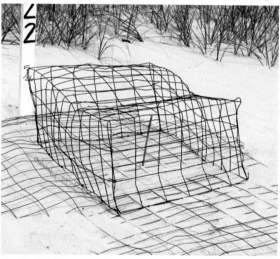

Workers bury loggerhead eggs in a protective on-beach hatchery

A self-releasing anti-predator cage in Georgia

In North Carolina, a runway helps emerging hatchlings orient

Nest and Hatchling Protection

On many nesting beaches, conservation workers provide sea turtle nests with protection from either natural or man-made threats. The threats vary, and so do the methods used to protect eggs and hatchlings. A spectrum of intervention ranges from leaving eggs where the turtle put them and doing nothing, to excavating the eggs and moving them into an artificial incubation facility, generally called a **hatchery**. Nests may be left in place (in situ) and protected by a variety of methods tailored to enhance egg and hatchling survival. A simple cordon (see page 211) can visually mark nests to deter vehicle and foot traffic. **Cages** (raised metal mesh) and screens (mesh flush with the sand surface) are commonly used to keep out predatory mammals like raccoons. The mesh is typically 2 in (5.1 cm) wide to allow hatchlings to escape from the nest. Restraining cages have a smaller mesh size that does not allow hatchlings to escape unaided. These cages are used where there is a threat to hatchlings on the beach such as driving or lights. Restraining hatchlings requires someone to tend the cage at night and collect hatchlings as they emerge. Where an artificial lighting problem comes mostly from distant urban sky glow, workers may leave hatchlings unrestrained, and install an **orientation runway** to guide hatchlings to the water.

One common way to protect nests is to move them away from a threat. This is the only way to protect nests from erosion and inundation, and is effective as long as the new location is not also threatened. Eggs must be excavated early in the morning following the night they were laid, and transported carefully. Then, workers must create an artificial nest at the new location, which involves digging an egg chamber, filling it with eggs, and covering them. When a beach location receives many nests, even if they are not protected by additional measures, the nests are considered to be in a hatchery. Sometimes, the new location is not on a beach. In these cases, the hatchery nests often incubate in insulated boxes. These efforts require special attention to incubation temperature, moisture, and collection of hatchlings.

To Intervene or Not to Intervene?

Protecting nests by intervention is a controversial practice. Some methods are effective, but many conservation scientists consider nest manipulation to be an incomplete, stop-gap solution to a threat. Some casually employed nest-protection methods can harm rather than help. For example, a poorly installed nest cage may attract predators (who learn what a cage means) without protecting the eggs. But the most controversial measures involve moving eggs and restraining hatchlings. Jostling and rotating eggs can kill them, and poorly constructed egg chambers (like those with a neck that is too narrow) can prevent hatchlings from escaping. Hatcheries add potential harm from crowding (like increased fungal pathogens), delay of hatchlings, and poorly timed mass releases. Grouping nests together defeats a female turtle's tactic of not putting all of her eggs in "one basket." Crowding effects extend to hatchlings that enter the sea at a single hatchery location. Research has shown that fish predators learn where these sources of hatchlings are, increasing hatchling mortality from predation in comparison to the survival of hatchlings from widely spaced nests. Any intervention also has an opportunity cost. Many conservation scientists feel that manipulating nests detracts from directly managing the source of a threat, like regulating beach driving, shielding lights, or controlling predator populations.

Conservation workers adhere to three principles guiding sea turtle nest intervention:

- Use the least invasive method to reduce a threat. Moving eggs (relocation) and restraining hatchlings are methods of last resort.

- When in doubt, trust the turtle's nest placement decision. Sometimes we can see the future. But often, we are no better than the turtle at predicting the fate of her nest.

- Don't allow nest-protection methods to reduce incentives for directly managing threats. Reducing a threat at the source provides long-term benefits. Leaving nests in place is a big step signalling that a beach is functioning as nesting habitat.

This low green turtle nest may do fine. Does mother know best?

An eroding beach where nests would be destroyed if left in place

Nest predation warrants caging as a minimal intervention

213

A storm blew in this post-hatchling loggerhead from the open sea

A live loggerhead gets a trip to the hospital and a data record

Red spray paint marks a dead stranded loggerhead as "counted"

Stranding Response

The study of sea turtles on land extends to the examination of stranded turtles (see pages 186–188). In addition to being a humanitarian act where injured turtles are rescued, conservation scientists rely on data from stranded sea turtles to understand their biology and threats to their survival. Some rarely seen life stages, like pelagic turtles from the open sea, offer glimpses into their lives when they strand on beaches. Other juvenile turtles and adult males are accessible to biologists studying them in coastal waters, but a stranded turtle presents additional opportunities for study. Just counting a stranded turtle, either live or dead, can result in valuable conservation clues. For example, the threat of shrimp trawling for loggerheads and Kemp's ridleys became abundantly clear when conservation scientists noticed a spike in dead turtles immediately following the seasonal opening of shrimp fishing season. As a result, fisheries management agencies enacted protective measures to reduce this threat (see page 243).

Dead turtles have important stories to tell. Samples of tissue can reveal their home nesting beach location and where they've traveled (by what elements they've acquired in their food). A complete necropsy (an animal autopsy) can also reveal the turtle's recent diet and the diseases and pathogens it had. The examination can also provide basic information like a juvenile turtle's sex and age. Recall that on the outside, males and females look alike until they mature (see page 97). Without an invasive sample of bone one would only want to take in a dead turtle, age would remain an important missing variable in understanding sea turtle population biology. Biologists can count the annual rings in sections of limb bones to estimate age. In this way, dead stranded turtles have contributed a wealth of information on age relative to size in our sea turtle populations.

A decayed loggerhead gets buried, but its data will live on

214

Fixing Problems

Many of the threats that sea turtles face on their nesting beaches have direct solutions. Although many problems seem large, they are often compound rather than complex. That is, solutions can often be reached in many small steps without the need of advanced techniques. The best example of this may be solving the problems caused by artificial beachfront lighting.

Lights on beaches deter nesting females and misdirect their hatchlings (see pages 192, 193). The solution to a lighting problem is often no more complex than finding a simple way to hide a light from the beach. Each errant light can be shielded, lowered, redirected, or turned off. Bad lights can also be replaced with better lights that are more efficient at directing light where it is needed. Of course, some beaches may have many visible lights, meaning that managing them all is a big job. This is where the individual diplomacy between a conservation worker and a beach resident requires a broader effort to inform the public and change human behavior. Because almost everyone likes sea turtles, its not too difficult to accomplish light management once people know what they need to do to help. But at the end of the day, each individual light shining on the beach will need attention. The greater effort to make a beach good for nesting turtles will involve lots of smaller efforts to recognize bad lights (from nighttime lighting surveys), to formulate remedies that make turtles safe and people happy, and to assist the owner of each light to hide it.

Other problems for sea turtles on nesting beaches are equally solvable. Beach furniture and other obstructing recreational equipment (see page 194) can be managed with the help of informed residents, and beach driving (see page 198) can have reduced effects if guided by regulatory authorities. A common theme among the solutions to these problems is that every small step can make a difference to sea turtle survival. Each light turned off, each beach chair removed, and each vehicle-free stretch of nesting beach means that additional hatchlings would recruit into a threatened population.

Bad floodlight

Better floodlight

Bad porch light

Better porch light

Conservation groups enlist the public to keep beaches dark

A no-driving zone to protect nests in North Carolina

A female loggerhead trapped in beach rocks awaits a rescue

Permitted volunteers measure a nesting ridley on a Texas beach

Nesting Beach Volunteers

Much of the information used to understand and protect sea turtles results from data collected by volunteers. This effort is essential to sea turtle conservation. Across the southeastern US, thousands of people survey beaches each morning of the nesting season to count the signs that sea turtles left during the previous night (see pages 153–167). This vigilance covers more than 1500 miles (2400 km) of nesting beach from Texas to Virginia. No budget could pay for such an effort without the diligent contribution of volunteers.

Sea turtle nesting beach volunteers tend to be organized locally by small non-profit groups whose mission is often focused on a single stretch of beach. There, the group is likely to handle all manner of sea turtle conservation needs. This generally includes nest counts, nest monitoring, recovery of stranded turtles, and rescues. For example, at the Blowing Rocks Preserve beach in southeast Florida, volunteers at first light check the natural rock formation on this beach for trapped turtles. Nesting females at night often get caught in the rocks and are unable to free themselves. Rescuing a 300-pound loggerhead wedged between a rock and a hard place often takes several sets of dedicated hands.

Apart from protecting nests, rescuing the occasional turtle, and supplying a critical data stream for management needs, volunteers are often the face of sea turtle conservation to the general public. Their work takes place on public beaches that receive a lot of visitors. People love beaches, but they may not realize how important beaches are for sea turtles. Visitors may also be unaware of how connected they are to these animals, even after they leave the beach. Outreach efforts from volunteers can deliver this message. And what better messenger than an enthusiastic volunteer so captivated by sea turtles as to donate one of their most valuable commodities—time. Whether these outreach efforts are organized morning walks (see page 207), or chance encounters during beach surveys, sea turtle volunteers are at the forefront of winning hearts and minds for sea turtle conservation.

Cute loggerhead + enthusiastic volunteer = conservation message

Sea Turtles Share the Beach

Beaches are special places, and are not just for sea turtles. These dynamic margins between land and sea attract other nesting animals, especially seabirds and shorebirds. Like sea turtles, these birds depend on beaches for reproduction, are prone to human disturbance, and are threatened with extinction. Solitary nesting shorebirds like **plovers** raise their young on the same beaches where loggerhead hatchlings enter the sea, and colonial seabirds like **skimmers** and terns also share these natal sands.

*Snowy plovers (*Charadrius nivosus*) nest on gulf beaches*

Nesting birds and turtles generally get along just fine, but conducting conservation activities for these species can be a challenge. Birds are present during the day, and are prone to disturbance from workers counting sea turtle nests. From an alternate perspective, cordoned-off seabird colonies can interfere with sea turtle nest counts needed for important population assessments. Thankfully, these multi-species conservation trade-offs are only occasional. Logistical decision–makers for birds and turtles typically share conservation philosophies as superimposed as the habitat needs of their respective species.

*Black skimmers (*Rynchops niger*) nest with loggerheads in SC*

For some organisms living on sea turtle nesting beaches, this thin, sandy habitat is the only place they occur on Earth. These include the **white beach tiger beetle**, which relies on sandy beach habitat for all its life stages. This handsome little insect occurs on beaches from Texas to Massachusetts. A northeastern sub-species of this tiger beetle has declined in number and is now endangered. The beetles are harmed by beach driving and nighttime lighting, threats that are also important to the sea turtles that share their beach. Other organisms unique to beaches include plants that grow only in salty, nutrient-starved sands. They are adapted to these beach conditions and benefit from a lack of plant competitors. These pioneering plants capitalize on the frequent natural changes that take place in these coastal systems, including the excavation of sand by nesting turtles. A turtle blasting sand out of her nest pit opens new real estate for many of these cascading plants.

*The white beach tiger beetle (*Cicindela dorsalis*)*

A sulphur butterfly sips from a beach morning-glory in a nest pit

217

Our Sea Turtles
in the Water

Mysterious Lives at Sea

Sea turtles spend most of their time underwater. Although we spend less time getting wet, it's not uncommon for us to find ourselves close enough to a swimming turtle to have a meaningful experience. Whether in a boat, SCUBA diving, snorkeling, or simply gazing out to sea, catching a glimpse of a sea turtle can provide an interesting perspective on their mysterious lives.

In this section, we offer some interpretation describing sea turtles at sea. We show what our sea turtles look like in the water, both at the surface and underneath, hoping this might aid in species and life-stage identification of turtles observed either from boats or through a dive mask. We also reveal how sea turtles behave in the water. In addition to satisfying the curiosity of those wondering what a turtle is doing, understanding behavior can help observers know when watching a sea turtle becomes harassment.

The sum of the human experience with sea turtles includes the ways that we threaten them. In this section, we describe how the human-induced challenges faced by sea turtles in the water are often evident in the turtles we see. These threats include plastics ingestion, entanglement, boat strikes, fishing interactions, and oil. Lastly, we describe the special experience with sea turtles that scientific research allows. Experiencing these animals through the biologists who work closely with them provides a vicarious experience for those who are merely spectators. A behind-the-scenes look at sea turtle science also helps to illustrate how we know what we know about these enigmatic creatures.

Above: Hatchling green turtles swim into the Atlantic and begin feeding in weedlines frequented by offshore sport fishers

Left: Loggerheads, like this subadult, are the most commonly observed sea turtles in our coastal waters

219

An adult green turtle takes a breath

A year-old juvenile green turtle in pelagic sargassum

An open-sea juvenile green turtle in offshore waters

A juvenile green turtle surfaces over a shallow nearshore reef

Identification at the Surface

All sea turtles occasionally linger near the surface and stick their heads out of the water to breathe. In this way, sea turtles present themselves for the most common encounters we have with them on the water. Even though only portions of a turtle may be visible at the surface, there are still ample clues one can use to identify who made an appearance.

Green turtles are recognizable at the surface by their unique profile. When most green turtles surface to breathe, their rounded head is upright, but little of the carapace is exposed. If some of their shell does rise above the water, it's smoothness allows waves to cleanly wash over it so that it is not very conspicuous. The head is easily noticed. If one is close enough, the rounded beak and large, dark brown scales of the face are a good indication that the head belongs to a green turtle.

The youngest juvenile green turtles are most likely to be observed in lines of sargassum floating in offshore waters. These surface-pelagic green turtles can be fairly dark, although they still bear the radiating scute pattern shown by larger green turtles in shallow coastal waters. These shallow-water juveniles may be dark if they are spending most of their time in shallow water, or they may be pale if their feeding areas are deeper than about 14 ft (4 m), or if the water is turbid.

Green turtles of all sizes spend little time at the surface getting their breath. Because green turtles forage along the bottom in relatively shallow water, they seldom need to acquire multiple breaths to recover from a long dive. A bout of surfacing commonly lasts only a second or two for most green turtles. After a breath, green turtles often dive quickly, giving the appearance that they are startled. This may be the case if one is close enough to be seen by the turtle. In general, surfacing green turtles seem skittish. Even though green turtles may be common in some waters, people unfamiliar with their brief surfacing pattern might not notice them. Old fishermen often tell of green turtles not liking to "show their backs" much.

Loggerhead sea turtles are more likely than green turtles to hang out at the surface, either breathing, basking, or searching for food. Adult and subadult loggerheads that show themselves up top have a number of visible characteristics to help us identify them. Their large head with yellow cheeks is a dead giveaway. In the right light, the bright yellow jowls of a loggerhead seem to glow. The carapace is typically exposed during a breath, which may show the extent of barnacle fouling loggerheads often have. In deep water, a loggerhead adult or subadult may spend 20 seconds or so at the surface collecting several breaths to recover from a moderate dive. Even in shallow water, loggerheads are often in no hurry to get away from the surface. When it's time to head to the bottom again, loggerheads will occasionally raise the rear portion of their carapace in the air before they descend into a dive. This reveals the hump in their carapace over their pelvis (the sacral hump) that is pronounced in most loggerheads.

In the Florida Keys and The Bahamas, loggerheads often live in clear-water seagrass habitat only a few feet deep. There, the turtles commonly acquire a coating of light, calcitic algae and sediment (**marl**) that makes them stand out against the backdrop of darker seagrass. Juveniles in the open sea have little of this fouling and often appear bright orange against deep blue waters.

The large, mostly yellow head of an adult loggerhead

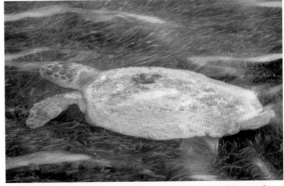

A Florida Keys loggerhead with its carapace covered by marl

A juvenile loggerhead basks in the open sea

The carapace of a loggerhead often has attached barnacles

On calm days during the hatching season (see page 28), especially off southeastern Florida, loggerhead hatchlings can be seen dispersing seaward. The thumb-length little turtles surface to breathe about once every 20 seconds.

A hatchling loggerhead swims seaward through nearshore waters

A juvenile hawksbill in sargassum shows its overlapping scutes

Young hawksbills have a serrated rear-shell margin

A juvenile Kemp's ridley in Florida's Big Bend near Crystal River

Pelagic ridleys are dark above with prominent carapace spines

Hawksbills are uncommon sea turtles in our region except where coral reefs occur. These waters are normally clear, which means that a turtle near the surface will show its colors even before it raises its head to breathe. The multi-colored streaks on a hawksbill's shell generally have a more contrasting pattern than that of a green turtle (see page 220). Especially in juveniles and subadults, a hawksbill's carapace seems rough due to the turtle's **overlapping (imbricate) shell scutes**. One might also notice the **sawtooth margin** of the rear shell that is more pronounced in juvenile hawksbills than in other sea turtles. In small hawksbills, the birdlike head profile is not always obvious as the turtle raises its head to breathe, but in larger hawksbills, this unique silhouette is a defining characteristic. In good light, the hawksbill's head can be seen to have the same highly contrasting colors of the turtle's shell. When breathing, hawksbills lift their heads quickly, take their air, and dive, all within a few seconds. Like green turtles, hawksbills in shallow waters seldom linger long at the surface.

Kemp's ridleys observed in coastal waters appear ghostlike. Their shallow estuarine habitat is frequently murky, which means that they are not likely to be seen until the turtle is at the surface for a breath. The pale, green-gray topside color of a ridley often presents a stark contrast with the turbid water surrounding it. Yet there are a number of locations where Kemp's ridleys can be observed in water clear enough to see the bottom, such as the seagrass pastures of Florida's Big Bend and Florida Bay. There, the discus form of the ridley shell clearly sets it apart from any other sea turtle.

Offshore fishers are the most likely observers of plate-size, pelagic juvenile ridleys. These turtles are occasionally found floating within sargassum algae in weedlines far from shore. Unlike older ridleys in shallow coastal waters, these little ridleys are at the surface nearly all the time. Their color is medium to dark gray, with a light margin to the carapace and flippers. Silhouetted at the surface, a young ridley's prominent **carapace spines** often stand out.

At sea, hatchling and post-hatchling Kemp's ridleys are closely tied to the surface. They are uniformly gray, a coloration that can overlap with that of little loggerheads. Location can separate these two species. Ridley hatchlings are not likely to be seen anywhere else but the western Gulf of Mexico.

A hatchling Kemp's ridley in blue waters off of Texas

Leatherbacks have a unique look and are not often confused with other species. These are turtles of the open sea, but some boaters may also see leatherbacks in waters close to shore if there is deepwater access. Only rarely do leatherbacks enter confined waters such as bays and lagoons. Clear oceanic waters often give boaters a nice view of the entire turtle. They are big. Nearly all leatherbacks in our region are adult turtles, which commonly exceed 1000 pounds (450 kg) and have a flipper span of 7 ft (2.1 m) or more.

Leatherbacks cruise in blue offshore waters

A leatherback turtle at the surface may take several breaths and keep its head and back exposed for several minutes. Their color is dark, even black, with their light spots only becoming visible upon a close encounter. Viewed from certain angles, three of the turtle's five **carapace keels** can be clearly seen. Each keel has a bumpy ridge, although the rest of the carapace is smooth. With the turtle's head up, its profile is noticeable as a rounded triangular shape, especially when seen from behind. This view also reveals the leatherback's signature **pink spot** (splotch) atop the turtle's head (see page 68). A leatherback observed in offshore waters may have returned from a dive that was more than a thousand feet deep. This type of exertion requires a recovery period during which the turtle will take in several breaths, lifting its head each time.

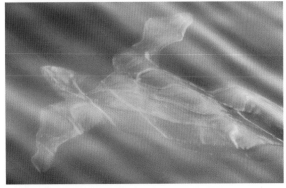

A leatherback lingers at the surface showing its distinct keels

Boaters should be aware that all sea turtles at the surface are vulnerable to being struck. Vessel-strike injuries are the most common, identifiable cause of death in stranded sea turtles. Cautious boaters never cruise without a keen eye out for floating objects that could damage the vessel's hull. Hopefully, the images and descriptions here will provide mariners an additional search image of things to throttle down for and steer around.

A raised head reveals a leatherback's pink splotch

An adult green turtle inhales with the aid of gular pumping

An adult loggerhead exhales before a big breath

Behaviors at the Surface

What is that turtle doing? Most often, a turtle at the surface is taking a breath (see page 90). For a green turtle or a hawksbill rising from shallow water, a single gulp is sufficient, requiring only seconds of air time. But for deep-diving loggerheads and leatherbacks, several breaths may be needed to replenish oxygen-starved tissues. In either case, a single exhale-inhale cycle takes only a second. Just before a turtle's head reaches the surface, it begins to forcefully exhale. The partially opened mouth lifts through billowing bubbles, or may spatter seawater just above the surface. Inrush of air is accompanied by inflation of the turtle's throat, which contracts and forces additional air into the lungs in a process called **gular pumping.**

Sea turtles also linger at the surface to bask (see page 102), mate (see page 110), and forage for food. Pelagic juvenile turtles (see page 115) may spend nearly all of their time near the surface, drifting along with floating sargassum seaweed.

One of several breaths taken by a deep-diving loggerhead

Other than breathing, which sea turtles must do with a regular frequency, some behaviors can be explained by conditions. For example, basking loggerheads are commonly seen when the water is cool and the day is sunny and calm. **Mating green turtles** are frequently encountered off southeastern Florida beaches in June, whereas mating loggerheads are most common at the western edge of the Florida Current in April and May. Basking and mating turtles are the most vulnerable to boat strikes, so mariners should be extra cautious when conditions favor these surface behaviors.

Mating green turtles just off a southeastern Florida beach

Post-hatchling Behaviors

As young of the year, loggerheads, green turtles, hawksbills, and Kemp's ridleys spend almost all of their time floating. Hatchlings of these species are active swimmers, but as the hatchling frenzy (see page 114) comes to an end, and as a little turtle finds itself far from shore, it gradually adopts a lower-energy lifestyle. The turtle is now a **post-hatchling**, which means it is largely finished with active dispersal, yet likely to move great distances as it is carried by currents. A post-hatchling has used up the residual yolk from its egg (see page 112) and must find food without using up too much energy and without drawing attention from predators.

Loggerhead post-hatchlings are the most common little turtles discovered by boaters in sargassum weedlines. Most of the time, these palm-size and smaller turtles are in a **tuck**. "Tucked" loggerheads are motionless at the surface, with their front flippers pressed against the sides of their carapace and their rear flippers folded tightly across their tail. This puts front flippers away from nipping fishes (see page 132) and allows the turtle to literally cover its butt with its rear flippers. A turtle in a tuck appears inanimate. Motionless floating is broken only a few times a minute by a head raised for a quick breath. Loggerheads may also go from a tuck into a low-energy swimming stroke called a **rear-flipper kick**. This behavior is similar to a tuck, except that the rear flippers stroke together to slowly propel the turtle at the surface. Little loggerheads can make pretty good progress by rear-flipper kicking. Hatchlings at the end of their two-to three-day frenzy period spend less time powerstroking (see page 107) and more time rear-flipper kicking, which still allows the turtle to maintain an offshore orientation. Post-hatchlings use rear-flipper kicks to "stroll" from patch to patch along a floating weedline. All post-hatchling behaviors are interrupted by periodic breaths during a brief dogpaddle. This water-treading technique employs the front flippers, allowing a small turtle to raise its disproportionately large head without sinking the rest of its front end.

A young loggerhead in a tuck, drifting within a sargassum patch

A loggerhead post-hatchling, rear-flipper kicking past sargassum

A loggerhead on a stroll showing a rear-flipper kick stroke

225

A royal tern feeds on a herring bait ball surrounding a loggerhead

A loggerhead post-hatchling floats in a tuck within a weedline

Dolphinfish school beneath a sargassum patch

Fishing and Sea Turtles

Experienced anglers know about sea turtles, because good fishing and turtles commonly coincide. Sea turtles, especially loggerheads, hang out over deep reefs, wrecks, and productive convergence zones that attract a wide range of fishes. This means two things. One is that spotting a turtle is not just a good omen, it's an indicator of fishing success. Another is that careless anglers run the risk of hooking a turtle.

Baitfishes (small fish species) occasionally cluster around a sea turtle as it involuntarily becomes the center of a **bait ball**. Fish form these swirling masses as protection from predatory fishes like tunas and billfishes, which attempt to feed by rocketing through the compact school. Apparently, there are accidental encounters between billfish and turtles, as shown by turtles found with a broken swordlike billfish rostrum penetrating their lower shell. Turtles also attract gamefishes like cobia (*Rachycentron canadum*) and **dolphinfish** (*Coryphaena hippurus*). Loggerheads and leatherbacks in deep water are most famous for this association, but juvenile green turtles and ridleys in coastal waters also have cobia tagalongs.

Because larger loggerheads feed on bottom-dwelling invertebrates that require structure, seeing these turtles at the surface often means there is a reef below that fish might like. And in blue water offshore, post-hatchling and juvenile turtles in a weedline often indicate that it is a productive one for gamefish.

The relationship between recreational anglers and sea turtles is largely positive, as long as fishers show a little reverence. Anglers should never cast lines close to a turtle, especially with multiple-hook lures. Turtles accidentally hooked should be de-hooked. A turtle released with trailing line is likely to die as its limbs become entangled. Pier fishers should use a bridge net to hoist a turtle for de-hooking, rather than pulling on the line. For deeply hooked turtles, fishers are urged to call their local stranding hotline for help (see page 188).

226

A Shared Community

Offshore weedlines are a common focus of both recreational anglers and nature enthusiasts interested in seeing pelagic birds, dolphins, and other charismatic marine life. These lines are typically formed at the surface where currents press together floating material, especially the golden-colored seaweed, sargassum. This alga forms the basis of a unique natural community. The presence of sargassum both signals and brings about the conditions that concentrate and foster diverse life in an otherwise featureless sea-surface desert.

The **open-sea juvenile stages** of green turtles, loggerheads, hawksbills, and Kemp's ridleys all depend on sargassum weedlines as developmental habitat. The lines provide food and cover. Much of the diet of these surface-pelagic turtles can only be found in the drifting sargassum community. Dozens of species are unique to this natural assemblage and are specially adapted to life within sargassum. In addition to sea turtles, this community is a nursery for many important game- and food fishes. The larvae of many valuable fish species, such as tunas, jacks, sailfish, marlin, and dolphinfish, share floating sargassum with little sea turtles. This open-sea resource also attracts birds such as storm petrels, shearwaters, terns, gulls, and even migrating sandpipers. Marine mammals also visit, including several dolphin species, pilot whales, and baleen whales.

Turtles share their weedlines with us too. These zones are the targets of recreational and commercial fisheries. But even people who live far from the sea end up shaping this natural community in important ways. The plastics we carelessly discard and the oil we demand as fuel often find their way to the sea and converge in the same weedlines that focus life for turtles and many other species (see pages 233–235). This unique sea-surface community is vulnerable to threats that develop far away.

A hand-size green turtle basks in a gulf sargassum patch

A loggerhead post-hatchling, drifting the western Gulf Stream

Hawksbill juveniles from southern Mexico drift into our waters

A post-hatchling Kemp's ridley in a weedline off Texas

227

Diving and Snorkeling

Sea turtles offer themselves in many ways, but one of the best ways to fully appreciate them as marine animals is to stick your head underwater. This means either breathing through a tube (snorkeling), holding your breath (freediving), or drawing air from a Self Contained Underwater Breathing Apparatus (SCUBA). In any case, you'll want to wear a dive mask that will allow a clear view of the underwater world.

A curious loggerhead on a shallow reef in the Florida Keys

Hawksbills are the quintessential coral-reef turtle

Green turtles use coral reefs as resting areas

Opportunities for an undersea experience with sea turtles vary by what kind of habitat one swims in. Coral reefs are the most popular dive spots, have clear water, and are great places to view loggerheads, green turtles, and hawksbills. Although most hawksbills are found on reefs with an abundance of living stony corals and sponges, they are occasionally seen on rock piles and less structured hardbottom. These areas of rocky bottom are favored by loggerheads and green turtles. Loggerheads may rest and forage within these habitats at depths far below safe SCUBA guidelines, but green turtles are commonly found in shallow hardbottom, including some patches that are just off of a sandy beach. The green turtles are attracted to these nearshore reefs because of the tufts of algae growing there (see page 19). Southern Florida has many opportunities to dive where sea turtles live, but additional locations also occur at deeper reefs off of Texas, Alabama, Georgia, and the Carolinas. Shipwrecks at a number of gulf and Atlantic sites create an artificial attractant for turtles, as do offshore oil platforms like those off Texas and Louisiana.

Snorkelers see green turtles on shallow reefs and seagrass beds

Behaviors Below the Surface

Sea turtles don't give us much change in facial expression, but their behavior can tell a lot. Hopefully, most of the turtles a diver might see are content. Any turtle calmly resting under a ledge could be described this way. Often, these turtles are sleeping. Like us, turtles need down time. A mellow sea turtle can hold its breath for hours. Feeding turtles show obvious signs, and are frequently accompanied by fish hoping for table scraps. Gently swimming turtles may be searching for food or commuting between foraging spots. A turtle that swims with its carapace toward you may feel a little threatened. Presenting the broadest possible look may be a way to signal a predator that the turtle is too big to eat. Green turtles close to the bottom sometimes react defensively by tucking their flippers underneath. Loggerheads are very mellow creatures, but if harassed, they may demonstrate their displeasure by presenting an open mouth. These are all varied signals that a diver has moved from admirer to stalker. Most turtles that become uncomfortable just glide away, but forcing this may deprive the turtle of a quiet meal or needed rest.

A green turtle turns its carapace toward a potential predator

A loggerhead rests under a reef ledge

Green turtles sit on their flippers to keep them unbitten

On occasion, it's the turtle that offers unwanted advances. More than one SCUBA diver has reported adult male turtles approaching them during the spring of the year. Sometimes, the turtle persists and attempts to mount the diver from behind. These males are, no doubt, under some intense hormonal control, but it is hard to see the attraction. Not that there is anything wrong with that.

A sleeping green turtle. They snooze at night, just like us

229

Turtles in Trouble

Sea turtles are threatened with extinction for many reasons. Historically, these threats were direct. Turtles were harvested from the waters where they lived, and were eaten or rendered into shell-jewelry or leather products. Much of this harvest took place on an industrial scale, and commercial trade in sea turtle products spanned international boundaries. Today, most of this intentional take of sea turtles is gone from our region, but important threats remain. This harm is largely unintentional. Although we may think of sea turtles leading their lives in a remote marine wilderness, there are countless accidental interactions between humans and turtles at sea.

Turtles at sea do not just swim about randomly. They feed in specific areas where they can easily find food and they travel along routes that help them get where they need to go. We frequent these same locations, and so does the waste we discard. By far, the most harmful encounters sea turtles have with us are with our fisheries. To catch our seafood, we use scores of methods that accidentally hook, entangle, and drown thousands of sea turtles each year. These fisheries are commercial and recreational, coastal and high-seas, and involve both small-scale artisanal and industrial-scale fleets. Hazards from fishing occur off the coasts of many countries and in international waters, and they involve fishing gear both deployed and discarded at sea. We humans on land demand seafood and our unintentional effects on sea turtles don't stop there. The plastics we throw away, the fertilizers and chemicals we use, and the petroleum we extract, frequently run off, leak, and spill, eventually reaching the sea. Each of these troubles for sea turtles seems to be increasing, but so is awareness, and numerous solutions are at hand.

The 2010 BP Deepwater Horizon *oil spill in the gulf oiled many thousands of pelagic sea turtles, like this juvenile Kemp's ridley*

Fishing Gear

We don't see most of the sea turtles killed by offshore fisheries. Dead turtles sink. Carcasses in shallow water may rise following decomposition and drift ashore, but deep-water deaths are unlikely to be observed. Except, that is, by "fisheries observers" who dutifully record captured turtles and other incidental, nontarget species (called bycatch). From the data supplied by these observers, fisheries scientists estimate that thousands of sea turtles die each year in the US shrimp trawl fishery. These numbers are far better than the tens of thousands of annual deaths before states enforced effective TED (see page 243) requirements in the late 1990s (although Louisiana still does not currently comply). Outside US waters, the mortality from fisheries is much higher. Longline fisheries from multiple countries in the Atlantic set tens of millions of hooks each year. Even though the hooks catch turtles at a low rate, the magnitude of the fishing effort influences mortality, which is estimated at tens of thousands annually.

Other fisheries close to home also kill sea turtles by accident. Deadly fishing gear includes **rope** on lobster, crab, and other traps (pots), and a variety of nets set to catch finfish, especially gill nets.

This green turtle drowned after becoming tangled in trap rope

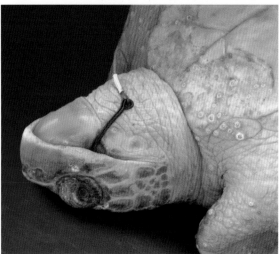

A loggerhead hooked by a commercial longline rig

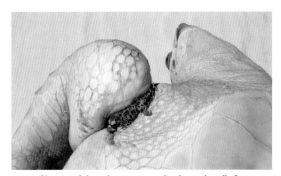

Monofilament fishing line cut into this loggerhead's flipper

Recreational fishing has a lower impact than commercial fisheries, but accidental **hooking** and **line entanglement** is still a common cause of mortality. Turtles drawn to fishing piers are particularly susceptible to injuries from recreational angling. All of these mortality factors affect turtles that are the some of the most valuable members of the population (see page 118).

Careful treatment helped this pier-hooked subadult loggerhead

A basking loggerhead is vulnerable to distracted boaters

Slashing propeller wounds severed the spine of this loggerhead

Boaters can help sea turtles by slowing down in turtle habitat

Boat Strikes

Most sea turtles spend about 3% of their time at the surface. They must breathe, of course, but they also **bask** in the sun or linger near the surface when feeding or traveling. This surface time makes turtles vulnerable to boat strikes.

It is difficult to know how many sea turtles are struck and killed by boats, but in our region, **propeller wounds** and other vessel-strike injuries are the most common identifiable cause of death in stranded turtles. The injuries seem to be from fast-moving watercraft, as well as from larger vessels. Turtles show injuries from both the props and skegs of outboards, from the larger propellers of sportfishing vessels, and from hull strikes by personal watercraft. No vessel appears to be "turtle friendly," except for any boat moving slowly enough for turtles to dive away from the threat.

Some sea turtles survive strikes by boats. Like manatees, many sea turtles bear the severe scars from old propeller cuts. Some of these turtles apparently were able to recover on their own, but many turtles wash ashore debilitated and become long-term residents at rehabilitation facilities (see page 251).

Turtles at the surface do respond to an approaching boat and will quickly dive. Vessels cruising below 15 knots have the lowest chance of striking a turtle. Faster-moving vessels increase the odds of striking a turtle, especially under certain conditions and in areas frequented by turtles near the surface. Conditions when mariners should pay special attention for turtles include calm sunny days, which tempt basking turtles to the surface. Even when surface water is warm, deep-diving loggerheads may soak up sun to warm themselves after a dive down to cold depths. Areas where boaters should travel slowly include any shallow water less than 6 ft (< 2 m), the waters just off of nesting beaches during the summer nesting season, and any location where multiple sea turtles have been sighted.

Plastics

Look around you right now and find all the throwaway things made of plastic. Now picture all of these things in ten years. Where will they be? Would you believe that some of these things may end up floating in a turtle's world?

Nearly all of our plastic stuff is not meant to last. Some things, like our plastic shopping bags, are made to be thrown away. The problem for sea turtles is not that our world is filling up with these plastics, it's that their world is. Appallingly, we're pretty terrible at managing our voluminous waste. Bags blow away like tumbleweeds, food containers wash out of landfills, and a kaleidoscope of plastic discards float their way to the sea. These plastics slowly degrade in sunlight, but this only makes things worse for turtles. The brittle, bite-size shards that float at sea become concentrated in many of the places where sea turtles search for food.

A joyous inland balloon release ends as harmful marine debris

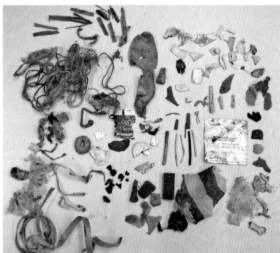

Plastics found in the digestive tract of a single dead loggerhead

Plastics in drifting sargassum, hundreds of miles from the source

And the turtles are easily fooled. Sea turtles evolved in a world where anything looking remotely like food should be eaten. In our modern age of plastics, this means that thousands of turtles suffer debilitation or death from the severe impactions caused by this ingestion. It's unclear how severe this problem has become, but the frequency of plastic ingestion is extremely high for some sea turtle life stages. Among young loggerheads and green turtles that strand following Atlantic-coast hurricanes, nearly 100% have evidence of ingested plastics. Other marine animals ingest plastics too, including seabirds and fishes like the oceanic triggerfish (*Canthidermis maculatus*).

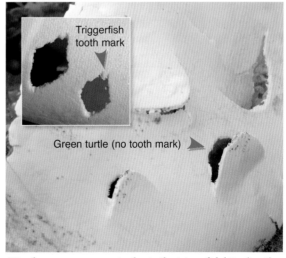

Triggerfish tooth mark

Green turtle (no tooth mark)

Bites from a young green turtle; similar triggerfish bites (inset)

233

Convergence zones collect lines of floating sargassum, and turtles

An oiled sargassum line during the BP oil spill

This oiled ridley was among the first rescued from the 2010 spill

Petroleum (Oil and Tarballs)

In the late spring and summer of 2010, sea turtles became a symbol of environmental harm caused by the BP *Deepwater Horizon* oil spill in the Gulf of Mexico. This was a massive event that spread over the northern gulf and mired thousands of pelagic juvenile turtles. These turtles were particularly susceptible to the oil because of their dependence on zones in the sea where floating material converges, like **sargassum weedlines**.

During the months-long spill, these lines became smothered by petroleum in varied forms—liquid oil with volatile fumes, emulsified oil, mats of grease, and tarballs of varied proportions. Because oil is sticky, the little turtles living where the petroleum collected became as oily as their surroundings. This included their insides. Most of the oiled turtles rescued during the event had ingested oil along with their food, to the extent that their throats were thickly coated. The rescue effort during the spill seemed large in terms of the hundreds of turtles brought in to rehab facilities in Louisiana, Mississippi, and Florida, but the exercise was small relative to the vast remote area of water covered by the spill. The full extent of sea turtle mortality from the oil spill is still being estimated by scientists.

The BP spill occurred during the nesting season on nearby beaches from Louisiana to the Florida Panhandle. Because of the clear threat to nests and hatchlings, the US Fish and Wildlife Service, state conservation agencies, and local non-profit groups made an unprecedented effort to move eggs out of harm's way. Nearly all the eggs laid on these beaches were relocated to a temporary hatchery near Cape Canaveral, Florida, where the hatchlings were released into the Atlantic Ocean. The move took place after careful deliberation among conservation scientists, and was felt to be a desperate measure brought on by desperate times.

Most of the effects from petroleum on sea turtles are not as dramatic as the BP spill. Other smaller spills have made headlines, but the majority of sea turtle oiling takes place in obscurity. These effects are from the many, smaller, everyday spills. And the "everyday" description is literally correct. The Bureau of Safety and Environmental Enforcement (BSEE) reports on about 1500 gulf oil platforms that are connected to land by a spiderweb of pipeline. These structures are pretty leaky. On average, each year sees one spill in the 50,000 gallon range, with thousands of smaller spills reported. Many more go unreported, and the **sheen** that spreads and drifts remains unidentified by its source.

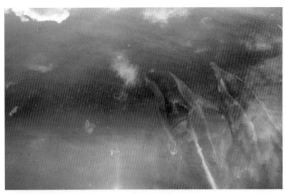
Rough-toothed dolphins in offshore oil sheen

Most oil spills go unreported

Tarballs like this may drift at sea for years

But the largest release of oil into the gulf by humans is from sloppy use of fuel petroleum. From freighters to jetskis, marine vessels spill millions of gallons of petroleum into the gulf each year. Just like other spilled oil, the "bunker oil" used as fuel by large ships floats at sea, weathers, and congeals into **tarballs**. These lumps of sticky goo drift at the surface for years and are a temptation to small sea turtles. The tar sticks in the jaws of young turtles and adheres to the bits of plastic that turtles also ingest. Much of this ingested petroleum has the hydrocarbon signal of bunker fuel oil.

Even during headline spills when resource agencies make a concerted effort to locate oiled turtles, the extent of damage to sea turtle populations is difficult to assess. This was especially true for the BP spill, which quickly spread into offshore waters where no search vessel could reach. No effort goes into locating affected turtles for most marine spills. For oiled turtles that are observed and represent the many turtles not seen, effects from oiling are still poorly understood.

Emulsified oil covers a juvenile loggerhead

Post-hatchling loggerheads commonly ingest tarballs

Dark water (arrow) signals a southwest Florida HAB

Floating fish are the first sign of an HAB like a red tide

Debilitated loggerheads may float for long distances

Mass Mortality

Sometimes, lots of sea turtles die and wash ashore. We don't always know why. These mass mortality events also involve debilitated live turtles that can be examined and treated. In both the living and the dead, varied clues hint at what happened to them.

Sea turtle strandings occasionally coincide with a local "red tide" or other **harmful algal bloom** (HAB). The algae in the bloom produce toxins known to kill fish, marine mammals, birds, and turtles. In the eastern Gulf of Mexico, frequent blooms of the dinoflagellate *Karenia brevis* coincide with dozens to hundreds of sea turtle strandings. The alga produces brevetoxins that affect the nervous system. Symptoms of live turtles include loss of coordination, head bobbing, nervous twitching, and coma. Affected turtles may breathe in aerosols of the toxin at the water's surface, and ingest the toxin along with food. It's unclear whether these HABs are brought about by our fertilizer runoff into coastal waters.

Other mortality events involve disease. Many remain a mystery until clinical investigations reveal a probable diagnosis. One example of a former mystery disease is a neurological disorder affecting loggerheads. Symptoms in affected turtles include weakness to the point where turtles cannot lift their head to breathe, which results in drowning. Necropsies (animal autopsies) of many of these loggerheads have found masses of parasitic, spirorchid trematodes (blood flukes) in vessels surrounding the brain and spinal cord. Why large numbers of loggerheads periodically suffer this affliction is unclear.

Throughout the southeastern US, loggerheads in significant numbers strand dead or moribund with debilitated turtle syndrome (DTS). These "Barnacle Bill" turtles (see page 241) still alive are emaciated, anemic, and heavily fouled with barnacles. Most strand dead or do not recover under care. A wide variety of pollutants, toxins, and disease organisms are suspect in this syndrome, but partial drowning from capture in trawl fisheries may also be a cause. Large numbers of dead turtles with no external signs of trauma often follow the start of shrimping season.

Research and Conservation on the Water

Without the researchers who study sea turtles and what threatens them, we would not know how to keep these animals around. Protection may seem to involve mostly "no-brainer" decisions, but the easily imagined solutions to sea turtle conservation problems are actually quite rare. Most often, the things we do to harm sea turtles are an incidental effect from an otherwise desirable activity. This means that a lot of evidence of harm is needed to change what we do, either in its location, timing, extent, or methods. For example, the way we fish for seafood kills sea turtles. Yet fishing is a desirable enterprise (it brings us food and makes money). To curtail our fishing, we need to be convinced by scientific evidence that, if we don't change our ways, we'll lose our sea turtles. So, what does the science tell us? How many turtles are killed? How does an alternative fishing method reduce mortality? Is the new mortality rate sustainable for the population? How do other threats compound with threats from fisheries? What is an acceptable rate of mortality that would not result in populations being lost? And, how do sea turtle population dynamics work anyway? How do reproduction, growth, survival, migration, ecological relationships, and changing climate drive the number of turtles we have? So many questions. … And these are just some that apply directly to conservation. Many more fall under the category of "basic" science, where the application of the investigation is not yet clear. This kind of science is sometimes esoteric, but it often teaches us critical concepts, like how sea turtles live their lives or how the rest of the living world works.

Biologists experience sea turtles like nobody else can. For this reason, we added research to this book's section on *Experiencing Our Sea Turtles*. Not only do researchers have the data, they've also had opportunities that can provide fascinating vicarious experiences for the rest of us.

Biologists release a captured loggerhead with a GPS computer tag that will transmit information on where the turtle travels, the depth and frequency of its dives, and the temperature of the waters it swims through

237

Biologists scoop a dip net ahead of a pelagic juvenile green turtle

A research crew tends a tangle net. Note the turtle-boarding dip

A hand-captured loggerhead is brought in for questioning

Capture and Study

How does one study a sea turtle in the water? You catch it. Even in our age of technological methods for remote observation, there is no substitute for laying hands on a sea turtle. This allows researchers to measure and weigh them, learn their sex, assess their health, and borrow a sample of blood, skin, scute, or poop. A captured turtle can also be tagged, which lets researchers recognize it next time it's caught.

The ways to catch sea turtles vary according to the size of the turtle and the nature of the habitat they are caught from. Post-hatchlings and small juveniles are captured by **dip net**. In shallow waters, especially those with limited clarity, researchers use **tangle nets** made of loose twine. Tangled turtles can still surface to breathe while they wait for the research boat.

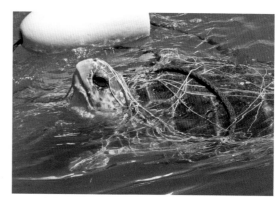

A tangled loggerhead takes a breath and awaits researchers

Shallow, clear waters facilitate turtle captures **by hand.** With this technique, a boat follows the turtle until a diver on the bow can plunge down to the turtle and grasp its carapace. Then, the turtle is pointed toward the surface where the boat crew can take it in for questioning. In deep water, the same trawls that accidentally catch turtles in shrimp fisheries are used with reduced tow-times to catch turtles live for research. Where leatherbacks are found foraging deep and lingering at the surface, they are caught by vessels deploying a breakaway hoop net, which is a bit like a giant dip net. Sea turtles are also obtained by researchers working with commercial fishers like those using trawls, longlines, and pound nets, which funnel fish and turtles into a netted "pound."

Measuring

The size of a sea turtle places it into a life-stage category and tracks the turtle's developmental progress. The ways to measure a sea turtle are standardized among biologists. Because the turtle's total length depends on how far out its neck extends, the most reliable size measurements are of the turtle's carapace and plastron.

Measuring minimum carapace length with a tree caliper

Straight measures of carapace and head. Abbreviations below

A caliper positioned at the nuchal notch

"Straight-line" carapace measurements are taken with a caliper (normally, one designed to measure the diameter of tree trunks). **Carapace width straight-line** (CWSL) is taken at the widest point of the carapace. **Minimum carapace length straight-line** (CLSL min) is taken from the nuchal scute to the pygal notch and is also known as notch-to-notch. A **standard carapace length straight-line** (CLSL) is measured to the tip of the longest pygal projection. **Head width** (HW) is the greatest width of the head.

A caliper positioned at the pygal notch

Like most other references to the size of a sea turtle, the general sea-turtle size notations in this book refer to standard carapace length straight-line. This is a pretty good measure with which to compare turtles of the same species and to register growth in an individual. But some problems arise when a measured turtle

A caliper positioned at the longest pygal tip

Measuring carapace width straight-line

Measuring carapace length over-curve, to pygal tip (inset)

Measuring carapace width over-curve, at the widest point

has its pygal scutes either broken off or worn down with age. Because calipers are bulky equipment to take into the field, carapace measurements are often taken with a tape measure. These are "over the curve" measurements. Most research projects take both straight-line and over-curve measurements. One never knows when a measured turtle will be seen again and what equipment the subsequent researcher will have. **Carapace length over-curve** (CLOC) is taken from where scute meets neck skin at the nuchal notch, to the longest pygal. **Carapace width over-curve** (CWOC) is taken from the widest part of the carapace. Because calipers large enough to measure leatherback carapace length are unwieldy (and hard to get), leatherback length is typically reported as over-curve.

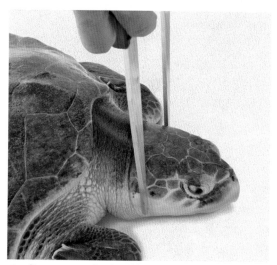

A caliper measures head width at the widest point

Plastron length is generally taken with a caliper along the midline spanning the anterior and posterior underlying plastron bones (not just the scutes). **Tail length** has two components—the length to the vent and the length to tip. The anterior reference point is the most posterior edge of the anal scutes. In maturing turtles, tail length begins to separate males from females.

Hopefully, the reader will appreciate the clean, calm, happy, and healthy Kemp's ridley that volunteered to be a model in these images. Measuring a sea turtle is not always like this.

Turtles as research subjects squirm, bite, claw, bear interfering barnacles, and have injuries making certain measurements impossible. This variation is why sea turtle biologists take so many measurements. Many research projects weigh their turtles, although this is tricky on the water, and of course, some sea turtles are really heavy.

Health Assessment

Captured sea turtles nearly always get a checkup. This can be as simple as a subjective report on body condition and injuries, or as extensive as a complete blood work-up and endoscopy (to observe reproductive state). Some captured turtles have obvious illness, such as **fibropapilloma tumors**, which are associated with a virus and poor water quality but have no certain root cause. Others may have debilitated turtle syndrome (DTS), characterized by anemia and heavy barnacle fouling, which is why those afflicted are called **"Barnacle Bill"** turtles.

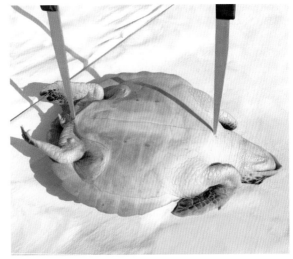
Plastron length measured with a caliper

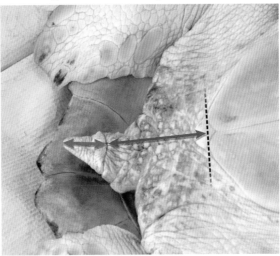
The tail is measured to vent (red) and to tip (blue plus red)

Fibropapilloma tumors are most common in green turtles

A weakened "Barnacle Bill" loggerhead

Checking for a PIT tag in a captured ridley

241

Stainless steel flipper tags have ID numbers and a return address

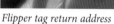

Flipper tag return address

Plastic tag ID code

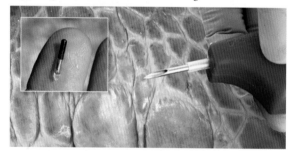

Pit tags (inset) are tiny radios applied under the skin

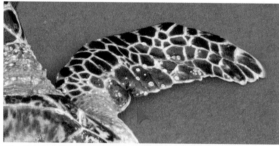

This hawksbill had its flipper tag tear out (arrow)

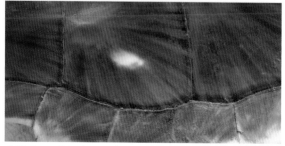

A "living tag" in the costal scute of a young loggerhead

Tagging and Tags

Sea turtles that become part of a research program nearly always get an identity. This allows biologists to recognize when individual turtles have grown or moved from other study locations. A sea turtle's identity is its "tag," which can take many forms. The stainless steel (monel or inconel alloy) **flipper tag** has been used by researchers since 1955. The tags pierce the inside trailing edge of the front (or sometimes, rear) flippers, and they bear a unique number/letter code and a return address. Plastic tags have similar markings. **Passive integrated transponder** (PIT) tags are rice-grain-size capsules inserted with a needle under a turtle's skin (flipper or shoulder). The tag is a tiny radio that emits an ID-coded signal to a scanner (see page 241). Although flipper tags often tear out after several years, PIT tags are thought to persist for the life of a turtle. A **living tag** is an exchange of a dark carapace skin/scute plug with light plastron tissue. The simple light mark in a uniform scute position identifies an entire year-class and lasts a lifetime.

A solar-powered Argos satellite tag on a juvenile ridley

Researchers use the number of turtles tagged, and the number of tagged and untagged turtles seen again, with some math, to estimate important things like turtle abundance and survivorship. Some tags are pretty fancy. Acoustic (sonic) tags broadcast a location-indicating ping. A passive archival tag (PAT) records location based on light cycles and saves the data until it can be broadcast to a satellite. Argos and GPS tags (see page 237) send information on position, temperature, motion, and dive patterns to orbiting satellites in real time.

Managing Fisheries

Because the way we fish for seafood has such a large impact on sea turtle populations, conservation researchers strive to monitor the incidental deaths from fisheries bycatch (see page 231) and the effectiveness of fisheries regulations.

Changing the Way We Fish

The most important gear change reducing turtle deaths in fisheries has been the use of **turtle excluder devices** (TEDs). TEDs are modifications to shrimp- and fish-trawl nets. Most are a metal oval of parallel bars sewn into the part of the funnel-like trawl net ahead of the net bag (cod end) where captured marine life collects. The bars are at an angle so that large items (like a turtle) are diverted through an open flap in the net. Smaller items like shrimp pass through the bars and are caught. Federal rules currently require TEDs in large trawls, but compliance varies. Researchers are interested in many questions about TED use, such as rates of compliance and effectiveness of various TED versions.

Biologists study many other fisheries that accidentally catch and kill sea turtles, hoping to reduce this mortality and understand its effects on sea turtle populations. In addition to trawls, turtles are also harmed by scallop dredges, gill nets, pound nets, and longlines set either at the surface or on the bottom. Next to trawls, longlines kill the most sea turtles. These lines are many miles long and dangle hundreds of baited hooks set to catch swordfish, tunas, and sharks. Millions of longline hooks are set in the Atlantic each year. Although the US and Canada manage these longline fisheries to reduce sea turtle mortality, many other countries fish longlines in poorly regulated international waters. Biologists struggle to understand how many loggerheads and leatherbacks are removed from our populations from this threat. Researchers also examine ways to reduce mortality by selective fishery closures and by use of alternative methods and gear, such as **circle hooks**. These hooks replace **J-shaped hooks** and are thought to lower the chance that a caught turtle is hooked in the throat, which is a more damaging injury than a mouth hooking.

Shrimp trawls without TEDs catch a lot besides shrimp

TEDs allow turtles to escape out through a flap in the trawl net

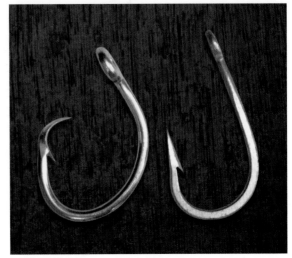

Circle hooks (L) may injure turtles less than J hooks (R)

243

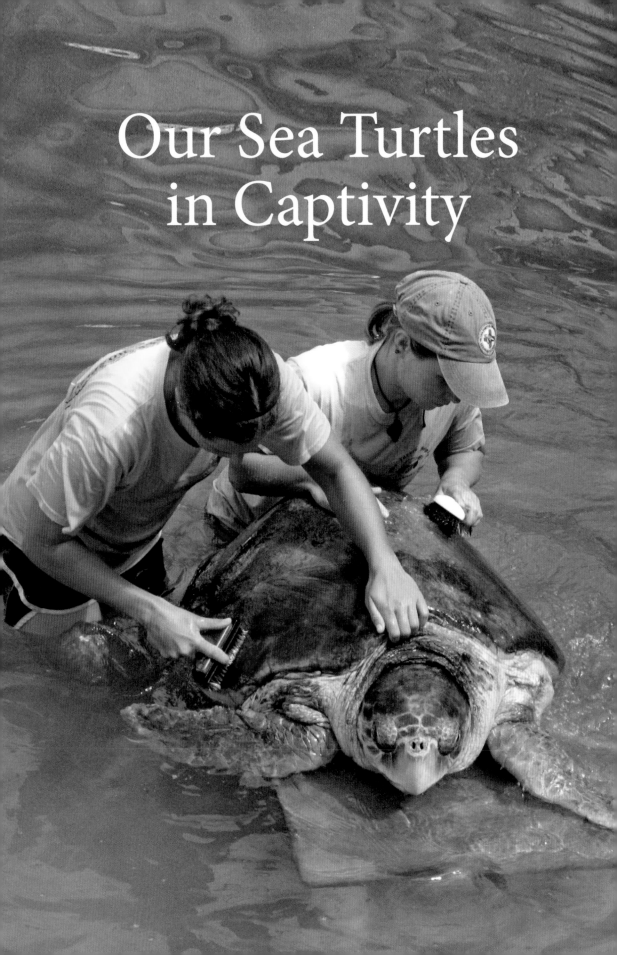

Our Sea Turtles
in Captivity

Why are Sea Turtles in Captivity?

So, whatcha in for? The answers vary. Some sea turtles are temporary captives of science, others are recovering from injury or illness, and a few are simply on display. All fulfill the role of representing their kind. Captive sea turtles educate us, inspire us, and serve as ambassadors of the marine realm.

Most of the sea turtles we keep in captivity are getting over some direct or indirect interaction with humans. They were struck, tangled, hooked, trapped, or ate some of our discarded junk that disagreed with them. Some convalesce in a matter of weeks or months, others suffer long-term effects requiring years to get better, and a few need extra help for the rest of their lives.

The majority of captive sea turtles are held at facilities that allow us to have an experience with them. Commonly, all but the sickest turtles are in open tanks or pools that provide a way of getting close enough to come eye-to-eye with their fans. Such an intimate experience with a turtle isn't required for the turtle to tell its story, but it helps. Each turtle represents numerous unseen turtles that don't receive such special attention. The stories are both heartrending and hopeful. They are tales of threats that take the lives of countless turtles, but leave lucky survivors who teach us about the possibility to change our ways and make the world a better place.

Some of these ambassadors of the marine world live at public aquaria, which receive thousands of visitors each day. The turtles are famous, and they become known as unique individuals. These are the special charismatic turtles that tell their stories broadly. But all captive sea turtles, whether elegant or ailing, represent their counterparts in the wild. They may await a return to the wild, or they may never return, but their contact with us should teach us about stewardship of the wilderness where sea turtles belong.

Above: Pale from its time in captivity, a loggerhead raised to test TED (turtle excluder device) effectiveness gets released into the Indian River Lagoon, Florida

Left: Rebel the loggerhead gets attention at the Turtle Hospital, Marathon, FL. He was struck by a boat, which paralyzed his rear flippers and caused him to float. Rebel has delivered inspirational conservation messages since 1991

245

A little loggerhead teaches us about its magnetic sensory abilities

Loggerheads like this are raised to a size useful in TED testing

A post-hatchling loggerhead awaits chow at the Galveston Lab

Captive Research

Understanding sea turtles helps us protect them. The scientific research that provides this information often takes place with captive turtles. Subjects take part in research designed to reveal what sea turtles need to survive and how the things we do affect them. The turtles stay under captive care for a relatively short time before they are released.

Hatchlings are probably the most studied life stage in captivity. They are easy to collect from beaches and don't require large tanks. Their swimming-orientation behavior and sensory abilities (see pages 95, 96, 120) are just some of the discoveries made from little turtles kept briefly in captivity. Hatchlings are also kept captive for longer periods of one to three years until they grow to a size large enough for certain procedures. These include endoscopy to determine the turtles' sex and trials with fishing gear to measure the gear's suitability for sea turtle protection. Dozens of loggerhead hatchlings each year are transported to the NOAA Fisheries Service Galveston Laboratory in Texas, so they can grow to the size of turtles susceptible to shrimp-trawl capture. At the right size (about 18 in, 45 cm, shell length), the turtles are released in front of trawlers pulling nets with TEDs (see page 243) in them. Divers record the escape times of the turtles and the information is used to judge suitability of the device's design. Before these "TED-testing" loggerheads are done with their stay in captivity, they may also be used for studies of sea turtle diet, toxicology, disease, sensory biology, physiology, and behavior, all in partnership with varied agency and university scientists.

On occasion, wild turtles are brought into captivity, studied, and let go shortly afterward. These turtles teach us about how sea turtles sense and move in their world in a way that could not be studied in the wild. Brief captivity also allows turtles to get a check-up so that they might represent the health of their population. An exam might include an adult's reproductive status, revealing the probability he or she will breed in the months ahead.

Sea Turtle Rehabilitation Facilities

These "rehab" facilities care for sick and injured sea turtles that strand on land or are discovered at sea. Dozens of organizations run these facilities (see page 253). They exist within a network of stranding recovery coordinated by state agencies that permit this work. Most rehab sites are coastal, but a few are located inland. Permit requirements for a sea turtle rehab facility specify minimum tank sizes, water quality, temperature, feeding methods, and veterinary experience.

The turtles brought into rehab have become debilitated due to entangling or ingested debris, other injuries, toxins, or disease. Many of these facilities have a limited clinical capacity and function mostly as convalescent homes for recuperating sea turtles. Sometimes, a little R&R, along with supportive care, is all a turtle needs. But some facilities are true sea turtle hospitals, with capabilities to diagnose patients with radiography and blood tests, and to conduct involved surgeries under anesthesia to remove hooks, excise tumors, clear blockages, and repair extensive wounds.

Because sea turtles are endangered species protected by both federal and state laws, the rehab facilities that care for them must have special permits. In many states, the federal government asks state agencies to oversee permitting and inspections. Almost all of the facilities that house rehabilitating sea turtles accept visitors and offer educational interpretation of the work they do. Rehab facilities offer unique glimpses of live sea turtles up close. Experiences like these can provide tangible demonstrations of many sea turtle conservation needs.

Sea turtle rehab facilities seek quality care for their sick and injured patients in the same way that any other veterinary clinic would. The big difference is, sea turtles do not have loving custodians ready to pay the bill. The turtles are charity

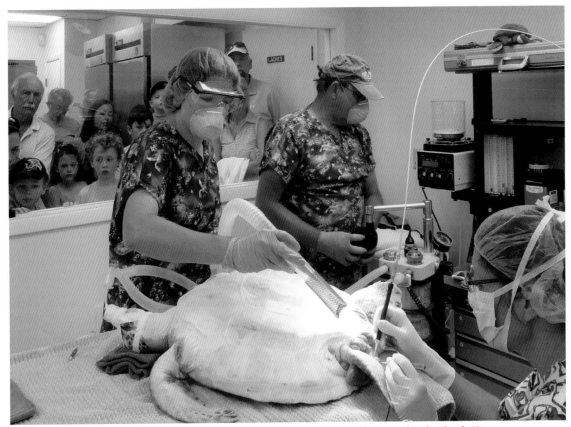

A juvenile green turtle has skin tumors removed before an audience at the Sea Turtle Hospital in the Florida Keys

Debilitated sea turtles are cared for by many local groups

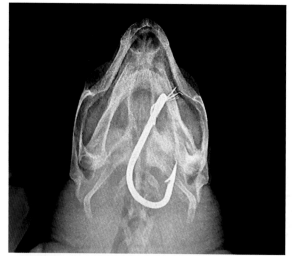

X-ray image of a hook in the mouth of a subadult loggerhead

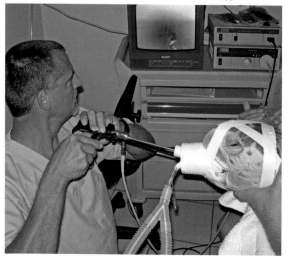

Dr. Mader removes a hook from a loggerhead under anesthesia

cases. Their treatment depends on a variety of dedicated non-profit organizations that run the rehab centers. These groups represent us all in acting as a provider of wildlife care. It's something to keep in mind when visiting a sea turtle rehab facility. Some benefit from the solvency of moderately sized philanthropic organizations, but most operate on a shoestring budget and rely on donations to continue taking patients. When you realize that nearly all the turtles in need of rehab were injured because of some human-caused woe, it's not hard to sense some obligation to chip in.

In the Florida Keys, sick turtles get an ambulance ride

All facilities depend on veterinarians who may volunteer their time. Most vets have had specialty training in treatment of reptiles and marine animals. However, the skills in treating sea turtles, with their many unique ailments and afflictions, can only be mastered after years of experience and insight gained from colleagues. Just like the human medical field, sea turtle medicine benefits from a disciplined record of clinical science. Every case is different, but there are a few types of sea turtle injuries that vets are getting much better at treating. One is removal of **fishing hooks**. Another is the treatment of fibropapilloma (see pages 241, 247). More frequently now, these skin tumors can be surgically removed so that they do not regrow. But some injuries continue to have troubling complications. Although shell injuries from boat strikes can heal given long-term care, these turtles are often left with debilitating buoyancy problems that prevent their release (see page 251).

Rescue, Rehab, and Release

This is the goal of every sea turtle rehab facility—to find turtles that need help, make them better, and put them back where they belong. It's work that requires a lot of dedicated people at every stage of the process.

This leatherback was disentangled from trap lines and released

The US Coast Guard rescues an adult green turtle

Accommodating a sea turtle in need begins with rescue, which may include capturing an injured turtle that is still able to swim. Turtles that are injured often fill their lungs and spend a lot of time on the surface, perhaps to prevent themselves from drowning. Weakened turtles may eventually strand on a beach. Unless the turtle is nesting (mostly at night, see pages 144, 145) a turtle on land is in trouble, so it is not helpful to push a stranded turtle back into the water.

Rescues are often initiated by good samaritans who recognize a turtle in trouble and make a call to a hotline. To find the emergency phone number for US states, do an Internet search for "sea turtle hotline." Top results will list phone numbers by state. In Canada, call the Canadian Sea Turtle Network at 1-888-729-4667. The biologist you reach through the hotline call can guide decisions on what the turtle needs. Sometimes, all a turtle needs is to be disentangled. Many heartening rescues result in the immediate release of a healthy turtle.

This large loggerhead rode a forklift to the hospital

Most rescued turtles require care. To get that care, they need to get out of the water or off the beach and into a rehabilitation facility. Transport is often not easy. Some turtles are large, strand in remote locations, or are found at sea. The complex transport logistics are worked out

Juvenile ridleys taken in during the 2010 BP oil spill

249

A juvenile loggerhead gets its final checkup before release

Leatherbacks are a big challenge for even the largest facilities

A rehabilitated loggerhead is homeward bound

between the original good samaritan and the hotline responder. Unlike the transport of human patients, there are few resources for turtle transport, which is generally undertaken by volunteers. Any extra assistance these folks can get from the public is greatly appreciated. The goal is to quickly transport the turtle to the closest facility with the capacity to hold and treat the animal. Some locations can't take large turtles or cases of infectious diseases, like fibro-papilloma. In cases of mass strandings, like cold stuns (see page 102), enormous transport help is needed and many facilities take part.

Impromptu green turtle transport during a mass cold stun

Once a turtle reaches a rehab facility, the next step is diagnosis and triage. Often, it's not clear why the turtle isn't well. X-rays, endoscopy, and blood work can reveal foreign bodies and other life-threatening conditions. Some turtles need immediate treatment, others can wait, and some, unfortunately, must be euthanized.

Treatment of a debilitated turtle may include surgery, wound attention, and a lengthy course of antibiotics or other medicines. The treatment stage can include extensive efforts to heal wounds, solve buoyancy problems, and regain weight and strength in the turtle.

After a successful rehabilitation, it's time for release. Because of the importance of returning turtles to wild populations, moderate disabilities do not disqualify a turtle from release. Limb amputations and shell injuries, as long as they are well healed, do not keep a sea turtle from returning home.

Long-term Care

Some sea turtles stay in rehabilitation for years. Those with the most prolonged needs include turtles with boat strike injuries to the shell. Carapace bone takes a long time to heal and the original damage to the turtle often involves scarring of the lungs or spinal injury. Because sea turtles use their lungs to control their buoyancy, lung damage can keep a turtle from diving like they should. Spinal injuries often result in paralysis, which can interfere with intestinal motility. When a turtle can't efficiently pass things through its gut, it gets gassy and bloated, and it floats. Sea turtles afflicted like this are often called "bubble butt" turtles, referring to the part of the turtle that rides high in the water. Experience tells us that turtles released in this condition often return after being struck once again by a boat.

Single limb amputations rarely keep a turtle from being released. Most sea turtles with only one missing flipper can swim in a remarkably straight line. But multiple missing flippers can hamper swimming and diving enough so that a turtle can't feed. A female with severely damaged rear flippers may have a significant challenge ahead in terms of digging an egg chamber for her eggs (see page 148), but these turtles are generally given their chance in the wild.

Blindness can keep a turtle from being safely released. In green turtles, the most severe fibropapilloma tumors in the eyes cause blindness that can't be addressed by surgery to remove the growth. Because all sea turtles depend on sight to find their food, a mostly blind turtle is typically considered to be nonreleasable. These same tumors can grow throughout a turtle's skin and are particularly debilitating in green turtles. The tumors can be surgically removed, but they often grow back. To watch for re-growth of fibropapillomas, turtles given a surgical tumor treatment are observed for a year.

Nonreleasable "lifer" turtles like **Kent** and **Montel** serve their wild counterparts well. They tell stories of limbs lost from line entanglement and disabling injury from boat strikes, and they inspire us to take care out on the water.

A green turtle waits to be declared fibropapilloma-free

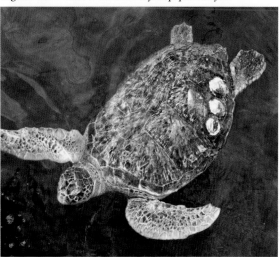

Kent floats high due to a boat strike. His weights offset buoyancy

Montel has one eye, half a front flipper, and a damaged shell

251

Tolstoy the loggerhead may be the oldest sea turtle in captivity

Sea turtles, young and old, intrigue us, young and old

Allison the green turtle allows some up-close questioning

Turtles on Display

Some sea turtles are cared for in exhibits. These turtles are not undergoing medical treatment and are held in aquaria for us to see them. Most often, there are technical reasons why the turtles should not be released, such as uncertainty over their genetic origin (and where they should be released). Many of these turtles were raised in captivity since hatchling size, or were taken in as adults back when the exhibition of healthy turtles was more commonplace. A few have moved between public aquaria for decades. Sea turtles live a very long time and can have extensive careers as celebrities. A loggerhead named Tolstoy, originally acquired by Marineland in 1964, currently lives at Disney's expansive Seas aquarium at Epcot. Given that the turtle was an adult when he was first taken in, Tolstoy is most likely over 80, making him possibly the oldest sea turtle in any aquarium. His youthful looks belie his age. Given his longevity and the number of daily visitors he gets, Tolstoy may have had a larger cumulative audience than the Rolling Stones.

Ocean Ambassadors

The role of an ambassador is to represent an unfamiliar place and make that place more familiar. Sea turtles in captivity, regardless of their length of stay, do this job well. They seem to have a special brand of marine-life charisma. Gazing at a sea turtle that returns the gaze can prompt questions from the shyest kids and most jaded adults.

Sea turtles are compelling and approachable, but they can't tell their story all on their own. The most effective sea turtle ambassadors represent their kind, and the ocean realm, with the help of interpreters. Educational interpretation is required for the display of endangered species, and many facilities go above and beyond this obligation. Charismatic turtles paired with a poised presenter and a provocative display can get across some heady messages about the conservation needs of our ocean world, instilling curiosity and conveying concise, sincere statements about solutions. It's just the kind of diplomacy our wild sea turtles need.

Sea Turtle Rehabilitation Facilities and Aquaria in Florida

1. **Gulfarium Marine Adventure Park**
   Fort Walton Beach

2. **Gulf World Marine Park**
   Panama City

3. **Gulf Specimen Marine Lab**
   Panacea

4. **Sea World Adventure Park**
   Orlando

5. **Walt Disney World, The Seas at Epcot**
   Lake Buena Vista

6. **The Florida Aquarium**
   Tampa

7. **Clearwater Marine Aquarium**
   Clearwater

8. **Mote Marine Lab and Aquarium**
   Sarasota

9. **Clinic for the Rehabilitation of Wildlife**
   Sanibel

10. **The Conservancy of Southwest Florida**
    Naples

11. **Key West Aquarium**
    Key West

12. **The Turtle Hospital**
    Marathon

13. **Theater of the Sea**
    Islamorada

14. **Miami Seaquarium**
    Key Biscayne

15. **Museum of Discovery and Science**
    Ft. Lauderdale

16. **Gumbo Limbo Nature Center**
    Boca Raton

17. **John D. MacArthur Beach State Park**
    North Palm Beach

18. **Loggerhead Marinelife Center**
    Juno Beach

19. **Florida Oceanographic Society**
    Stuart

20. **Environmental Studies Center**
    Jensen Beach

21. **Brevard Zoo***
    Melbourne

22. **Marine Science Center**
    Ponce Inlet

22. **Marineland**
    St. Augustine

* Rehabilitation only, turtles not on display.

Other Sea Turtle Rehabilitation Facilities and Aquaria in the US

1. **Sea Turtle Inc.**
   Padre Island, TX

2. **Texas State Aquarium**
   Corpus Christi, TX

3. **Grapevine Sea Life Aquarium**
   Grapevine, TX

4. **Galveston Sea Turtle Lab**
   Galveston, TX

5. **Audubon Nature Institute**
   New Orleans, LA

6. **Institute for Marine Mammal Studies**
   Gulfport, MS

7. **Georgia Aquarium**
   Atlanta, GA

8. **Georgia Sea Turtle Center**
   Jekyll Island, GA

9. **South Carolina Aquarium**
   Charleston, SC

10. **Ripley's Aquarium**
    Myrtle Beach, SC

11. **Sea Turtle Hospital**
    Surf City, NC

12. **North Carolina Aquaria**
    Roanoke Island,
    Pine Knoll Shores,
    and Fort Fisher, NC

13. **Virginia Aquarium**
    Virginia Beach, VA

14. **National Aquarium**
    Baltimore, MD

15. **Pittsburgh Zoo**
    Pittsburgh, PA

16. **Adventure Aquarium**
    Camden, NJ

17. **Marine Mammal Stranding Ctr.**
    Brigantine, NJ

18. **Riverhead Foundation**
    Riverhead, NY

19. **Maritime Aquarium**
    Norwalk, CT

20. **Mystic Aquarium**
    Mystic, CT

21. **National Marinelife Center**
    Bourne, MA

22. **New England Aquarium**
    Boston, MA

23. **ATMAR**
    Maunabo, Puerto Rico

PART THREE

Saving Our Sea Turtles

Above: Because we've stopped harvesting green turtles in our region, there has been an increase in the number of green turtle hatchlings leaving our beaches each year. This species has shown us that saving sea turtles is well within our grasp

Left: A young hawksbill rescued from the BP oil spill in the northern Gulf of Mexico. Only rarely can we save sea turtles by direct heroic action. Most sea turtles are saved when we heroically decide to stop doing things that harm them

Why Save Sea Turtles?

Because they are valuable. It's a common theme for the things we strive to save. Money, time, prized possessions—all are valuable to us as individuals. But what about the things that belong to everyone? These are valuable too, but in a way that is hard to describe in terms of what we would be willing to pay to keep them around.

Wild, living sea turtles belong to all of us. No one person or group can buy or sell our living sea turtles in a direct way, and they have no price on the open market. Sure, dead sea turtles and their parts continue to be a marketable commodity in some places, but the price paid is for a turtle that is used up and not available for anyone else. It's easy to understand price, supply, and demand, for someone purchasing turtle-egg tapas or a pair of tortoiseshell eyeglasses, but what would we all be willing to chip in to keep a sea filled with turtles?

The value of living sea turtles can be an elusive measure. We do sometimes pay to use them, albeit in a non-consumptive way. This is the case wherever sea turtles are an attractive feature of an eco-tourism enterprise. As such, sea turtles contribute significantly to local economies. People who travel for a sea-turtle experience stay at hotels, eat at restaurants, and buy gifts and mementos, all because of these charismatic animals. Exchanges of money are pretty easy to add to our sea turtle's value ledger. What's harder to itemize is what a common resource like sea turtles is worth to the general public altogether. Do we receive value from simply knowing that sea turtles exist? Do they have an intrinsic worth?

Part of the non-consumptive value sea turtles have is their ecological value. This value extends to sea turtles and their genes, to populations, to species, and to grand sea turtle phenomena, like their mass-nesting *arribadas* (see page 53). Ecological value comes from the influence of sea turtles on the fundamental ways that ecosystems

The Inwater Research Group rescues a leatherback trapped in the intake canal of a nuclear power plant

Oil spills and other catastrophic events for sea turtles have resulted in large-scale efforts to try to save them

function, influences that are just beginning to be understood. Some examples include the important role of green turtles in the cycling of nutrients within seagrass communities, and the role of unhatched eggs in providing energy, nitrogen, and phosphorus to nutrient-starved dunes. Much of this sea turtle influence occurs within ecosystems we depend on for food, that protect our property from erosion, or that provide pleasant places to visit. This valuable influence on keeping the world just the way we like it may require not just some sea turtles, but lots of them.

The economic and ecological benefits we receive from sea turtles, along with other aspects of their value, need to be demonstrated if sea turtles are to be saved. This is because of competing interests. Many of these interests have their own definitive value—for example, commercial fisheries. We fish for valuable seafood, and we accidentally kill sea turtles in the process. We could fish so that we kill fewer turtles, but this costs money.

A balance point between killing an acceptable number of turtles and killing too many is driven by demand from seafood consumers and by political pressure to regulate seafood producers. Sea turtle advocates have an opportunity to effect change in this interplay by providing information. Informed consumers, producers, and regulators, who recognize the civic value of wildlife and the long-term, cost-effective nature of conservation are our best chance for a future with sea turtles.

Perhaps by now you are viewing this book as a rather extensive sales brochure. You'd be right. This attempt to showcase the mystery, beauty, and intriguing nature of sea turtles is indeed meant to be a testament to their value. Much of this value can't be easily measured and will not satisfy cynics, but the worth is distinctive and discernible nonetheless. Why save sea turtles? Because they make our world a much more interesting and pleasant place to live.

An 1870s depiction of a green turtle in a Paris restaurant

Green turtles gave the illusion of being an inexhaustible resource

By 1900, nearly all our southeastern green turtles had been canned

Why Do Sea Turtles Need Saving?

Our history of using sea turtles began simply. The native people of the Americas were nourished by sea turtles, as evinced by turtle bones in coastal middens (trash piles). But it's unlikely that this use had a significant effect on sea turtle populations. These people had no capacity to capture and transport large numbers of turtles. Although they had access to both eggs and adult turtles on nesting beaches, coastal tribes may not have spent much time there during the summer nesting season, thanks to the viciousness and former abundance of the saltmarsh mosquito.

The Great Green Turtle Plunder

Times changed for sea turtles with the European colonization of the wider Caribbean. Through the sixteenth and seventeenth centuries, the Spanish, English, Dutch, and French sailed the Caribbean, vied for island colonies, fought with local populations of Arawak and Carib Indians, and became very hungry. Their desire for meat was met by the discovery of a profoundly abundant local resource—the green turtle. In 1503, Christopher Columbus reported on the green turtles he experienced as he sat anchored off the Cayman Islands, noting that the islands were "… full of tortoises, as was all the sea about, insomuch as that they looked like little rocks. …" To hungry sailors and settlers, the green turtles of those tiny Caribbean islands were as profound an example of divine providence as anyone could hope for. Nesting turtles were carted to ships and stacked below decks where they would persist for months as a supply of fresh meat. Like the turtles' persistence as living cargo, the green turtle population seemed unending. By the late seventeenth century, British vessels were shipping out an estimated 13,000 turtles each year. For decades during which nearly every turtle ashore was killed, green turtle nesting on the Caymans persisted. Then, in what could easily be predicted now, the Cayman Island green turtle began a steady slide toward oblivion. By the early 1800s, a time when eating green turtle had reached its peak in European fashion, the Cayman nesting colony was essentially gone. Estimates are that the colony once numbered several million green turtles. Today only a handful of green turtle nests are recorded there each season.

The history of green turtle overharvest in the southeastern US did not begin until the 1800s. In both Texas and Florida, juvenile green turtles in shallow lagoon waters were the subject of an extensive net fishery taking tens of thousands of turtles per year. Key West, Florida, was a focal trade port for this industry, but by the turn of the century, nearly all of the local green turtles had been fished out. For the Key West "turtle kraals" (turtle corrals) and cannery to keep busy, turtle fishers expanded their operations into the western Caribbean. By the 1920s, most green turtles shipped through Key West were from Nicaraguan waters. This kept the market open for increasingly rare local turtles.

Modern Problems

By the Great Depression in the 1930s, eating sea turtles of all species was common throughout the southeast, and **collecting eggs** from beaches was familiar to coastal families. Egg harvest on the Kemp's ridley nesting beach in northeastern Mexico was massive, right up until the 1960s when the population crashed to about a hundredth of its size just 15 years before. An additional major threat to both Kemp's ridleys and loggerheads was mechanized trawling. After World War II, the number of diesel-engine trawlers that could pull large nets dramatically increased. These vessels began to harvest shrimp where ridleys and loggerheads congregated, and sea turtle drowning deaths increased to tens of thousands per year.

Wanted: For Being Beautiful

Many sea turtles have suffered for their beauty. **Turtle curios** were once common in tourist shops, and they continue to be sold in many countries. The hawksbill turtle has seen the worst of this commerce. Trade worldwide in decorative hawksbill tortoiseshell products has brought perilous declines in hawksbill populations, a threat that continues today.

Egg collectors worked our region's beaches through the mid-1900s

Female loggerheads taken from a SW Florida beach, early 1930s

Stuffed hawksbills in a curio shop. They are much prettier alive

Current Threats to Sea Turtles

In our western Atlantic region, many of the threats that depleted our sea turtle populations have eased. This is especially true for commercial harvest. In The Bahamas, US, Canada, Mexico, Cuba, and Bermuda, sea turtles are now protected by law. So are sea turtles off the hook? Unfortunately, no.

The principal threats remaining for our sea turtles are accidental. Although it may seem that the world is a much safer place for sea turtles now that fewer of us are killing them on purpose, the incidental mortality we cause is often no less devastating. Foremost among these incidental threats is the capture and drowning of sea turtles by nets and hooks set to catch our seafood. Although

national fisheries regulations and international agreements have begun to moderate this mortality, the enforcement of regulations is hampered by the vastness of the open sea.

In our coastal waters, boat strikes, debris entanglement, and other threats incidental to human activity kill significant numbers of turtles each year. And on nesting beaches, light pollution, seawalls, and construction of poorly made artificial beaches continue to reduce hatchling production and deter nesting females. Yes, some big threats that sea turtles once faced have been reduced, but the prevalence and complexity of threats remaining presents a set of big challenges to conserving our sea turtles.

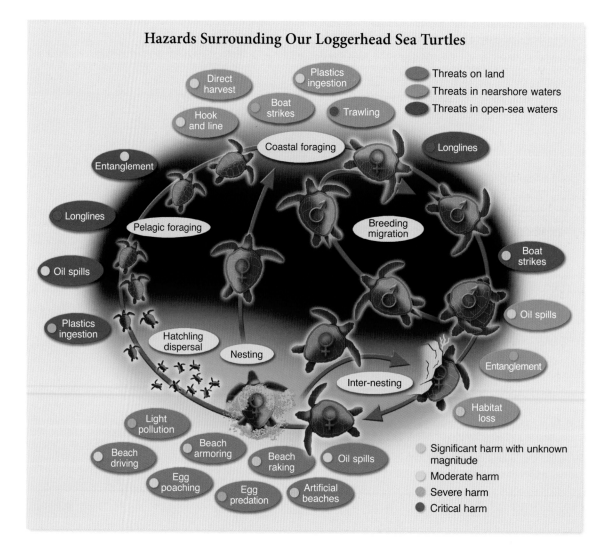

Hazards Surrounding Our Loggerhead Sea Turtles

Some Threats are More Important than Others

The **threats to loggerheads** listed below affect all sea turtle species, and are examples of how population effects can vary. Each threat is color-coded by the magnitude of its effect. The ratings are based on the loss to the population, determined by numbers of turtles lost and their "reproductive value." For more information, search online for "loggerhead recovery plan."

● Significant harm with unknown magnitude ● Moderate harm ● Severe harm ● Critical harm

Threats on Land

Light pollution (see pages 192, 193) deters nesting females and misdirects hatchlings, killing hundreds of thousands each year.

Beach driving (see page 198) creates hatchling-trapping ruts and occasionally kills turtles.

Beach raking (see page 198) removes dune-building seaweed and plants, and contributes to problems from light pollution.

Artificial beaches (see pages 199, 200) present unnaturally wide and unstable beach profiles that deter nesting and contribute to egg loss and hatchling disorientation.

Beach armoring (see pages 195–197) blocks nesting and contributes to egg loss from erosion. Includes hard structures like seawalls and rocks, but similar effects come from sand fences, sand bags, and other obstructions.

Egg poaching (see page 172) takes eggs, mostly in south Florida, Cuba, and Mexico.

Egg predation (see pages 131, 170–172) from introduced and subsidized predators destroys hundreds of thousands of eggs each year.

Oil spills (see pages 234, 235) cause harm even when nests are moved away. But catastrophic spills are uncommon.

Threats in Coastal (Nearshore) Waters

Plastics ingestion (see page 233) causes slower growth rates and mortality.

Boat strikes (see page 232) are the most common recognized cause of death in stranded loggerheads.

Entanglement (see page 231) in fishing debris and trash injures and drowns turtles.

Trawling (see pages 231, 243) drowns thousands each year. TEDs reduce this, but not all trawls use TEDs.

Hook and line (see page 231) injuries come from recreational and commercial fishing.

Direct harvest (see page 259) occurs in isolated areas, although it is illegal.

Oil spills (see pages 234, 235) occasionally cause high mortality.

Habitat loss (see page 135) results in reduced foraging opportunities, lower growth rates, and higher mortality.

Threats in Open-sea Waters

Plastics ingestion (see page 233) affects a high proportion of young turtles.

Boat strikes (see page 232) kill some turtles, but this threat is difficult to measure.

Entanglement (see page 231) injures and drowns pelagic turtles.

Longlines (see pages 231, 243) kill tens of thousands each year from hooking injury and drowning.

Oil spills (see pages 234, 235) kill thousands during catastrophic events. Frequent small spills leave tarballs as an ingestion hazard.

Archie Carr in 1984, on the refuge beach now named for him

Peter Pritchard

Karen Bjorndal

Who Saves Sea Turtles?

They are numerous. Such an enormous and ongoing challenge could not be met by only a few. Saviors of sea turtles include wise pioneers in conservation, diligent scientists, effective educators, key innovators, advocates, coordinators, managers, and, of course, you. No person effective at saving sea turtles has ever worked alone. Yet there are some who should be known for their unique contributions to sea turtle conservation in our region.

Archie Carr—University of Florida Graduate Research Professor, prolific author, and subject of the biography *The Man Who Saved Sea Turtles* (see page 273). He was immensely influential at a time when our understanding of sea turtles was basic and conservation biology was in its infancy. Professor Carr left us in 1987.

Peter Pritchard—Student of Archie Carr, director of the Chelonian Research Institute, author of *Encyclopedia of Turtles,* and the world's foremost authority on turtles. His pioneering work on Kemp's ridley and other species set the stage for current conservation efforts.

Karen Bjorndal—Student of Archie Carr, distinguished professor, and director of the Archie Carr Center for Sea Turtle Research, University of Florida. She has advanced the science of sea turtle biology and conservation in pivotal ways, led authoritative conservation policy efforts, and fostered numerous influential students.

Anne Meylan—Another student of Archie Carr, and leader of the Florida Fish and Wildlife Conservation Commission's sea turtle research program. She has been instrumental in managing long-term nesting data and in informing efforts to protect hawksbill turtles.

Jim Richardson—Ecology faculty, University of Georgia. Central to the long-term project at Little Cumberland Island, GA, he described an initial loggerhead population model.

Sally Murphy—Former leader of South Carolina's sea turtle conservation program during three critical decades when nesting and stranding information were essential to saving sea turtles from trawl fisheries.

Llewelyn (Doc) Ehrhart—Professor Emeritus, University of Central Florida. His long-term nesting information justified the Archie Carr Refuge in Florida. He has also fledged dozens of students into the field of conservation biology and sea turtle protection.

Sinkey Boone—Shrimp fisherman and sea turtle advocate who perfected and promoted the modern TED, the most important sea turtle–saving device ever used.

Barbara Schroeder—National Sea Turtle Coordinator for NOAA. In the hotseat of sea turtle diplomacy, she has coordinated important achievements in the regulation of fisheries that harm sea turtles.

Jack Woody—Former National Sea Turtle Coordinator for the US Fish and Wildlife Service, a skilled conservation statesman who achieved crucial goals for Kemp's ridleys and the requirement of TED use in trawlers.

Earl Possardt—US Fish and Wildlife Service champion for the federal funding for sea turtle conservation at home and abroad.

Many others have made major regional contributions to sea turtle conservation—scientists like Alberto Abreu, Alan Bolten, Brian Bowen, Charles Caillouet, David Caldwell, Ray Carthy, Debbie Crouse, Larry Crowder, Carlos Diez, Ken Dodd, Scott Eckert, Sheryan Epperly, Bob Ernest, Allen Foley, Nat Frazer, Jack Frazier, Matthew Godfrey, Harry Hirth, Elliot Jacobson, Mike James, Charles LeBuff, Ken Lohmann, Peter Lutz, Sandy MacPherson, Kate Mansfield, René Márquez, Erik Martin, John Mitchell, Nicholas Mrosovsky, Jack Musick, Felix Moncada, Larry Ogren, Dave Owens, Pam Plotkin, Carol Ruckdeschel, Mike Salmon, Jeff Seminoff, Bob Shoop, Jim Spotila, Ed Standora, Roldán Valverde, John Watson, Thane Wibbels, Ross Witham, and Jeanette Wyneken; tireless advocates like Carole Allen, Gary Appelson, Marydele Donnelly, David Godfrey, Ila Loetscher, and Mike Weber; caregivers like Tony Amos, Jean Beasley, Richie Moretti, and Jack Rudloe; and leaders like Fred Berry, Pat Burchfield, Richard Byles, Michael Coyne, Mark Dodd, Karen Eckert, Rod Mast, Chuck Oravetz, Laura Sarti, and Donna Shaver. Yet most heros go unsung.

Doc Ehrhart

Sinkey Boone

Barbara Schroeder

Customs confiscated this stuffed hawksbill, illegal under the ESA

Mexican marines guard the Tamaulipas ridley arribada in 1968

A US coast guardsman inspects a TED aboard a shrimp trawler

Protections for Sea Turtles

Intentionally harming a sea turtle can get you in trouble. Protection for sea turtles also extends to actions that cause unintentional harm. Our good intentions range from local ordinances to international treaties.

Local Ordinances

Many coastal communities have codes to protect sea turtles on their nesting beaches. These ordinances include regulation of artificial lighting and bans on bonfires and beach driving.

State Laws

Many US states where sea turtles occur have statutes that protect them. Some states also regulate fisheries to protect turtles, banning certain fishing methods that kill them, like gill nets. State legislation and agency rules govern development near nesting beaches. Most states discourage the construction of armoring that prevents nesting.

Federal Laws

Sea turtle harvest and trade is prohibited by law in the US, Canada, Mexico, Cuba, Bermuda, and The Bahamas. The US Endangered Species Act of 1973 (ESA) and Canada's 2002 Species at Risk Act (SARA) require additional protections from incidental harm or "take." In the US, incidental take may be permitted if there are steps to minimize the take. Steps for fisheries include use of **TEDs** in certain shrimp trawls and requirements for large-diameter circle hooks in longline fisheries (see page 243). More specifically, the US Magnuson–Stevens Fishery Conservation and Management Act (MSFCMA) and the Pelly Amendment to the Fishermen's Protective Act aim to manage fisheries and bycatch of US protected species wherever they occur. Although these acts can mandate trade sanctions, bycatch concerns are typically addressed with diplomacy. Other national actions have established nesting beach refuges in Florida, St. Croix (USVI), and **Tamaulipas, Mexico** (the principal Kemp's ridley nesting beach). The US government has also defined areas of "critical habitat" for some sea turtle species on beaches and in the water.

International Treaties

Several treaties between nations have benefitted sea turtles as international animals and have encouraged conservation efforts within and among countries. One of the farthest-reaching agreements for sea turtles is the 1975 Convention on International Trade in Endangered Species (CITES), with over 145 countries as signatories. The treaty restricts international trade in sea turtles or their products, and is especially important to green turtles and hawksbills, two species that have suffered immensely from international trade. An additional regional treaty, the Inter-American Convention on Sea Turtles (IAC), commits 15 contracting countries in North, Central, and South America to implement domestic measures to reduce threats to sea turtles. Measures include prohibiting harvest of sea turtles or their eggs, use of fishing practices that reduce turtle bycatch (including mandatory TED use), designation of protected habitat, and promotion of sea turtle research and education.

Another treaty that protects sea turtles along with other animals that move between nations is the Convention on the Conservation of Migratory Species of Wild Animals (1979), also known as the Bonn Convention. As of 2014, the Convention had 120 Parties. Additional treaties benefitting sea turtles include the 1978 International Convention for the Prevention of Pollution from Ships (MARPOL), which bans ocean dumping of oil and plastics among its 152 signatory states.

Do These Protections Work?

Yes, in the same way that speed limits protect us from danger on our roadways. Have you ever seen someone speeding? You probably have, but our hope is that traffic laws curtail the most flagrant and threatening of violators. Our most valuable sea turtle conservation tools remain inextricably wrapped around well-intentioned, compromising laws like the ESA and international agreements like CITES. These instruments are essential, notwithstanding their reliance on limited enforcement, and their constraints, which allow some harm to legally continue. Despite harvest bans in all our regional nations, illegal taking still occurs. But the days of commercial sea turtle harvest on a massive industrial scale are behind us. For that, we can thank the rules that curb our pernicious tendencies.

Wave wash immerses a loggerhead sea turtle as she enters the sea after nesting on a protected refuge beach in Florida

Dozens of groups coordinate a continental sea turtle network

In 2010, responders rescued over 5000 cold-stunned green turtles

The 2010 oil spill response required a multi-state network

Conservation Networks

Many work to save sea turtles, and their effectiveness is coordinated through networks. These allow connections between people on beaches and in the water, and those in offices, meetings, and deep within digital data streams.

Stranding networks mobilize when someone seeing a stranded turtle (see page 214) notifies a US state coordinator through a hotline. Coordinators contact local participants trained and permitted to respond to strandings. Responders comprise a largely volunteer force of thousands. The 18 state coordinators are organized by NOAA fisheries, one of two federal agencies responsible for sea turtle conservation. Responders receive guidance from coordinators in transporting rescued turtles to rehab and in collecting data and samples from dead turtles.

Nesting networks in each of the southeast states organize data collected by the hundreds of organizations that survey beaches. Like stranding responders, nesting beach surveyors are trained and permitted by state coordinators.

Data and information networks meet the global need for sea turtle resources. The State of the World's Sea Turtles (SWOT) organizes population status information through the expertise of the Marine Turtle Specialist Group (MTSG) and the data-management of OBIS-SEAMAP. Seaturtle.org makes available useful contact information, data and mapping tools, nesting and stranding data, images, and publications. The Canadian Sea Turtle Network coordinates information in eastern Canada, and WIDECAST oversees a sea turtle network for the wider Caribbean. Other networks include the sea turtle tag identification database at the University of Florida (UF).

Response networks rely on all the networks above to assemble rescue teams during severe cold stuns or oil spills.

Idea networks promote sharing. Scientific presentations at the Annual Symposium of the International Sea Turtle Society, and communication on the cturtle listserv (see page 273), have initiated important conservation guidance.

How to Save Sea Turtles …

If you live on or visit the coast—Keep nesting beaches naturally dark and safe for turtles during their nesting and hatching seasons by turning off, shielding, and redirecting outside lights, and by closing curtains in beachfront windows. Satisfy your curiosity by attending a guided sea turtle night walk, rather than searching for nesting turtles on your own. Remove recreational equipment like chairs, umbrellas, and boats from the beach at night so that nesting turtles are not turned away. Let the proprietor of your beach hotel know when lights, beach furniture, or human disturbance from the hotel are likely to harm sea turtles. Reduce or eliminate your use of lawn fertilizers that pollute coastal waters.

If you fish or have a boat—Be alert at the helm, slow down, and steer around sea turtles. Reduce hooking and entanglement risk by casting lines far from any observed turtles. Remove as much line as possible from hooked turtles and get help for those that are injured. Avoid running in shallow seagrass beds and anchor away from coral reefs. Be fastidious about your trash disposal, making sure that plastics and fishing line stay out of the water.

If you travel abroad—Let traveling companions know that buying sea turtle eggs, meat, curios, or jewelry made from their parts is an important reason why we may lose our sea turtles.

If you eat seafood—Choose sustainable seafood types caught by methods and in places that don't harm sea turtles. Ask for this information, and visit **seafoodwatch.org** for guidance.

If you simply care—Properly dispose of plastic litter. Much of the plastic and entangling debris harming sea turtles, including balloons released into the sky, comes from places far from the sea. **Clean up** a nesting beach. On Elliot Key, FL, the Coastal Cleanup Corporation removed tons of trash, which allowed nesting sea turtles to access the beach. Learn about the varied threats to sea turtles and teach others what you know. Speak out if you are moved to do so, letting government leaders know what you think. Contribute to sea turtle conservation groups who can represent your concerns.

A healthy dune free of obstacles attracted this nesting green turtle

Seafood Watch is a guide for those with discriminating tastes

After trash was removed, nesting returned to Elliot Key, FL

Whose Sea Turtles are They Anyway?

A social dilemma hampers the conservation of community resources. This was ecologist Garrett Hardin's argument outlined in "The Tragedy of the Commons," published in 1968. The misfortune is in the failure of individuals to act in the public interest. It's a tragic story in the classic sense, in which culpability rests not with villains, but with well-meaning people who share their communities' interests.

A tragedy might begin with an individual's decision to take a turtle from the ocean commons. The decision has both negative and positive effects on the taker. The positive effect is the benefit gained from one turtle eaten or sold, and the negative effect is the loss of one turtle from a population benefitting many people. A different positive effect could also come from the sale of seafood caught by methods risking the accidental death of turtles. But whether accidental or intentional, the loss of a living turtle's value is spread widely over all who value sea turtles, so that the negative effect on the taker is tiny. Thus, every rational taker's cost-benefit analysis justifies taking each community turtle, even as extinction nears. Loss of the resource is tragic, but the concept of permanent loss has little effect on an individual's decision to take (or to do something that accidentally takes) just one more turtle.

Ownership is the way to turn tragic loss into a negotiated settlement. Owners have standing, represent their interests, and seek social solutions from the rule of law. These rules include the agreements between nations that help us all get along, agreements that acknowledge claims to community resources and allow redress of grievances. Rules give weight to objections, such as, "Pardon me, but you're hurting my turtles."

A juvenile loggerhead hatched on a US beach drifts in international waters. Who claims this turtle?

They are Ours

Belonging to all of us is vastly different from belonging to none of us. As owners, it's up to us to look out for our interests.

In the introduction to this section on saving our sea turtles, we proposed a number of ways that they provide value. One value is in what we might gain from simply knowing that sea turtles exist. What evidence could there be that this value is realized?

A good place to begin understanding the value of our sea turtles that swim the ocean commons is with a sea turtle person (turtle girl, turtle guy, turtle nerd …). They (we) have meetings, each drawing a thousand or more people from all over the world. There is an annual international symposium, meetings within the southeastern US, and meetings in Latin America and many other world locations. The gatherings attract experts, conservation advocates, and aficionados, all with one thing in common—they love sea turtles. This love is demonstrated in the passion expressed, time devoted, money spent, and careers chosen. Such affection is felt by millions more, albeit with slightly less fervor. Sea turtles are widely recognized as charismatic facets of nature that are worthy of art in a variety of forms—sculptures, toys, cinema, paintings, literature, mosaics, tattoos, and jewelry (but not from real turtles). Even those who may never experience a sea turtle firsthand often demonstrate the most tangible measure of turtle-worth we know, which is to pay for them. People confirm sea turtle existence value in the marketplace by contributing to conservation organizations. But we also invest emotions in our sea turtles. We give them names, we feel their stories, and we follow their lives as best we can with the aid of Internet access to maps interpreting data from satellite-tracking technology.

Deservedly so, we invest in our sea turtles. We devote money, time, and emotion. The returns we receive vary, but on balance, the contributions to our happiness and spiritual well-being seem obvious.

A little loggerhead kindles curiosity and delight

A young girl wears her love for sea turtles on her back

Sea turtles are the subject of countless forms of art

269

Challenges and Opportunities Ahead

The first humans to wander near a warm sea came to know sea turtles, animals that were here an enormity of time before us. There are billions more of us now. Our numbers have spread over every continent, and our presence spans oceans. We've consumed a lot of what was, and the planet we had thought of as infinitely hospitable now seems small. Our familiar climate is changing, our seas are rising, and these waters contain diminishing diversity to nourish us. Much has been taken on purpose, and much by accident. Total bummer, right?

To be plagued by conservation problems is indeed misfortune. A "problem" is a matter involving doubt, uncertainty, or difficulty. Alternatively, we might accept our circumstances as a "challenge," or a call for special effort. Problems are endured by those who fret. Challenges are met by those

who act. Despite adversity from the many threats sea turtles face, the challenge of conserving them involves numerous opportunities. These opportunities are the prospects for incremental success. Yes, this is a pep talk.

Beyond accepting a semantic spin on our conservation situation, we should recognize hope. Take for example, our green turtles. In 1957, several decades had passed since the massive commercial fishery for green turtles in US waters collapsed due to overharvest. To that date, no green turtle had been recorded nesting on a North American beach. Records of two nesting green turtles in Florida, one in 1957 and one in 1958, so excited Archie Carr and Robert Ingle that they published the records as a unique scientific contribution. Then, in 1973, President Richard Nixon signed the US Endangered Species Act (ESA) into law

Green turtles nesting on southeastern beaches had become extremely rare. Now, they are part of a conservation success story

A hatchling leatherback enters the Atlantic. Our heirs may see her return to nest on her beach, with all the interest she has gained

and put into effect the CITES treaty restricting trade in endangered species. The Florida green turtle population was listed in 1978 as endangered, which effectively stopped any legal harvest. Were they saved? Not yet.

Sea turtle conservation takes time. Their generation time spans many decades. Juvenile green turtles that survived their formative years during the disco era thanks to the ESA might not be expected to show up on nesting beaches for another 20 years or so. But on a turtle time scale, things happened fast. In 1979, there were 62 reported green turtle nests on Florida beaches. The count surpassed 500 nests in 1985, then 5000 nests in 1999, then 10,000 nests in 2008, and spiked just beyond 36,000 nests in 2013. We stopped killing them, and they came back. The challenge of recovering a sea turtle that was nearly gone was met by bold steps taken despite uncertain political times (Nixon's release of Watergate

tapes, his Vice President's resignation in disgrace, ending days of the Vietnam War, and the doubling of oil prices under OPEC, all in 1973).

Many opportunities to save sea turtles lie ahead. Our sea turtle conservation philosophy has matured, and more than ever, we have programs in place to meet the challenges of protecting sea turtles from ourselves. In a way, we might even consider the present to be a golden age in our relationship with sea turtles. They may have declined, but our advancing technology allows us a greater familiarity with them and a greater flexibility to improve our behavior. Our golden age comes at a crossroads. Along one path, our descendants may both envy us for our experiences with sea turtles, and curse us for not doing more to save them. On another path, our kids and their kids would delight in the wonders we leave for them. Sea turtles can contribute to this inheritance of happiness we leave, but we'll have to earn it.

A Turtle's Courage

Unlikely journeys commence with hope;
with a little help from friends,
we whittle walls and best we cope,
during moments we depend.

Unsure steps strike stray and feckless,
our footing is not sure.
But excitement tests, however reckless,
a pace we can endure.

Brothers on our passage fall,
their lives beget more lives.
Sisters lost no longer crawl,
their entrusted spark survives.

The foamy green, the mountain sea,
the crush consuming ardor,
can propel us unexpectedly,
and compel us to try harder.

An endless trial of ocean blue
deludes as struggles never ending,
but life's much more before we're through,
than a wait for fates impending.

A turtle's courage is one of pluck.
Adversities don't hinder.
No moment wasted lamenting luck
in a hundred years of splendor.

~ Blair Witherington

Resources and Suggested Reading

Popular Books

Carr, Archie F. *So Excellent a Fishe: A Natural History of Sea Turtles*. Gainesville, FL: University Press of Florida, 2011 (1967)

Carr, Archie F. *The Windward Road: Adventures of a Naturalist on Remote Caribbean Shores*. Gainesville, FL: University Press of Florida, revised edition, 2013

Davidson, Osha Gray. *Fire in the Turtle House: The Green Sea Turtle and the Fate of the Ocean*. New York, NY: Public Affairs Press, 2001

Davis, Frederick R. *The Man Who Saved Sea Turtles: Archie Carr and the Origins of Conservation Biology*. New York, NY: Oxford University Press, 2007

Gulko, David, and Karen Eckert. *Sea Turtles: An Ecological Guide*. Honolulu, HI: Mutual Publishing Company, 2004

Perrine, Doug. *Sea Turtles of the World*. St. Paul, MN: Voyageur Press, 2003

Ruckdeschel, Carol, and Robert Shoop. *Sea Turtles of the Atlantic and Gulf Coasts of the United States*. Athens, GA: A Wormsloe Foundation Nature Book, 2006

Safina, Carl. *Voyage of the Turtle: In Pursuit of the Earth's Last Dinosaur*. New York, NY: Holt Paperbacks, 2007

Spotila, James R. *Saving Sea Turtles: Extraordinary Stories from the Battle against Extinction*. Baltimore, MD: Johns Hopkins University Press, 2011

Spotila, James R. *Sea Turtles: A Complete Guide to Their Biology, Behavior, and Conservation*. Baltimore, MD: Johns Hopkins University Press, 2004

Witherington, Blair E. *Sea Turtles: An Extraordinary Natural History of Some Uncommon Turtles*. St. Paul, MN: Voyageur Press, 2006.

Witherington, Blair E., and Dawn E. Witherington. *Florida's Living Beaches: A Guide for the Curious Beachcomber*. Sarasota, FL: Pineapple Press, 2007

Witherington, Blair E., and Dawn E. Witherington. *Living Beaches of Georgia and the Carolinas: A Beachcomber's Guide*. Sarasota, FL: Pineapple Press, 2011

Technical Books

Bolten, Alan B., and Blair E. Witherington, ed. *Loggerhead Sea Turtles*. Washington, DC: Smithsonian Books, 2003

Bjorndal, Karen A., ed. *Biology and Conservation of Sea Turtles*. Washington, DC: Smithsonian Institution Press, revised edition, 2009

Committee on Sea Turtle Population Assessment Methods, Ocean Studies Board, Division on Earth and Life Studies, and National Research Council. *Assessment of Sea-Turtle Status and Trends: Integrating Demography and Abundance*. Washington, DC: National Academies Press, 2010

Lutz, Peter L., and John A. Musick, ed. *The Biology of Sea Turtles*. Boca Raton, FL: CRC Press, 1996

Lutz, Peter L., John A. Musick, and Jeanette Wyneken, ed. The *Biology of Sea Turtles, Vol. II*. Boca Raton, FL: CRC Press, 2002

National Research Council. *Decline of the Sea Turtles: Causes and Prevention*: Washington, DC: National Academies Press, 1990

Plotkin, Pamela T., ed. *Biology and Conservation of Ridley Sea Turtles*. Baltimore, MD: Johns Hopkins University Press, 2007

Wyneken, Jeanette. *The Anatomy of Sea Turtles*. Miami, FL: Southeast Fisheries Science Center, 2001

Wyneken, Jeanette, Kenneth J. Lohmann, and John A. Musick, ed. *The Biology of Sea Turtles, Volume III*. Boca Raton, FL: CRC Press, 2013

Movies

Stringer, Nick, dir. Richardson, perf. T*urtle: The Incredible Journey*. Springdale, AR: Hannover House, 2011, DVD

Websites and Listservs

conserveturtles.org

myfwc.com/research/wildlife/sea-turtles/nesting/

nmfs.noaa.gov/pr/species/turtles/

seaturtle.org

cturtle listserv (hosted by the Archie Carr Center for Sea Turtle Research, University of Florida)

Each resolute stroke matters